1964

THANK YOU FOR HAVING ME

C. A. LEJEUNE

THANK YOU FOR HAVING ME

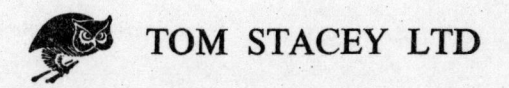

TOM STACEY LTD

© C. A. Lejeune 1964

This edition published 1971 by
Tom Stacey Ltd.
28–29 Maiden Lane, London, WC2E 7JP
England

All rights reserved

SBN 85468 0667

Printed in Great Britain
by Biddles Limited, Guildford

CONTENTS

	Foreword	7
1	A Tall, Yellow House in Manchester	9
2	A Very Odd School Indeed	18
3	'A Gaim of Crickit and Other Storeys'	27
4	Mr. Scott Drops in for Tea	36
5	Growing Up	45
6	Who Fished the Murex Up?	54
7	First Ventures into Print	63
8	And so to London	71
9	A Column of My Own	79
10	'Charmante Soirée!'	88
11	Home and Abroad	100
12	A House of Our Own	113
13	The *Observer* and the Talkies	127
14	'C. A. Lejeune is on Holiday'	140
15	'Company at Lane End'	153

CONTENTS

16	The Amazing Mr. Korda	166
17	Wartime and Leslie Howard	178
18	War's End and Arthur Machen	191
19	Cliveden and Horses	203
20	Recreation of a Feuilletonist	216
21	Writing for Television	232
22	It's Never Too Late to Begin	242
	Index	251

FOREWORD

I SHOULD like to make it clear that this is not a book about films, but the personal story of a girl from the provinces who grew up at the same time as the cinema and spent some forty years as a film critic.

It might be subtitled: 'How to be Happy though Middle-class'. I have led a typically middle-class life and been extremely happy. I have enjoyed a number of things as well as films, and all of them find their places in this story.

Perhaps I should add one thing in particular. Like many fortunate people, I had a most remarkable mother. I have often wanted to write something about my mother, and here, in a small way, I have had a chance to do so. It is not my intention to belabour any point in these slight memoirs, but I hope that, by implication at least, her character breaks through.

I

A TALL, YELLOW HOUSE IN MANCHESTER

I WAS born during a paper-chase on a Saturday in March 1897. My sisters had been panting across the sooty Lancashire fields after a trail of newsprint (almost certainly the *Manchester Guardian*) when they stopped at a house for tea and found a telegram announcing my arrival. I don't know why, but this has always seemed to me a funny story. One way and another, there was to be a good deal of newsprint in my life.

I had four older sisters and three brothers, all born within a year or so of one another. Their names, in chronological order, were Franziska, Marion, Juliet, Helene, Alick, Russell and Arnold. Father had come from Germany as a young man to learn the cotton business. Mother, although born in Manchester, was a full-blooded Scotswoman. *Her* father, Dr. Alexander MacLaren, was a rather well-known nonconformist minister who had married his first cousin Marion; a eugenic lapse condemned to her dying day by another female MacLaren cousin, who felt she should have married him herself.

Franziska was nineteen and Arnold nine when I arrived. I rather think I was an accident, but everyone was very nice about it, and because I was so much younger than the others I came in for a lot of spoiling.

I never knew my father, who died in Switzerland before I was two years old. I have a dim memory of a stranger who once came into my nursery and tossed me up on top of an immensely high toy cupboard. It was every inch of four feet tall, and I knew I never, never should get down again. Apart from this, Father remains for me a photograph of a fair man in a bow tie and bowler hat. It hung over my bed, and every night I had to kiss it with the mysterious words, '*Gute nacht, lieber Vater.*' I didn't like this much, particularly in winter, when the glass was very cold to the tip of a child's nose.

One does not miss what one has never known, and to me it seemed quite natural to grow up in a home without a father: a home where Mother was in charge of everything; paid all the bills, arranged the family holidays, held morning prayers, sat at the head of the long dining-table and carved the Sunday joint, dealt deftly with the vast turkey and blazing plum pudding at Christmas.

Mother was a most unusual woman, as you will find if you pursue this story. In fact, it would be no exaggeration to say that my story is largely Mother's story. She influenced a great many people without their knowledge. She never asked questions, never interfered, but somehow what she intended would be done.

Her formal education had been sketchy. She went to what was known then as 'a dames' school', and was 'finished' abroad in homes of French and German pastors selected and approved by Grandfather. She married very young, and for the first ten years of marriage was kept busy with childbearing.

But she had the sort of lively mind which never stultifies, but seeks for and finds its own education. She grew with the changing times: was keenly aware of current concepts, although she did not always conform to them; could weigh an opinion as well as any man, and, what was more unusual, she could keep her counsel. She was the repository of many secrets. I can guess now at the gravity of some of them, but they remain secrets to this day.

Mother must have been in the early forties as I first remember her, but there wasn't a trace of grey in the long rope of black hair which I used to watch her comb out at the dressing-table. Every morning, winter and summer, she took a hip bath in cold salt-water.

I suppose she was still in mourning for my father, because I can clearly see her dressed for dinner in a black lace teagown. She never wore black in later life. Brown was her colour; brown or a soft mole-grey with just a tinge of brown.

Her clothes were very much her own. They were chosen for comfort, not for fashion; yet somehow they never looked out of place, because they were so characteristic of her. All her life she favoured soft materials and loose fittings; comfortably low necks with lace or frilling; wide sleeves with ruffles falling to the wrist; short boleros for the winter. She found a style that suited her and stuck to it, with only slight modifications to do credit to her friends and appease the anguish of her dressmaker.

She went to some 'little woman round the corner' for her dresses, but her loose coats and capes were man-tailored to her own design, and she must have spent a lot of money on her feet. She suffered from varicose veins and had to wear elastic stockings. Long skirts hid these to a great extent, but for comfort she had her shoes hand-made on her special last by one of the best shoemakers in England. For outdoor wear these were of the softest kid; in the house, except on formal occasions, she wore sandals.

In many people these affronts to fashion would have seemed odd and ostentatious. In Mother's case they were taken quite for granted. It would indeed have seemed a little shocking to find her dressed in any other way.

We lived in a tall, yellow brick house in Manchester, halfway between Withington and Fallowfield. From the nursery windows you could watch the trams rattle by across the cobbles; horse trams in my sisters' and brothers' childhood, electric trams in mine.

Number 10, Wilmslow Road, known in my sisters' youth as Lyndhurst, was an ugly house, four storeys high and replete with every Victorian inconvenience. The rooms were large and draughty; gas lighting left the lofty ceilings and cornices in shadow. Coal for the open fires was carried up in scuttles from the cellar. The only bathroom was a cramped cubby-hole under the roof, with a very nasty, narrow bath, a gurgling cistern and no light all day long except one feeble gas jet.

I have sometimes wondered why the bathroom was put in such an inconvenient place, and have come to the conclusion that by the time a bathroom was considered necessary there was nowhere else to put it.

My eldest sister used to recall that in her childhood the house had no sort of indoor sanitation. Every month a notice would arrive for Father, bearing the sinister words 'The Night Cleaners will call' on such-and-such a date. 'Please Leave Your Garden Gates Open.' Franziska, who loved to dramatize, would make my flesh creep with this story.

The Night Cleaners had ceased to call by my time, although there was still a rather loathly ashpit in the garden for the disposal of all household refuse. Plumbers had been at work and partly modernized the house. As well as the bathroom underneath the roof, there was a sumptuous lavatory one floor lower. This was an L-shaped room with stained-glass windows. A step led up to the immense mahogany throne, where a child could sit at ease and read a book (strictly against all the rules, of course), with background music of choir or organ practice from the Presbyterian church next door.

It has sometimes puzzled me to know where everybody slept at 10, Wilmslow Road. As well as eight of us and Mother, and any odd relation who might be visiting at the time, there were Cook, the housemaid and Lizzie to be fitted in.

Cook was not a person but a personage, who ruled the lower regions beyond the green baize door. I was taught to treat her with the utmost respect, never to go into the kitchen without knocking.

She had a larder where huge bowls of milk stood on a stone slab waiting for the cream to rise; where there were whole hams and cheeses, moulds and jellies by the dozen. She had a wash-house with copper and mangle; not to be confused with the room known as the laundry, where bicycles were kept and a trapeze hung from the roof, and later I used to help Mother count the bag-wash. The kitchen itself, the holy of holies, was a wonderful and mysterious place, with its rag rug, open range, rocking-chair, fat tabby cat and kettle singing on the hob.

That was where the bells hung in a row, with their curled springs like question marks; and that was where the 'hoist' started on its upward journey to the pantry, laden with sirloin, Yorkshire pudding and vast gravy-boats. The kitchen fascinated me, and Cook, in her august way, was kind, but I never got to know her very well because of the black beetles.

The housemaid wasn't very fond of me, and I'm not surprised. It can't have been much fun carrying those coal-scuttles upstairs when I was kept in bed with a bad cold, which happened often in the winter. We called her Beatrice, but the name printed on her apron-strings was 'SHARKEY'. It reminded me of *Peter Pan*, a cross between Starkey and the crocodile, and I was very much in awe of her.

Now Lizzie never minded what she did. Lizzie was my nurse. She had a voice like a steel file and a profile like Savanarola. I doubt if she had been to school, but she was one of the finest gentlewomen I have ever known, and I loved her dearly.

She had come from Oldham many years ago as nursemaid to the little boys. By the time Arnold was nine, and there was nothing left to do for him but darn his socks, she was preparing to pack up her traps and go, when Mother gave her the glad news that there was to be fresh nanny-fodder for the nursery.

I don't know how the household would have managed without Lizzie, with a wailing infant in the cot (I was always what was called a masterbit at crying), the seven other children growing up and Mother increasingly concerned with Father's illness. Lizzie had the grim Lancashire ability to cope. She was at once a dragon and an angel; an erect, formidable little figure dressed in grey, with high, whaleboned collar, white lace front and a thin coil of hair securely skewered on the top of her head. She had dry, firm hands and a rough edge to her tongue. She ruled the nursery absolutely, and would stand no nonsense from anybody.

She did everything for me in the early days. I can dimly remember sitting up to tea in a high chair, with a tray purposely designed for banging on, and watching Lizzie's fingers twirl the syrup spoon. I can remember, still very dimly, splashing in a flat tin bath beside the fire, my wincey nightgown warming on the guard, and Mother coming up to say good night.

Later, when I was promoted from the nursery cot to Mother's bedroom, Lizzie remained my help and mainstay. She pushed me to 'the village' in the pram. She made my frocks, with exquisite hand-smocking at the yoke and wrists. She dressed my dolls, and made a new coat for my beloved toy dog Brownie when he began to come to pieces at the seams.

She curled my long hair round her fingers into fat brown sausages, made the 'loose pockets' to go under party frocks and starched my frilly pinafores. She came with us on all our holidays, keeping a bucket handy in the train in case one wanted to be sick.

Lizzie was an essential part of home, and I shed bitter tears when it was time for her to go away, to be replaced by an Austrian fräulein with one blue eye and one brown. I needn't have grieved. Fräulein soon vanished from our lives, but Lizzie was to come back into them again and again, even in foreign parts like London.

I have mentioned visiting relations. They were lodged, by another of 10, Wilmslow Road's vagaries, in an uncomfortable spare bedroom in the attics, next to the bathroom with the gurgling cistern. Considering the four flights of stairs that had to be climbed in order to get there, it was a good thing that most of the visitors were young and active.

There were various male MacLaren cousins, personable young men who pursued Franziska, and were in their turn pursued by Helene. There was Uncle Arthur, Mother's widowered brother-in-law, who lived in London, had a ruddy face and bushy eyebrows and gave really understanding presents.

There were his two small boys, Graeme and Cecil, who often came to stay with us in the holidays. They wore Eton suits and toppers and almost always spoke in unison. The story goes that when their four-wheeler first pulled up at our gate the cabby gave them an astonished glance, did what is known in stage circles as a double-take and asked, 'Pray where did you two young gents spring from?' To which they replied: 'Four Holly Terrace. West Hill. Highgate. London.' The story was Franziska's, so I take it with a grain of salt.

I do remember, though, the solemn chant with which they were wont to describe their method of dealing with an orange.

> 'First We Cut the Top Off,
> Next We Suck the Juice Out,
> Then We Spit the Pips Out,
> Last We Tear the Flesh Out.'

This duet, graphically illustrated, was the young Wests' party-piece, and never failed to entertain a grown-up audience. I, several years younger than my cousins, used to sit and listen fascinated but alarmed, waiting for the wrath of heaven to descend on them. Lizzie, whose word was law, had taught me to eat an orange in a very different way, far less spectacular and almost dull; peeled and divided neatly into sections, or 'pigs' as they were known in Lancashire.

It's odd how large a part food plays in memories of childhood. There are grown men and women who still shudder at the sight of spinach, or turn away with loathing from stewed prunes and tapioca. For me the worst horror is the thought of lukewarm rice pudding with a thin skin on top, or perhaps a slab of fat boiled mutton with carrots and caper sauce.

Luckily, however, it's the good tastes one remembers best. Crispy brown sausages for Sunday breakfast. Bread sauce. Thick onion soup. Kedgeree, for which I had a passion. A jolly sort of red sauce called tomato chuckney ('chuckney' has remained my favourite colour). Rissoles. Ginger-snaps with cream. Thin, hot pikelets swimming in butter.

An old customer of Father's used to send us tins of Guava jelly. This was supposed to be a delicacy, but it tasted to me like indiarubber flavoured with scented soap (and most children are experts in the taste of soap and indiarubber). A much more welcome gift was the Edinburgh rock which came from MacLaren aunts in Morningside, and the chocolates at Christmas from other aunts in Switzerland: noisettes, creams, dragées, cat's-tongues and my favourite nougatines. Helene and I kept a sharp eye on each other over the nougatines. We were the only members of the family who went for hard chocolates in a big way, and neither of us was above a spot of quick exchange when nobody was watching.

On Sunday afternoons Mother kept open house, and I have fond, greedy recollections of the cakes provided for her visitors. Manchester at that time was famous for its confectioners, and Mother patronized the best. There were vanilla slices, oozing yellow cream; Eccles cakes, rich with fruit; and éclairs—where can you find such glorious éclairs today? The chocolate ones with white spots were called Othellos. The vanilla ones with brown spots were Desdemonas.

Before I leave the absorbing subject of food I ought to tell you about a rather shameful thing that happened to me when I was eight or nine years old. I had been invited out to tea at one of the rich German-Jewish houses which flourished at that time in Manchester. Most of them were very welcoming, and made a child feel thoroughly at home. This house was an exception.

High tea was served, but not in the friendly, pot-luck Lancashire way to which we were accustomed. Servants in uniform came round with dishes, and suddenly I was aware of a Personage at my elbow offering a silver dish piled with asparagus. There was no sign of any spoon or fork, only a mysterious pair of silver nippers. I had no notion how to use them, and the Personage made no attempt to help me. I was in despair. My face grew hotter and hotter. I imagined the eyes of the whole table on me. Suddenly a once-heard remark came to my rescue. I waved the asparagus away and said, in the most grown-up voice that I could manage, 'Thank you, but I never touch greens.'

I am writing this at Christmastime, and it seems no bad thing to end a chapter of early recollections with a few thoughts on Christmases of childhood. Of course, I can tell only of what I knew myself, but to have been young and happy and surrounded with affection once at Christmas is an experience many of us hold in common.

Strange how few years it takes to form a pattern, when the mind is young and eager and belief unshaken. No matter how time shatters the illusion; how keenly we may realize, as years pass by, that we were the fortunate ones in a world of suffering; it seems to me neither unnatural nor unrealistic to rejoice in our memories of Christmas, and give wholehearted thanks for what we have received.

My father's German upbringing had left its mark on the way we kept Christmas at the old house in Manchester. The continental custom of having the tree on Christmas Eve had been abandoned, but the tree itself remained an object of mystery. No child was allowed to catch a glimpse of it before the great unveiling. The ornaments and candlesticks had all been brought from Germany: coloured balls, fragile as eggshells; tiny glass cages, holding feathered birds; candlesticks shaped like butterflies; chains of bright beads, like rosaries of soap-bubbles.

The songs we sang round the piano were the *Weihnachtslieder* of Peter Cornelius: 'Christbaum', 'Die Hirten', 'Simeon' and the favourite 'Drei Könige', which has now found its way into the service of Nine Lessons and Carols at King's College Chapel.

Although we were not allowed to dress the Christmas tree, we always helped to decorate the house. Evergreens came in a large hamper from somewhere in the Lake District: holly, ivy, mistletoe, bay, laurel and every kind of conifer. These were spread out on a dust-sheet, and we were free to take our pick. It was long past dark on Christmas Eve before we had finished fixing sprigs along the mantelshelves, larger branches behind the pictures, and winding ivy round the grandfather clock. Almost time for bed and hanging up one's stocking.

The night before Christmas was a mixture of bliss and agony. I remember the sound of carol-singers in the dark; the dreadful certainty that I should never go to sleep; the fear, as I grew older and belief in Santa Claus less certain, that I should catch someone in the act of filling up my stocking. Then the half awakening in the small hours, to grope down the bed and find a stocking fat and bulging; the blessed security of real sleep at last.

The presents in the stocking, between the crackers at the top and the tangerine in the toe, were only little things: small toys, small dolls, small books—ranging from *Little Black Sambo* to Gems from Scott or Tennyson—puzzles, pencils with different colours at each end, and once, I remember, a kaleidoscope. But they were enough to keep a child happy and occupied until the great moment in the afternoon when darkness fell, the curtains were drawn and we all filed into the drawing-room, youngest first, to see the lighted Christmas tree.

Our presents were laid out on separate tables. Mine was a low table just beneath the tree. I have it to this day. Our television set stands on it now, but then it bore a far more glorious burden. Books mostly; the Andrew Lang coloured fairy-books, the Brown, the Green, the Olive and the Yellow, filled with delightful pictures for a child to paint with her new sable brush and paintbox. Light blue Mrs. Molesworths, *The Cuckoo Clock, The Tapestry Room, The Children of the Castle*. Those two glorious blue-and-gold volumes, George Macdonald's *The Princess and the Goblin* and *The Princess and Curdie*, and all the E. Nesbits as they came out in their original scarlet bindings.

Once I got down to the new books the world was quite forgotten. My Christmas picture ends with that as the happy fade-out: a tall, gas-lit room, the scent of spruce and candle-wax, a small girl in her Sunday frock crouched on the floor enrapt by illustrations, and background music by Peter Cornelius from the Celestial Choir.

2

A VERY ODD SCHOOL INDEED

I WENT to school when I was three years old. This was equally unfortunate for me and for the school. During the long years of our association we never managed to get on together. Other past pupils speak of Lady Barn House with reverence, with pride and even with affection. Most of the time I just plain hated it, and brought no credit to the school at all.

The headmistress, Caroline Herford, was my godmother. That was the root of all the trouble. For many years she had been a devoted friend of Mother's. They read Italian together; they went on holidays together; they shared a passion for the pre-Raphaelites, and doted on Ruskin, Froebel and William Morris wallpapers.

From earliest infancy I resented Miss Herford's presence in our house. According to Mother's notes—she kept notes scrupulously about her children—I screamed at the mere sight of her. 'C.H. came to tea today. Our Caroline refused to go to her, but turned away and made wry faces.' 'The other day someone said something about Caroline Herford, and our Caroline at once said "naughty (or nasty) girl".' 'Once when we were on a holiday at Salcombe Lizzie took C.H. to bathe and helped to dry her, while our Caroline was left playing on the sands. She made an ugly face and scolding noises. I think she was jealous.'

Of course I was jealous. I can't remember the incident at Salcombe, because I was only eighteen months old at the time. But it seems to me entirely reasonable. Why should I be left playing on the sands while *my* nurse helped to dry a grown headmistress?

I don't have to pay a psychoanalyst to tell me that jealousy of my godmother had a blighting influence on my character. Sometimes I fancy that my cattiest reviews as a film critic were subconsciously addressed to her. Nor was I the only member of our family to feel resentment. In an old diary of Franziska's, dated 1890, I find the bleak entry: 'Miss Herford came to stay. Father and I went for a long walk.'

The friendship between Mother and Miss Herford had cooled off a good deal by the time that I was sent to kindergarten. Mother had discarded Ruskin for the 'modern' novelists. She was too busy running the house to spend her afternoons in art galleries, gazing at Rossettis, and Holman Hunts and Burne-Jones. She had found a woman who could teach her Russian, and another who yearned to teach her Swedish cooking. In fact, she was beginning to outgrow Miss Herford, as all through her life she was apt to outgrow her contemporaries.

Nevertheless, Miss Herford was my headmistress, and at school she had me at her mercy. No doubt she was a very worthy woman. She sat on multifold committees, and ended as a J.P., much respected, in some foreign part of England. I'm sure she acted on the strictest principles, one of which was to show no favouritism to children who might be thought to have some claim on her affections.

The result was that her godchild and her various nephews came in for some pretty rugged treatment. The boys grinned cheerfully and bore it. I used to scurry for shelter behind the trailing skirts of little Miss Retallak, a battling Cornishwoman who stood all of five foot high, taught us arithmetic, feared nobody and still enjoyed life vigorously on her hundredth birthday.

But Miss Retallak was not always handy. She had other things to do at school as well as championing the weak and bullied. Miss Herford *was* a bully, and the shrewd thing would have been to stand up to her. I know that now, but at the time her bluster petrified me.

'Write Oxe up on the blackboard, Caroline.'

With fumbling fingers I wrote Oxe and broke the chalk.

'Join the O properly to the x.'

A pause. Where ought the join to be? Top, bottom or in the middle?

'Quickly now, I'm getting tired of waiting.'

A longer pause. Somehow the big O and the little x didn't seem to *want* to come together.

'Caroline, you're not even *thinking*.'

I was past thinking.

'Very well, then. If you don't join the O to the x before I count five you'll be sent to bed. One—two—*three*—FOUR . . .'

I was sent to bed. I suppose that expiated my sin. But it didn't make me any fonder of my godmother, and to this day I have no notion how to join the O to x in Oxe. (Not that I often have occasion to.)

Lady Barn House was rather a famous school. It had been founded by Miss Herford's father, an immensely energetic Victorian with liberal and advanced views on education. He was, I fancy, less of the scholar than the man of action. His talents lay in organizing. The only things I personally saw him organize were tremendous games of Turn the Trencher and General Post at Christmas parties. But what a master hand he was at that!

The school was co-educational in the fullest sense. From the ages of three to eleven, boys and girls did all their work and play together. This led to a rather healthy indifference between the sexes. There was no sentimental nonsense about 'boy-friends' and 'girl-friends'. We didn't think much of one another, which at that early stage is to the good.

It was undeniably an odd school. Ian Hay, who was at Lady Barn with my sisters, described a school *very* much like it in his novel *Pip*. Under the Herford régime there were some curious customs. That business of the labour tickets, for example.

At the beginning of term we were issued with a number of slips of paper, known as labour tickets, one or more of which were confiscated each time we misbehaved. I never did find out what happened when all the tickets were exhausted, because there was a compensating system by which we could earn extra labour tickets for good behaviour.

With a little calculated virtue we could buy our way out of almost anything. The most reliable bankers were voluntary jobs such as Rain Gauge, Ink, or Pigeon Monitor. These jobs were all well paid, and lasted for a week. Personally, I always thought Pigeons was the softest option. Ink was tedious and rather messy. It takes a certain amount of skill to read a rain-gauge, but absolutely none to sprinkle a window-sill with Indian corn.

Another Lady Barn House peculiarity was the system of cash payments for prowess in the gym. You were paid a penny the first time you climbed the rope. Twopence the pole. Sixpence the rope ladder.

A VERY ODD SCHOOL INDEED

When I say sixpence the rope ladder I may be falsifying figures. It could have been a shilling easily. I never got beyond the rope myself. I was clumsy with my feet and hands. A candid friend once told me that I danced like a grasshopper in a fit. I could catch a cricket ball when it fell directly into my hands, but I was always much happier at longstop in the outfield where I could go on picking daisies.

I did once win a race, though. It was in the kindergarten. I won it by running very slowly in the right direction, while the rest of the field of twelve, following an intrepid leader, ran very rapidly the other way.

Setting all personal prejudice aside (if that is possible for other than the saints), I should say that Lady Barn House was a remarkably good school. It still flourishes in South Manchester under the old name, though not at the old address; and to have survived for three-quarters of a century in these changing times seems no mean record for a private preparatory and kindergarten.

The teaching on the whole was excellent; the curriculum imaginative and wide. We were taught to read by the straightforward Cat Sat on the Mat method, pronouncing each letter separately, until the taste was familiar to the tongue. A—S—S, Ass. The left hand doubled into a fist for A. The right hand doubled twice for S. Bring the hands together and there you were. It never seemed particularly difficult, and we were all reading freely by the time we were seven.

We learnt to write a very decent hand, no printing and no back slope. It wasn't copperplate, but it was legible and fluent, with a lighter upstroke and a heavier downstroke. I have heard people say that old Lady Barn House pupils can always be recognized by their handwriting; or could, before the arrival of the ballpoint pen.

There was a great deal of handwork: clay-modelling, basket-making, something that was called Sloyd but seemed to me like woodwork, and sewing. We made all our own school exercise books, and very neatly too. We learnt how to twist strands of coloured thread, double them and beat them on a chair back until they turned into a bookmarker. (I can't *describe* the way that this was done, but I can *do* it any time you like.) We bombarded our families with cross-stitch kettle-holders and pen-wipers edged with blanket stitch.

I wish I could claim that my sewing has shown marked progress since those days. Pen-wipers are no longer in demand, and blanket stitch does have its limitations. Through sheer necessity I have learnt to darn, and at a pinch I can turn up a hem in a rough-and-ready way.

But put me down in a big store with a new dress which needs a simple tuck or two ('Just a *little* lifting on the shoulder, madam. I'll put the pins in, you can do it yourself in five minutes'), and do I give a big, bright smile and reply yes of course I can? I call madly for the fitter.

Lady Barn House drew most of its pupils from South Manchester's middle-class professional families, although the rich merchant houses (like my hosts with the asparagus) were also represented. There were doctors', dentists', lawyers' and bankers' children, with a large sprinkling of offspring from the University, the *Manchester Guardian* and the Hallé Orchestra.

My two particular friends were both professors' daughters. Margaret Tout's father was an historian, whose books were used in almost every English school. He was a shortish, stocky man with a tremendous head, a rolling walk and a face of quite endearing ugliness. Everybody liked him. His lectures, as I found in later years, were amongst the most popular in the University; for, as a fellow-historian, Professor Tait, once said of him, '*Tout comprendre c'est tout pardonner.*'

Margaret's mother was a tall and handsome woman, with flashing black eyes and a skin like a camellia. Her patience with small children was inexhaustible. Sunday after Sunday she would 'hear' our bible verses, or the poems that we had to learn for school out of M. A. Wood's *First Poetry Book*.

I think her greatest triumph must have been the day when Margaret and I were chosen as joint soloists for the kindergarten at the annual school concert.

Hand in hand, we tottered to the front of the platform; Margaret in a smocked red velvet dress, myself in a white muslin frock made by Lizzie out of an old cot cover. Miss Waddell, the kindergarten mistress, struck a chord and we piped up, almost in unison.

>'Pitter *pat*ter, pitterpatter,
>Pitter *pat*ter, *on* the pane,
>Pitter *pat*ter, pitterpatter——'

(a tremendous breathing, then with a triumphant rush)

>'Pitter patter falls the rain.'

Sylvia Hickson's father was professor of zoology. Her mother was fair and young, and wore a djibbeh. The Hicksons would have been our next-door neighbours if it hadn't been for the Presbyterian church between. Our back gates, though, were opposite each other, and Sylvia and I spent most of our young lives in and out of each other's houses.

I always called Sylvia by her second name; which was Kema, after an island Professor Hickson had visited in the Celebes. She was a heavy, pale child who wore glasses, and at an early age made up her mind that she was going to become a doctor. She *did* become a doctor and a very good one, well known in Manchester as a baby specialist under her married name of Guthrie.

My friendship with Sylvia has lasted all my life. We seldom meet nowadays, but that's of no account. For more than twenty years, through two schools and university, we shared experiences, and there is very little about me that Sylvia doesn't know. She comes into my dreams casually but constantly, like a person who has a perfect right to be there. You'll find her coming into this story too, like Mother and Franziska, time and time again.

During my early years at Lady Barn House I was more often absent from school than present. I kept on catching colds, which went on to my chest and obstinately stayed there. The old family doctor used to lay his beard against my nightgown and cluck in a disapproving way: 'More wheezers and sneezers? Tk, tk, tk.' He prescribed liquid ipecacuanha, taken with sugar in a teaspoon. They called it 'ipecacuanha wine', but *that* didn't fool me for an instant. He recommended hot mustard plasters, which tore the skin off a child's chest, and another invention of the devil known as Chili Paste, which did the same thing, only faster.

In spite of all these remedies the wheezing went on, and presently it was decided that what was wrong with me was asthma. Regrettably, this diagnosis proved to be correct. I did have asthma, and it has stayed with me all my life. Not all the time, of course, but on and off. 'Don't worry, Mrs. Lejeune,' the doctor would say cheerfully to Mother, 'she'll grow out of it in time.' Doctors were prone to talk like this to mothers. Now my experience of asthma—and I can't be the first person to have noticed this—is that once you have the thing you *have* it.

Naturally there are exceptions. One of them was an elderly cousin of Mother's, who claimed to have cured his asthma by a special diet. I was put on to Cousin John's diet, and cursed the day when Cousin John was born.

It was a very simple diet, most of it prohibitive. I was to have no butter, milk, cream, bread, potatoes, cakes, eggs, sweets, nor any kind of fruit. This came as a real hardship in the strawberry season, when all the other children at summer parties were gulping down great helpings of strawberries-and-cream. Once, moved by my sufferings, Mother did write to Cousin John about it. Might Caroline have a *few* strawberries for a treat? Back came the inexorable answer, 'Only if she takes them with bicarbonate of soda.' Humiliation piled upon abstention! Fancy going to a party with a packet of sod. bicarb.!

The positive part of the diet consisted of grilled chops or steaks, served with boiled rice and very, very dry. Now there is nothing basically wrong with chops and steaks, even with boiled rice and very, very dry. But chops and steaks for lunch and supper, every day and in all seasons, can be too much of a good thing. They might have been endurable if they had helped my asthma, but they did nothing of the kind.

One memorable day Mother plucked up her courage and took me to see a specialist. Like everybody else he said that Time Alone Would Cure. Mother might as well have saved her money but for one thing. The specialist smiled indulgently at Cousin John's diet sheets, and observed in a voice like honey that they were not *quite* the treatment he would prescribe himself, but Mrs. Lejeune must use her own discretion.

Mother used her discretion like a flash. She whisked me off for tea at the Manchester Art Gallery. It was the first real tea that I had had for months, and I shall always associate 'The Light of the World' with white bread-and-butter, cut extremely thin.

There is no need for me to tell people who have suffered from it that asthma is a beastly and a baffling thing. In spite of all the research that has gone into the subject, it remains as much a mystery as the common cold, and if a doctor tells you he knows all about it you can promptly strike him off *your* medical register.

Asthma attacks different people in different ways, and heaven alone (so far) knows just what causes it. There are people who get asthma on one side of the street, and not on the other. There are people who get it in damp air, others in frost. I once knew a Londoner who could stop an attack by simply plunging into the nearest Underground. I have a friend who claims that the worst thing she knows is a flock of really wet sheep bleating round her. Fortunately in towns this is not very common.

'It's all a matter of allergies,' they say. 'You're probably allergic to feathers' (or wool, fur, cats, dogs, rubber mackintoshes, strawberries —ah, perhaps old Cousin John had something there!—horses or golden rod).

The implication is that once you know what you're allergic to, you can do something about it. Well, sometimes you can. There really isn't any *need* to keep a horse, and you can always move (or move away from) a vase of golden rod.

But take the case of the woman at a party who feels an attack of asthma coming on the moment a total stranger sets foot in the room. It's probably another allergy; the effect of clashing auras, some would say. But what in the world is she to *do*? Keep her own aura out of circulation? Refuse all invitations to parties? Carry an atomizer in her handbag? (Contents 'specially formulated (1) to relieve attacks of asthma with great rapidity, (2) to check impending attacks promptly'.)

Asthma can be a social embarrassment, as well as a physical disability. In my case it's mostly an affair of pillows. I like, when I can, to sleep banked up on four pillows, practically horizontal. That's all very well at home, even if it comes hard on pillow-slips, but extremely awkward in other people's houses.

In the days when I used to go about and do a lot of lecturing, kind hostesses would rally to my aid, their arms piled high with cushions from the lounge. (Their word, not mine.) But most hotels, I found, took a much dimmer view. One guest, one pillow, was the general rule. Sometimes, with luck, you might find a knobbly sausage covered with striped ticking firmly tucked underneath the bottom sheet. There were, of course, ways and means of wrenching an extra pillow out of an obliging chambermaid. But on the whole it was always preferable, if you could, to make a rush for it and catch the last train home.

After the episode of Cousin John, Mother and I worked out our own formula for asthma. Or, rather, she worked it out and I followed it. We found it possible, on the whole, to let the days look after themselves. I never had much asthma in the daytime. It was the nights that were the trouble.

Every night, almost without exception, I woke up with an attack of wheezing. I would sit up in bed and burn some aromatic powder in a saucer. Then I would read for a bit, or Mother, her head nodding with sleep, would try to read to me. We got through the whole of *Ivanhoe* and most of *Quentin Durward* in that way, and I can still recall my fretful interruptions when her voice trailed off. 'Mother, wake up, *wake up*, you're reading nonsense!' (What callous little brutes children can be!)

After an hour or so the asthma wore itself out, and Mother would make tea for both of us, with water boiled on a small spirit lamp, and biscuits. She kept the tray constantly beside her bed, and it was the most delicious tea I ever tasted. Then, in the small hours, we really settled down to sleep. I was allowed to 'lie in' until eight o'clock after a particularly bad night, though Mother was always up and about by seven.

On the whole, once we had got rid of mustard plasters and Cousin John, I think I quite enjoyed those nights of asthma. There was something private and confidential about them. They provided a chance to do a lot of reading. It was nice to have felt bad and to be feeling better, and there was always the young sense of security that everything would come all right because this was home.

3

'A GAIM OF CRICKIT AND OTHER STOREYS'

ONE of the best of all books for a child to read in bed was *The Adventures of Robin Hood* by Howard Pyle. It was romantic, it was big and had the most fascinating illustrations. I always longed to paint them, but I couldn't, because the book was not my own. It was lent us, with special injunctions to be Very Careful, by an old lady of whom all I can remember is that she wore black mittens. I borrowed it at least a dozen times, and thought it rather mean that I wasn't allowed to keep it. After all, the book was *important* to me, and what could an old lady want with the adventures of Robin Hood?

To my great joy, I discovered it again some thirty years later, and was able to buy it for my son. (Or so I *said*, but I think it was mostly for my own delectation.) That was the first time I realized that Howard Pyle was an American. The singing simplicity of the words enchanted me, and this still remains to my mind the most beautiful and nostalgic account of the Sherwood Forest legends ever written.

I said something of the kind in an *Observer* review of Hollywood's talkie *Robin Hood* in the middle 1930s. (Not the silent Douglas Fairbanks version, which was a really rousing piece of screen acrobatics.)

The notice brought an unexpected letter from Arthur L. Bailey, librarian of the Wilmington (Delaware) Institute Free Library. He wrote that he was sending the review on to Mrs. Howard Pyle, 'the sprightliest octogenarian that I have ever known'.

'Howard Pyle', he said, 'was born in this city and lived here practically all his life. In 1910 he and his wife went to Florence where he died suddenly in the spring of 1911.

'Delaware and Wilmington consider him famous as an artist. All of his old friends thought that his writing was done in spare moments and that it was not important. I am quite sure, however, that throughout the rest of the United States he is far better known as the author of *Adventures of Robin Hood*, *Story of King Arthur*, *Man of Iron*, than he is as an artist. Furthermore, artists today consider that his best work appears in the pen-and-ink drawings that he made for his books.'

Well, one way and another, Howard Pyle of Wilmington, Delaware, managed to capture the heart of an English child half a century ago. Other fine, fat books for reading in bed were bound volumes of *Little Folks* and the American *St. Nicholas*. These were inherited from senior members of the family.

Little Folks, of course, was easy enough to come by. You could buy the current issue on any bookstall, and so I did when I could coax the money out of Mother. (My own pocket money was already spent on a twopenny classic, published in green covers, devoted to the adventures of one Prince Pippin and his horse Fly-by-Night.)

How we came by all those volumes of *St. Nicholas* I can't imagine. They gave me a certain social standing, though, a great while later. When we were shown a film (or one of the several films) called *The Little Princess* it was pleasant to be able to remark, in an offhand manner: 'Oh yes, *Sara Crewe; or What Happened at Miss Minchin's*. I read it when it first came out as a serial.' This was barefaced lying, but it sounded fine.

I find myself associating the books of childhood with the places where I first read them. Probably most people find the same, for none of us are quite such individuals as we like to think we are. I remember starting Charlotte Yonge's *The Little Duke* on the top of a step-ladder in Professor Tout's study. I remember finishing *What Katy Did* in a railway carriage on the way to Llanfairfechan; holding the book upside down, the better to make it last out the journey.

I fell in love with Rupert of Hentzau within sight of the Langdale Pikes, discovered *The Four Feathers* on a Yorkshire moor and devoured most of *The Scarlet Pimpernel* before breakfast in a house at Steep near Petersfield, lent us for the holidays by a Bedales schoolmaster.

The Prince and the Pauper is regrettably associated with Something Nasty in the Grapenuts in lodgings somewhere close to Snowden. *The Black Arrow* suggests Church Stretton and an exciting little stream where we raced the corks which bobbed down in flotillas from a nearby cork mill.

Kidnapped belongs to a village near Morecambe Bay called Yealand Redmayne. My sister Juliet was in charge of me, and there wasn't much to do there *except* read; the rain fell inexorably.

'I have been reading *Kidnapped* by R.L.S.', I wrote to Mother, 'and I perfectly revel in it (if you don't mind my using such awful language). I think it is perfectly *glorious*, and it doesn't do me any harm at all, for I understand it *perfectly*, so you needn't be frightened it will be bad for me to read.'

I fancy this letter may have been prompted by a sense of guilt, in connection with my discovery, a year or so earlier, of a battered copy of *Danesbury House* in a Welsh farmhouse that we had taken for the holidays.

It was rather an intimidating farmhouse, with texts tucked into every bedroom drawer admonishing us to 'Flee from the Wrath to Come' and 'Prepare to Meet Thy God'. Nobody specifically told me *not* to read *Danesbury House*, but a certain native prudence suggested that it might be wiser to read it privately in the hay-loft. I got my due deserts, of course. Red spiders bit my legs while I shuddered over the accounts of pink elephants and gin palaces. The hay made me sneeze violently and revealed my hiding place. I was caught climbing down the ladder with the book in my hand. That farmhouse certainly gave a child no chance to flee from the wrath to come.

Mother was a firm believer in regular holidays away from home. From early days I can remember, dimly, a great family exodus in August. We travelled in two or more reserved compartments, with Lizzie, Cook and at least fifteen pieces of luggage; linen, silver, cutlery, bundles of rugs and all the bedding. Later, as the family grew up and scattered, the journey became less spectacular. The biggest trunk, the one we called the Ark, was relegated to the attic and filled with 'dressing-up clothes'. The laundry hamper was reserved for laundry. We managed to make do with one reserved compartment. But the Lejeunes still went away regularly twice a year.

Easter holidays were mostly spent at Silverdale, a tiny village close to Morecambe Bay, and just as pretty as its name. It boasted a single shop-of-all-work, where you could buy groceries, stamps, bolts of cloth, paraffin, bacon, boots, bull's-eyes, waders, glass marbles in matchboxes and snakes with red flannel tongues curled up in Easter eggs. It had an intoxicating smell of kerosene, unbleached calico, rubber and cheese, and was lit by a single swaying lantern.

I adored those holidays at Silverdale. It was an enchanted place for children. Not far off stood the ruins of Arnside Tower, which I don't suppose were haunted, but I liked to think they were. There was something eerie, too, about the shore. Grim tales were told of people swallowed in the quicksands, like 'Mary, Call the Cattle Home'. And every now and then a mysterious tidal wave came roaring up the estuary. The people thereabouts called it The Boar. (Don't tell me the proper spelling was The Bore, or you will break my heart.)

Close by our house was a gorsy common, with a steep ridge of rock. Footholds had been worn into the limestone, and the place was known as The Fairy Steps. I can't remember whether I was told or whether I just imagined that you might find *anything* at the top of The Fairy Steps on the right day.

At any rate, one April morning Sylvia and I scrambled up the steps, and climbed through a gap in a hedge into an unknown wood. It must have been the right day, for we found ourselves in a paradise of primroses. Never in our lives had we seen so many primroses. We simply stood and gaped. To pick would have been sacrilege.

Presently we were accosted by a tremendous hound, followed by a man in gamekeeper's leggings with a gun. (We had seen pictures of gamekeepers, so we knew.) He called off the hound (it was a very gentle hound) and asked us, not unkindly, who we were.

I answered, 'Please, I'm Caroline Lejeune and this is Sylvia Hickson and we come from Withington, Manchester, and please we're only looking at the primroses because we've never seen so many primroses before.'

The gamekeeper looked us up and down and said, 'Come along then, and I'll show you some more of them.' He took us through a hundred miles of woodland, along rides foaming with white cherry blossom, and carpeted with primroses, anemones and tiny curling fronds of bracken, until we reached the drive of an enormous house, with sloping lawns and vineries and pineries.

He picked us each a bunch of primroses and said, 'Next time you come, come straight to the front door and ask for Mr. Alexander.'

'But won't Mr. Alexander mind?' I said.

'No,' said Mr. Alexander.

For a long time he remained the hero of my dreams, but we never went back to that wood again. Perhaps we climbed The Fairy Steps on the wrong day, but somehow we could never find it.

Summer holidays were more promiscuous. We never went twice to the same place in August, Mother believing in the virtue of a change of scene.

I can remember staying near a lighthouse on the Isle of Wight; the sweeping searchlight of the beam and the hot, coconut scent of gorse along the Undercliff. I remember a moonlight climb up Chanctonbury Ring from Steyning. Bouncing balls on a thread of elastic along the quay at Robin Hood's Bay. A pierrot called The Honerable Edward on the sands at Littlehampton. A concert party at Alnwick with a golfing song in Scots, which inexplicably made Mother laugh aloud. And in particular a month at Brough in Westmorland, in a farmhouse just a stone's throw from the ruins of Brough Castle.

The castle was practically in our garden, and Margaret Tout and I earned ourselves a lot of sixpences as self-appointed guides to tourists. We were both of us historically minded, both handy with a child's bow and arrow. We had mugged up the whole history of the castle, and when people wanted to know more about the defence value of double arrow-slits we *showed* them. I reckon that as labourers we were worthy of our hire.

One fine September I was taken up to Scotland, to stay with Grandfather at his summer home at Carr Bridge near Inverness. It may seem odd that so far I have hardly mentioned Grandfather, who, as I am only too constantly reminded, was the one *important* member of our family.

The reason is quite simple: I scarcely knew him. He lived with his married son, my Uncle Alastair, not far away from us in Fallowfield, but to the best of my recollection there was no close contact between our two households. I have a fancy there was no great love lost between Mother and Aunt Maggie. I can just remember Aunt Maggie as a pale person with a cat, who always gave me asthma. It may have been her aura *or* her cat.

I used to embroider smoking-caps for Grandfather at Christmas, and every now and then was taken to pay visits to him in his study. The study was a big upstairs room, reeking of pipe smoke, with a roaring fire and books up to the ceiling.

He was always very kind to me in his grave way; allowed me to blow down the speaking-tube connected with the kitchen, and even to strike a key or two on the mysterious machine he used for writing sermons. He was a very tall, wrinkled man, dressed in a frock-coat, with keen blue eyes and a jutting chin beard; something, to my mind, between a Mosaic god and Abraham Lincoln.

Grandfather was certainly in residence at Carr Bridge the year we went to stay there. I know that, because I was taken once to hear him preach at chapel. His sermons were famous at that time in the non-conformist world, but I'm afraid I paid little heed to that one. The sun was shining, the hills were purple with the last of the ling and I was thinking how lovely it would be to go out and gather blaeberries.

My memories of Carr Bridge are largely of the kitchen, where I used to help Grandfather's cook Bella to make girdle cakes, potato scones and sheets of crumbly, speckled oatcakes.

I remember being invited, with grave Highland courtesy, into a low, stone beehive of a cottage, with beds built into the walls and a warm, glorious fug of peat smoke. I remember drinking ice-cold water from the burns; filling a milk-pail with ripe scarlet cranberries; and the rumour that the old veteran Wild Cat was roaming the woods behind the house again.

Most vividly of all I can remember the day when I was lost in a pine forest. I had strayed away from the others, who were picking berries, and was busy with my own ploys when suddenly it seemed that the straight red trunks on every side were no longer friendly but were closing in on me. I didn't know which way to turn. There were no landmarks; every tree looked just the same and *hostile*. I was seized with atavistic panic. I screamed, and after an unbelievably long time people came. The whole thing was like the grimmest sort of fairy-tale, and I remember it more clearly than I remember yesterday.

I think Grandfather must have died not long after that Carr Bridge holiday. At least, we never went there any more, and he was an old man at the time, well on in his eighties. I wish now that I had known him better. I like to remember the last thing I ever heard him say.

Mother had told him she was taking me to the theatre to see *Peter Pan*. Grandfather sighed and shook his head. I was afraid that for a moment he was going to upbraid; but no. 'It is one of my deepest regrets,' was what he said, 'that I never set foot inside a playhouse. I am sure that I have forfeited a great deal.'

One of the first things I always did on coming home from holidays was to snatch a tennis racket and a ball and go into the garden.
'Where are you going, Caroline?'
'Only to play against the wall.'
'You've still got to unpack your box.'
'I know. But this is terribly important.'
The exercises known as playing against the wall began as soon as I was big enough to hold a racket. The racket was an old one of Helene's, with two or three strings broken. The wall belonged to the Presbyterian church, which turned an inviting bare back on our garden. (When I say 'bare' I use the word comparatively. High up, there were a number of small, leaded windows which went in with a *plunk* when the ball hit them.)
At first I clutched the racket tightly with both hands, standing close up on a flower-bed and trusting the ball would come back to the racket and not drop. This didn't last for long. I found it too much like a kindergarten game.

> '*Thy* little hand my chi-ild sho-ow me,
> *I* give the pretty ba-all to-o thee.
> *Now* close it up and *let* i-it rest,
> *Like* birdie in its cosy-y nest.'

We had been taught to play 'catch' with that song at Lady Barn House.
Now I discovered it was more fun to stand back and let the ball *bounce*. The farther back the better. After a year or so of practice I was battering the church wall vigorously from the full distance of the garden. I was using my backhand and forehand indiscriminately; volleying and placing with some accuracy (to avoid those windows); and acquiring quite a working knowledge of the rudiments of tennis, which was later to stand me in good stead.

At the time I never thought of tennis. My one object was to keep the ball in play while I made up stories.

Most imaginative children make up stories, and most children, heaven help them, are imaginative. A great many of them like to have some accessory to occupy their hands while the mind is roaming. A piece of wood to whittle. A daisy chain to make. A hank of bast to plait ('Rapunzel, Rapunzel, let down your hair!'). A battered Roman soldier, a small meat-skewer and a burnt matchstick to fumble with beneath the blankets.

My own accessories were racket and ball. When it was too wet to play against the church wall I played down in the laundry or among the aspidistras of the half-landing. (I was always careful of the aspidistras. In a way they were my special charge, since I had to sponge them every week.) On Mother's At Home days the half-landing was out of bounds. Then I played in the morning-room, unless it was in possession of the sewing-woman who came in by the day to do the mending, and was so unbelievably called Miss Button.

The stories I made playing against the wall were very private; disjointed I-stories like dreams, and never meant for publication. Before long, though, I decided to make some that were. I had the example of Franziska's output to inspire me. As a child she had written prodigiously; and she kept all her stories, including a novel with the memorable sentence, 'The gentlemen were taken to the bathroom by the housemaid, to wash their hands and brush their hair for dinner.'

My efforts were less dashing than Franziska's. The other day I was turning out a cupboard, and came across a mottled penny exercise book with the words 'Caroline Alice Lejeune Age 7' sprawled in broad pencil on the label. Inside is the title, 'A Gaim of Crickit and other Storeys'. The *pièce de résistance* is one of the other Storeys called 'A Party'. If you will allow me to quote a few extracts from this essay in contemporary reporting it may give you some idea of the way that children entertained themselves in Januaries of nearly sixty years ago.

'Once there was a familly and the youngest of the familly was a little girl called Nora. One day Nora went to her Mother and said Mother can I have a party. Yes said Mother I think we will have it on the 9.'

There follow the formalities of sending out the invitations, until 'at last the day came and it was just three'.

'A GAIM OF CRICKIT AND OTHER STOREYS'

'Nora heard the bell ring and Olive came in. How do you do said Nora, how do you do said Olive. Then there came another ring at the bell and in came Lizzy till at last they wear all in the room. What shall we play said Olive. Blind mans buff said Laura, Who will be blindman. I will said Jenny. Soon she caught Robert. When everybody had been it they thought they would change the gaim.'

At this point Nora pulls out of her 'loose pocket' (which every little girl wore under her party dress) 'a card on which the gaims that had been decided to be played were written'. They were:

> 'Blind mans buff,
> Hiss and Clap,
> Tea.
> Honey Potts,
> Dum Crambo,
> Musical chairs,
> Supper.

'Maud's side was out. She was wrong. She bowed to Olga and it ought to have been Robert. Just then the bell rang for tea and they all went into the dining-room. The table looked lovely.'

Unfortunately we cannot reproduce the illustration of the table, rather sparsely laid on trestles, with a king-size teapot, crossed knife and fork, a cake with a couple of smoking candles, three cautiously drawn cups without saucers, and a banana.

'There was a fern in the middle,' continues this enthralling chronicle, 'and crackers of all kinds caps and mottos. Nora poured out the tea they all had a very good meal. When tea was over they all went back and played honeypotts. When they had it twice it was suppertime.'

By this time I think the writer was getting a bit bored. At all events, she hurries on:

'Soon someone came for Lizzy. Then someone came for Robert. The rest were all sent for at the same time. They said Thank you very much for having me.'

And then, with an ecstasy that only writers know, the two triumphant words, 'THE END'.

4

MR. SCOTT DROPS IN FOR TEA

I WAS twelve years old when we left Wilmslow Road. The tall, yellow brick house was much too large for our diminished family. Franziska and Marion were both married. Russell had gone to Australia to do sheep-farming. Alick had become a parson. Helene was teaching at a school in Sheffield, and came home only for holidays.

Holland House, or 8, Burlington Road, as the Post Office preferred to call it, had been the property of Judge Parry, the man who wrote that fascinating play for children, *Katawampus*. It was a square-built, rather ugly house on the corner of two back streets in Withington. Its only claim to elegance was the South Room, which had obviously been an afterthought on somebody's part, for it seemed to belong less to the house than to the garden. It was a fine large room with a parquet floor and windows on three sides, so that it was almost always filled with sunshine (for the sun does shine in Manchester, whatever the old jokes may say).

Ugly or not, 8, Burlington Road was a convenient house; for 1909, comparatively up to date. I always thought it a bit odd that you had to go right through the only bathroom to reach one of the best bedrooms; but, on the other hand, it was nice to have a bathroom within reach of everybody, and the plumbing worked without a gurgle.

There was a tennis court; not a particularly good one, but still a court. There was electric light all over the house, and one of the first things I was taught, when I reached years of discretion, was how to mend a fuse. There was also a telephone; not a speaking-tube like the one in Grandfather's study, but a real machine that answered when you turned a handle.

From the beginning a regular visitor to the house was C. P. Scott, the great editor of the *Manchester Guardian*. Two or three times a week I would come home from school and find his bicycle parked in our hall. This was part of life in Burlington Road; something that I took for granted.

Mr. Scott and his wife had always been close friends of Mother's. Their daughter Madeline (later Mrs. C. E. Montague) had been at school with my sisters, and the Montague children, although slightly my juniors, were at school with me.

When I first became aware of C. P. Scott he was a widower, and one of the handsomest old gentlemen I have ever seen. He had a full grey beard and keen hawk's eyes, which, when he talked to children, as he loved to do, softened and grew extraordinarily kind.

He wore loose, light grey tweeds with the real peaty smell. Every afternoon, wet or fine, he used to take a three-mile bicycle ride round the grimy but still comparatively open spaces of South Manchester; what we called 'the fields'. Several times a week it was his custom to drop into our house for tea before his evening appearance at the *Guardian* office.

I can't remember ever thinking of C. P. Scott as an important editor, although it did seem peculiar now and then to hear that he was late for tea because he had been having breakfast with Lloyd George in London. I simply regarded him as the familiar 'Scottie', a reliable tennis partner with a tricky underhand service, and Mother's special friend.

Mother's relationship with Mr. Scott was very close and very durable. It was, perhaps, unusual, but they were both unusual people. Each summer they would go away together, and spend a fortnight in the Lake District, or a fortnight in Devonshire. They set great store by these quiet, annual holidays, and seemed to find strength and refreshment in each other's company.

This long-term intimacy with C. P. Scott undoubtedly made things much easier for me when I decided to become a journalist. 'Contacts' are of prime importance to a young writer, and I already had the finest contact in our drawing-room.

It was easy enough to get Mr. Scott to *read* what I had written, but of one thing I am certain. His integrity as an editor was such that he would never have given me a job on his beloved *Guardian* unless he had felt confident that I deserved it. His work and his private life were utterly divorced. I had grown up almost like one of his own grandchildren, but he judged what I put down on paper with an impersonal, a stranger's, eye.

During those early years at Burlington Road I was much too busy to consider what I meant to be when I grew up. Growing up is quite a business in itself, particularly when you've just gone to a new school. For the first time in my life school had become important. I could hardly wait to set off in the morning, and dawdled unconscionably on the way home.

'Caroline, why are you so late for tea?'

'I was only walking home with Freda' (or Gertrude, or Adèle, or Marjory).

'But that couldn't take you a whole hour.'

'I know, but then I had to walk back again.'

Withington Girls' School was my notion of a *proper* school, where there were no boys to interfere, and we could get on with the things that mattered, like tennis and hockey, the school plays and taking flowers to the current mistress of our affections.

All my sisters had been at Withington before me, and the headmistress of my time, Miss Grant, had been chosen from 'the short list' at a meeting in our house. This was still the old house in Wilmslow Road. I remember watching through the banisters as the discarded candidates ('Thank you, we'll let you know') were shown out one after the other. Miss Grant stayed for lunch. Eyeing her over the soup and halibut, I got the impression she was someone to be reckoned with.

She was. She turned out to be one of the great headmistresses; conservative by training but naturally venturesome; fair but disciplinary; imaginative but impartial; a good historian and a born organizer. Her mind was full of plans for enlarging and developing the school. She had a genius for adapting space; for adding on or cutting up. At the beginning of a new term you were never certain what changes you were going to find.

'I *say*, Mother, Miss Grant's built a new corridor'; 'I tell you what, Mother, Miss Grant's put in a staircase'; 'Do you know, Mother, Miss

Grant's found two old bedrooms and turned them into classrooms?'; 'You must listen to this, Mother: Miss Grant's cut an *enormous* piece out of the front garden and built a new room for the Lower Fourth.' To all of which Mother would reply with just the right shade of enthusiasm, 'How *very* nice, dear; yes, I know.'

She knew because she was one of the school governors, and Miss Grant made a habit of consulting her on most things. The other governors were C. P. Scott, Miss Herford and Mrs. (later Lady) Simon. The four houses in the huge Withington Girls' School of today are named after them.

In my day there were just over a hundred girls. We wore claret-coloured ties and hatbands, with the badge '*Ad Lucem*'. We humped our satchels on our backs like boys, and thought it highly dashing to possess a Koh-i-Noor propelling pencil.

The Sixth Form girls turned up their hair in 'door-knockers', or tied it back with broad, black moiré ribbon. The clothes we wore successfully for games would seem incredible by modern standards. I can still see a vivid picture of my friend Freda Drew, our most brilliant hockey forward, dribbling the ball through an opposing field with almost contemptuous ease, in spite of a tubular tweed skirt to her ankles and a dangling silver watch-chain.

I scraped into the hockey team as an assiduous but somewhat ineffective inside-right. I had a technique to which I rigidly adhered: not to take pot-shots at the goal myself, but pass the ball to someone else as soon as possible.

My real game was tennis. From the beginning I found myself handier at tennis than most girls of my age. Those years of playing against the wall were paying off. None of my young opponents seemed able to return a ball as fast as the rear elevation of the Presbyterian church, and I had learnt some tricky placing from those leaded windows.

When I was fourteen I beat the champion of the school at singles. This was diplomatically passed over as a fluke. I'm inclined to think it was. In fact I'm sure it was, for I could *feel* right through the game that she was much the better player. In any form of single combat a contestant knows these things by instinct. I'm positive that any of those knights of old, happening to tilt against a visored Tristram or a Lancelot, *knew* that he was dealing with a seeded jouster.

Luckily my prowess as a singles player was never put to public test. For match purposes, doubles were the things that mattered, and it wasn't long before I found the ideal partner in a girl in my own form, Carol Samuels.

Carol and I were great friends in and out of school. Both of us took our tennis very seriously, and from the age of fifteen upwards we were tenderly nursed as a couple by the games mistress, Miss Casswell. All through the summer term we practised tennis in the evenings; sometimes at school, more often on the courts at Mr. Scott's house, The Firs; which (except for weekends, when he liked to play himself) he put entirely at the school's disposal.

We came to have a perfect understanding of each other's game. Broadly speaking, this amounted to the tacit knowledge that Carol would do the hard work along the baseline while I performed my pyrotechnics at the net. I was erratic: she was utterly reliable. On a good day I could take a love game on my service, but Carol never served a double fault.

As I see it now, it was an arrangement by which she did all the give and I the take. However, the combination worked. For two years in succession we won 'The Shield', the coveted trophy of the Lancashire Girls' Schools Lawn Tennis League. This tournament was the grand climax of the season, played at the Northern Tennis Club, on turf hallowed by the feet of stars from Wimbledon.

I have just found a snapshot of the pair of us, holding the Shield and grinning all over our young faces. We are wearing piqué skirts of the new length for sport, hem no lower than the bottom of the calf; white cotton stockings and serviceable cotton blouses, with high collars and long sleeves.

The sight of our costumes would undoubtedly give Mr. Teddy Tinling a heart attack, but I hope our court tactics would have been approved by Mrs. Sterry, the redoubtable player who won the Ladies' Single Championships at Wimbledon in 1895, 1896, 1898, 1901 and 1908 under her maiden name of Charlotte Cooper.

A few years ago, at the age of ninety-one, Mrs. Sterry gave a sprightly television interview about her impression of the current crop of girls at Wimbledon.

'There are some fine players these days,' she admitted, 'but I don't think they use enough of *this*' (tapping her forehead). The interviewer

MR. SCOTT DROPS IN FOR TEA

mumbled something and her voice rose sharply. 'Yes, head is what I said, young man. *Head*, not legs.'

Apart from the League, the big occasion of the school year was an entertainment in the spring term known simply as The Function. The function of The Function, I suppose, was to show our parents just how bright their children were, and how wisely their money was being spent. To this end there was acting not only in English but in French and German, and a great deal of enthusiastic singing.

Our music mistress, Mrs. Bridge, was the wife of Frank Bridge, leader of the second violins in the Hallé Orchestra. (Sometimes they would both come to supper and play for Mother in the South Room.) Mrs. Bridge was a first-rate pianist and a wonderfully inspiring teacher. There was something infectious about the way she played accompaniments that made even the least musical children want to join in and sing. 'The Old Superb', 'The Skye Boat Song', 'D'Ye Ken John Peel?', 'Rolling Down to Rio', 'Forty Years On'; we loved them all.

'Ich weiss nicht was soll es bedeuten
Das ich so traurig bin',

we sang joyously in chorus, to accompany a German play.

We may not have understood the half of what we sang, but what we learnt stayed with us and we made a happy noise. Mrs. Bridge had a knack of choosing music for The Function which could be made to sound exciting by mass enthusiasm in support of one or two good voices. Her cleverest find, perhaps, was George Rathbone's setting of the Longfellow poem 'Vogelweid the Minnesinger', a rich but simple piece of music well within the scope of young soloists and chorus. 'It's an oratorio,' I told Mother, 'all about monks and birds and a cathedral. It makes you feel *religious* somehow.' Secretly I thought it better than *The Messiah*.

I learnt my own way about the piano keyboard early, thanks to the efforts of Milly Cureton, my sister Juliet's friend. She was an admirable teacher, who liked her pupils to *enjoy* their music lessons, and never made the mistake of regarding all her geese as swans.

I was a goose as far as solo playing was concerned. It soon became apparent that I would never make a star performer, and had neither the talent nor the inclination to get beyond the easier Chopin preludes. The thing I really loved to do was play accompaniments. There was something deeply satisfying about that: to sit down at the piano and make a pleasant background noise to singing. So Miss Cureton taught me how to play accompaniments by every means within her power.

In piano duets I was allowed to play the bass, which is a form of accompaniment in its way. I learnt to use the pedals and read music fairly well at sight. I was taught to transpose and anticipate a singer's pauses. I was encouraged to buy or borrow vocal scores, and find my way freely about them. Above all, I was introduced to Gilbert and Sullivan opera, which was to play a big part in my life.

The first opera I saw was *Iolanthe*, done by an amateur society on the pier at Colwyn Bay. I knew the words; I knew the music; but nothing had prepared me for the *bulk* of all those dainty little fairies, tripping hither, panting thither in the opening number. (I learnt later that the professional trick is to put the more glamorous fairies into the chorus line, and infiltrate the larger ladies later.)

However, after a few moments of initial stupefaction I managed to adjust myself to this strange new form of spectacle. Long before the end I was madly in love with the local tailor who played the part of the Lord Chancellor.

For at least three days I haunted the neighbourhood of his shop in the Station Road, but to no avail. At last, in desperation, I tore a button off my coat and went into the shop to have it mended. I received prompt attention from a minion tailor, and left without a glimpse of the Lord Chancellor. And probably a good thing too.

About a year later Mother took me to see what I described in my diary as 'my first *real* Gilbert and Sullivan opera'. This was *The Mikado*, done by the D'Oyly Carte Company at the Prince's Theatre, Manchester.

'Oh, it was glorious!' I wrote with passion. 'The man who took Ko-Ko's part was the best of all, and Yum-Yum was awfully pretty. I'm terribly happy now, because I have the complete opera of my own, songs and words. We bought a copy of the words with our programme.'

I may have been terribly happy, but I was by no means satisfied. I began to collect and learn the scores, one after another. Sylvia had a pretty, true soprano, and I could take a light and fairly accurate second. We spent hours over those scores together, at the baby grand in the Hicksons' drawing-room, or the old upright in our South Room.

Every year the D'Oyly Carte Company came to Manchester; the sight of the red-and-black posters on the hoardings was synonymous with the arrival of spring. We went to see everything we could afford; booked seats when our parents were feeling extra generous, otherwise queuing for the pit. It was an exciting company in those days. 'The D'Oyly Carte Company includes,' I learn from a current programme,

'Fred Billington	Sydney Granville
Leicester Tunks	Elsie McDermid
Dewey Gibson	Nellie Briercliffe
Lyon Mackie	Phyllis Smith
Frederick Hobbs	Bertha Lewis
Leo Sheffield	Henry A. Lytton'

I became a passionate follower of the Company's progress, wherever it might take them up and down the country. I remember my blind rage one morning in the Rusholme Free Library when I read the horrible things a critic called Ernest Newman was writing about the Gilbert and Sullivan operas in the *Birmingham Daily Post*. He described W. S. Gilbert as 'a cumbrous joker', 'a manipulator of words', and suggested that the Savoy operas would stand a better chance of survival had Sullivan 'not been so unfortunate as to collaborate with Gilbert'.

In a round, fair schoolgirl hand I wrote a letter to the editor. When this was understandably ignored I wrote to Henry Lytton. 'Dear Mr. Lytton,' I began. 'Have you ever heard of a newspaper called the *Birmingham Daily Post*? We in Manchester are simply furious at the virulence with which Sir W. S. Gilbert was attacked. It seems scarcely credible that he should be spoken of with such obvious ignorance. Could not you or Mr. Billington intimate officially that Sullivan at least appreciated the libretto of *The Yeomen of the Guard*?'

Lytton replied promptly with a charming letter, handwritten, on the notepaper of a Birmingham hotel. It began with the intoxicating words 'Dear Madam', and went on with the perfect Jack Point idiom, 'Oh, the pity of it all.'

That letter is the prize exhibit in the fat, black exercise book which contains all my records of the Gilbert and Sullivan operas. There are programmes, cuttings from the *Manchester Guardian* and, attached to each programme and cutting, my own personal review of the performance. For by that time my pen was itching, and I knew more or less that I had to be a writer, and more or less the sort of things I meant to write.

GROWING UP

LET nobody suppose I had abandoned writing after the first, fine careless rapture of 'A Gaim of Crickit' and 'A Party'. These early works were followed by a book of fairy-tales (fully illustrated, in hard covers), a three-volume school story in penny notebooks, and a powerful contribution to non-fiction entitled 'The Seasons; or Spring, Summer, Autumn, Winter'; hand-sewn, as we had been taught at Lady Barn House.

Then there were all my gems of poetry. These are collected in a limp, red leather volume with the words 'Writing Album' inscribed in gold letters on the cover. The pages come in various pastel shades, and on the flyleaf I find the legend: 'F. M. Lejeune and C. A. Lejeune. VERY PRIVATE.' Franziska's contribution to Writing Album consists of two water-colour sketches, one of a wood anemone, the other of three primroses, marked neatly 'Silverdale, April 1895'.

My own work opens with a lyrical description of a sunset, which Helene used to refer to as 'The Bruise'. There follows a rather naughty piece named simply 'Farewell to Ladybarn House!' The exclamation mark presumably represents a note of personal exuberance. It was the custom, upon leaving Lady Barn, for every child to mount the platform where the teachers sat and make a speech. These speeches followed a prescribed pattern. 'I am very sorry to leave this school I have been very happy here I hope I shall be as happy at the next school I am presenting a few books to the library which I hope you'll like.' Merciful escape and loud applause.

When it came to my turn to leave I determined to have neither part nor lot in this sycophancy. I composed a poem for the occasion, and bullied poor Sylvia into delivering it on behalf of five of us. So she climbed the platform steps, looked at the assembled school over her owl spectacles and falteringly spoke the shocking words:

> 'When we first came to this school
> We very often broke a rule,
> And still, I'd have you understand,
> Though we are better, we're not very grand.
> We hope you will win every match,
> And never miss a single catch,
> Don't drop the ball and never say
> "Bad luck!" when really it's bad play.'

(This was an outrageous piece of parody, which made the staff look cornerwise at their headmistress.)

> 'Some books to the library we present
> And though you mayn't like them you must be content.
> Sylvia Hickson, the speaker, who
> Thinks this as silly as all of you,
> Sybil and Caroline, Margaret and Jeanne
> Have made this as short as they possibly can.'

The poem was received in an almost tumultuous hush, and Mother told me gently afterwards that I must learn to be more considerate of others.

Between the ages of twelve and eighteen I was a prolific versifier. Turning the delicately tinted pages of Writing Album, I find girlish effusions of every sort, from the wildly romantic 'The Phantom of Adventure' to the grimly realistic 'The Dentist', with its sinister refrain:

> 'Drill and stoppings and looking-glass,
> Glass and stoppings and drill,
> The years may pass and the ages pass,
> But these memories never will!'

There are Odes, Incantations, Valentines and Sonnets, addressed promiscuously to Night, Spring, Carol Samuels, a Dandie Dinmont,

E. Nesbit, Easedale Tarn, Arcadia, Daylight Saving and Sydney Carton. This last effort (on a pink page) is distinguished by a 'coda':

'It is glorious to live for one's country, to fight for one's faith
   and king,
But to give up one's life for a rival is a far, far better thing.'

Many of these poems were read aloud to the curate, for whom I had conceived a schoolgirl passion, when the poor fellow came round to play tennis and have tea at our house at Mother's somewhat reluctant invitation. There was one poem, however, which I never read him. I felt he would be shocked by its stark, outspoken daring. It was entitled 'Saturday Afternoon', with the odd acknowledgement 'after Walt Whitman'.

'Four o'clock and December. A heavy sky
With not one cloud to break its dull monotony.
A damp and chilly wind that seems to come from nowhere,
Bringing with it a drizzling rain.
The air is murky with yellow haze,
Hardly fog, but of the consistency of thin pea soup.
The distant houses are indistinguishable in the dim half-light.
Nearer at hand, rising from the haze, are rows of chimney pots and
   leafless trees.
The pavements are black and greasy, the road is a sea of mud.
There lies a bedraggled silence over all.
Even the sound of passing wheels is muffled.
Our back street is deserted, save for two errand boys carrying
   baskets,
The postman, a lamplighter and one quickly passing milk-cart.
On such a day as this the public houses are full.'

I quote this anti-poem, written in 1914, in its entirety, to show that youth changes very little through the generations, and that we old fogey sentimentalists enjoyed our dustbin period too.

In spite of this proliferance of verse and fiction, I doubt if anything of this kind that I wrote in schooldays did much to further my career. The big, green scrapbook was another matter.

Into this scrapbook I pasted the programmes of every play or pantomime to which I was taken, together with the *Manchester Guardian* reviews and my own attempts at criticism. (The Gilbert and Sullivan operas, as I have mentioned, had their separate volume.)

Here I find a notice of my first *Peter Pan*, with Zena Dare as Peter, and a little girl called Ela Q. May as Wendy. (She was familiarly known as Queenie, she had a doll almost as big as herself, and for some reason I was invited out to tea to meet her.) The Michael on that occasion was a curly-haired boy known as Master Philip Tonge. More than forty years later he wrote to me from Hollywood, where he was playing elderly character parts, thanking me for remembering him in a review of some film or other.

Here too is a glowing report of James Welch in *When Knights Were Bold*, and a somewhat dubious one of Florrie Ford as principal boy in *The Babes in the Wood*, singing 'Who, who, *who* is your lady friend?' I never really enjoyed pantomine, and I found Miss Ford's bust and thighs a trifle overwhelming.

Now comes an impression of the veteran Sarah Bernhardt, when she topped a variety bill at the Manchester Hippodrome, and a record of a Forbes Robertson's *Hamlet* during the actor's farewell tour. This had more than academic interest for me, since it turned out that Forbes Robertson was an old acquaintance of Professor Hickson's, and Sylvia and I were taken 'round behind' to meet him. My chief recollection of that first of countless visits backstage was the intoxicating smell of size and greasepaint. The actor himself I considered handsome, but rather disillusioningly small.

Later I find reviews of Martin Harvey in *The Only Way*, Lewis Waller in *The Three Musketeers*, most of Miss Horniman's productions at the old Gaiety and several plays I saw with Franziska during my first visit to London. Doris Keane in *Romance*, Renée Kelly in *Daddy Long Legs*, and *Dorothy*, a spectacular musical, with 'Chorus of Hop Pickers, Peasants, Huntsmen, etc., and FULL PACK OF ENGISH FOXHOUNDS.' I adored the foxhounds, but was a little shocked by the ethics of the hit number, 'Why should we wait till Tomorrow? You are Queen of My Heart Tonight'.

All my reviews are appallingly florid and lacking in any sense of moderation; for where I loved, I loved intensely, and when I hated, I hated hard.

But I notice with interest that they are always independent, often in direct contradiction to the official criticism pasted up beside them. For example, I seem to have detected something spurious in the quality of the applause for Sarah Bernhardt in that final Hippodrome appearance. 'Was it,' I wrote, 'the great actress we were cheering to the roof, or the lamed, courageous Frenchwoman triumphing over her disability?' I was beginning to use my own judgement, even if that judgement was often wrong.

What is more important, perhaps, in the story of what was to happen later, is that my comments gradually settled into the pattern required of all useful newspaper reviewing. I began to state facts first and give opinions second. This I am sure I learnt from a study of the *Manchester Guardian* cuttings. From them I also learnt to keep reviews in compass. I didn't count the words as I would later, but subconsciously I grew to know that curtness and overwriting are both bad habits.

There are no reviews of films in this early scrapbook, because when I first became aware of these exciting things they were still considered to be not quite proper. In spite of *Punch*'s daring couplet,

'Please take off my pinny, Ma,
And take me to the cinema',

well-conducted ladies were expected to attend only such classics as *Cabiria*, *Quo Vadis*, *Les Miserables*, and later on *The Birth of a Nation* and *Intolerance*.

My early visits to the local cinema were not exactly clandestine. That is to say, Mother knew about them, and was generally prepared to give me sixpence ('for one of the *clean* seats') on a Saturday afternoon, when I insisted that I *must* see that week's instalment of *The Perils of Pauline* or *The Exploits of Elaine*. But they were made with caution, and involved a good deal of concealment behind cardboard cut-outs, when one of our At Home Day callers was sighted in the distance. Mother wouldn't have minded in the slightest, but something told me that the callers would.

Apart from serials, my taste in films at that time ran to sweetness-and-light or Westerns; Mary Pickford, Marguerite Clark, William S. Hart and the newcomer Douglas Fairbanks. A little later I was captivated by the romantic profile of the young John Barrymore (what girl wasn't?) and the exotic, almost sinister allure of the actress whom we knew as Nazzimova.

The one sort of film that I could not abide was slapstick comedy. I loathed the Keystone Cops and fretted through the antics of the screen's greatest comic genius. I didn't find Charlie Chaplin funny. I thought him rather low.

In time my brain taught me to correct these first impressions. I learnt to acclaim the art of slapstick in the cinema, but I never really learnt to like it.

This is something I tried to keep dark all through my tenure of office as a critic. I find it very difficult to laugh aloud, except when something like an Osbert Lancaster cartoon takes me by surprise, or at some particularly fatuous TV commercial. I salute the unique skill of Chaplin. I recognize his supreme importance in the early history of the cinema. I know that in his time he was one of the world's most subtle drolls. But, since this book is meant to be an honest book, I'm bound to say that with the exception of *Monsieur Verdoux* I never wholeheartedly enjoyed a Chaplin film.

The First World War broke out when I was seventeen, heralded (or so I chose to think) by a setting August sun the colour of a blood-orange. I can still recall that sunset, and the way it stained the pale walls of our South Room; but looking back on the war as a whole, it is strange to realize how very little impact it had on the life of a provincial schoolgirl.

We played our tennis matches and sat for our examinations. I went on writing theatre notices and poems; including a special poem for the curate, who had succeeded in shaking off his female adorers in the parish by joining Kitchener's Second Army as a chaplain.

I read the war news sometimes and glanced at the long casualty lists with a due sense of solemnity, but there was no name in particular that I dreaded finding. I had no friends of military age. Of my three brothers, only Arnold was involved. Alick, the clergyman, was attached to a railway mission in South Africa. Russell, the sheep-farmer, tried to join up in Australia, but was rejected by the medical board. (Varicose veins, the family heritage, exacerbated by much hard riding.) Arnold did reach the trenches, but didn't stay there very long. He was an early victim of a gas attack, which mercifully left no lasting effects, but brought about his discharge as unfit.

One day I found Mother crying very bitterly, and she told me, as she splashed cold water on her face, that my cousin Graeme West was killed. I felt sorry, but no more than that. I hadn't seen Graeme since he was a little boy, and performed the orange-sucking act with his brother Cecil in our old dining-room at Wilmslow Road. He was a kind and gentle little boy, and as a baby I was fond of him. But that was fifteen years ago. It would be another twenty years until I read *The Diary of a Dead Officer*, and learnt from Professor Joad, Graeme's closest friend at Oxford, the full pity of his story.

Life, for a girl of my age in a northern city, went on very much as usual. I can recall no sense of danger. We did hear a maroon once, when a Zeppelin was sighted far away, but no 'incident' followed, and I was quite annoyed to be hustled out of my warm bed for nothing. There was rationing, of course, but that was our parents' problem and not ours. Personally, I was far too busy with my own affairs to notice any difference between butter and margarine.

The time had nearly come for leaving school, and the question of my future was still undecided. I think there must have been some idea that I should follow Franziska to Somerville, or Helene to Lady Margaret Hall; for instead of sitting for matriculation, like most of the Sixth Form girls at Withington, I was sent up to Oxford to take responsions.

We were lodged in Oriel, during the men's long vacation. Everyone was very friendly, particularly the Principal of Somerville, who invited me to coffee, and seemed eager to find a place for Franziska Lejeune's young sister.

But I hated every moment of my stay there. It rained and thundered for three days. I was going through one of my worst monthly periods, which racked me with pain and made me very sick. The narrow bed and confined cell of a student's room filled me with claustrophobia. If this was college life, I thought, I wanted no part of it. The train that took me back to Manchester seemed like a rescuing and kindly dragon.

Of course I was glad, some ten days later, to get the telegram that told me I had passed responsions. I took a long walk in the smutty fields to celebrate the news. But there and then I determined not to go to Somerville or any other residential college. Home was the place for me, I decided; home as a base for work, home to come back to in the evenings. I have never found cause to change my mind.

This obstinacy left Mother with an awkward problem. What *was* to be done with me when I left school? For some reason, writing was never considered seriously as a profession, although Miss Grant did suggest that I might try my hand at 'one or two nice little things for *Punch*'. (What a hope! Never in my long career did I reach such heights of glory.) Teaching was out of the question without a degree. A hopeful attempt to make me useful about the kitchen was thwarted when our invaluable and usually forbearing cook threatened to give notice. (Or 'warning', as we called it in those days.)

As a measure of desperation it was decided that a secretarial course would do me no harm for the time being. I had no particular objection. It left me strictly uncommitted, and free to go on with my private writing.

So I took the train daily into Manchester, and at the excellent establishment of one Miss Wilkinson (a lady of discreet demeanour whom I shall always associate with the scent of cachous) learnt to type reasonably well and take Pitman's shorthand at reporting speed. The less said about my attempts at book-keeping the better. I was the despair of the frock-coated chartered accountant who came once a week to instruct us in the mysteries of double entry. 'Tut-tut, little lady,' he would say, breathing heavily down my back. 'Tut *tut*, we can do better than that, little lady. We're not *thinking*, are we now?'

We weren't and we couldn't be. Figures have always been blind symbols to me. For years Mother had struggled in vain to make me keep accounts correctly. Sylvia always helped me with my arithmetic homework. An odd nought here and there seemed to me of small importance. In spite of my defaults of book-keeping, I left Miss Wilkinson's after a few months with a scroll known as a Teacher's Diploma, and landed a plum job as private secretary to Mr. Fiddes, the Registrar of Manchester University.

Looking back on it, I can only think that the appointment was largely an affair of nepotism. My qualifications were good enough, but no better than those of several of Miss Wilkinson's young ladies. However, Mr. Fiddes had a niece, Jean Campbell, who lived with him and the sister who kept house for him. At that time she was my most intimate friend. We were constantly in and out of each other's homes.

So I suppose it was only natural that the Registrar should consider me when I was looking for a job and he was looking for a secretary.

Jean was a rare girl with a grave, attractive face, and the most brilliant and responsive mind I had ever yet encountered. Ours was an intimacy of the imagination. We revelled in the same books, enjoyed the same turns of phrase; our letters to each other were full of shared allusion.

She introduced me to Du Maurier's *Trilby*, and the still more treasured *Peter Ibbotson*. I can't remember which of us discovered Murger's *Vie de Bohème*, but it was another common bond.

We collaborated on a novel, to be called *Equal Thanks*. We wrote alternate chapters, keeping them secret to surprise each other. The scene was the Latin Quarter of Paris. The characters, though outwardly bohemian, were at heart obstinately and whimsically English. They might live in sin; they might paint freak pictures upside down; but there was always a jar of bronze chrysanthemums reflected from the polished surface of the table.

This novel kept us busy for the best part of a year. (Since neither of us had ever been to Paris, it involved a deal of topographical research with maps and guide-books.) Fortunately, perhaps, it was never finished. Before we could write our way to the bitter-sweet conclusion both of us were claimed by other interests. Jean went up to Newnham; and I was spending all my spare time watching and listening to grand opera, with which I had fallen head over heels in love.

6

WHO FISHED THE MUREX UP?

THOSE were the great days of the Beecham Opera Company, and what a company it was! Mullings, Radford, Allin, Austin, Ranalow, Brandram, Thornton, Licette, Nevada, Ellinger. Beecham himself to conduct, among other things, the Mozart operas; young Eugene Goossens, the Puccini; Albert Coates for *Boris Godounov* and *Prince Igor*.

We had a long season every winter, and usually another in the summer. Manchester, with its proud tradition of the Hallé, has always been a music-loving city. Except for one or two operas, such as *Samson and Delilah*, which never seemed to catch the public fancy, there was seldom an empty seat in the house.

Somebody gave me a ticket for a matinée of *Tosca*, and from then on my devotion to opera has never wavered. It is still my favourite form of entertainment; but in the theatre only, not the living-room. I can't endure to have it hacked about and edited, presented with huge, gaping close-ups and filmed inserts of scenes which the composer rightly left to the imagination, to provide a 'version' for the television screen.

Within a couple of years I had run through the Beecham repertoire from end to end; from *Faust* to *Falstaff*; *Carmen* to *Coq D'Or*, *Tannhäuser* to *Parsifal* and *The Mastersingers*. My favourites, notably *Otello*, *La Bohème* and *The Marriage of Figaro*, I saw time and time again.

With Beecham at the conductor's desk, *Figaro* was as exhilarating as dry champagne. (A modern simile; we didn't drink champagne in Burlington Road.) *Otello* remains my first love among operas; *Un bacio* the most moving of all operatic themes. And I still cannot resist another nibble at *La Bohème*'s frosted mixture of meringues and cream.

54

The thin ice-tinkle of music at the beginning of the third act, out in the snow, waiting for the gates to open, sends a delightful shiver down my spine. Even though *Equal Thanks* was left unfinished, I never quite outgrew my taste for Murger.

I daresay my interest in the Beecham Company would have remained academic but for something that happened at this time in our home life. *I* may not have felt the pinch of war, but others had.

'About a fortnight ago,' I wrote to Jean, 'Mother suddenly decided that this house was too big for us, and we should move into another on the spot. After a considerable amount of trouble I dissuaded her, but out of the ashes of that plan has risen the phantom of A Paying Guest. The wife of someone on the *Manchester Guardian* thinks she knows someone we should like.'

The Paying Guest duly arrived, and my report continues:

'She comes for a month on appro.: she works in some Government department: she brings an extra ton of coal and more food coupons: her sister—hold your breath now—is our favourite Mimi, Bessie Tyas. I didn't manœuvre this; the Fates did. Comments, please.'

I have no record of Jean's comments, but in any case they would be superfluous. The month on appro. proved a great success and Dora Tyas became a permanent boarder for as long as her job lasted. She was a charming and considerate person, devoted to Mother and invincibly cheerful. I don't think she was musical herself. I can't remember that she went much to the opera. But it was natural that through her we came to know her sister Bessie, and many other members of the Beecham Company.

Bessie was a darling. She was young and slight, with a sudden, sparkling smile, a gentle voice and big, brown eyes like a doe's. Her taste in clothes was exquisite, and I shall never forget the filmy lingerie that she passed on to me when, as far as she was concerned, its day was over. These wisps of silk and lace needed only a tiny darn, a catch of thread here and there, which I duly gave them. I never used them, but kept them wrapped in tissue paper simply to admire. Nothing in my Jaeger-clad and bloomered youth had taught me that such underwear existed.

Apart from Bessie Tyas, the members of the company whom I knew best were Frederic Austin and Frederick Ranalow, Sylvia Nelis, a pint-sized coloratura who sang the Queen of the Night in *The Magic*

Flute, Edith Clegg, whom I think of as the eternal Suzeki, punching holes in the backcloth for Madam Butterfly to watch through, and her room-mate, Clytie Hine, a long-legged mezzo-soprano from Australia, who looked well in tights and seemed doomed to play such thankless parts as the lovelorn Siebel in *Faust*.

Mother didn't share my enthusiasm for grand opera. In one of the diaries that she kept during her finishing-school days abroad I find the entry: 'Elberfeld, September 1874. Last Tuesday we went to the opera and I have made the resolution not to go again. I think it is a waste of time and money.' To the best of my belief she never did.

All the same she welcomed the Beecham singers to our house, and even invited Frederic Austin's daughter, Freda, to stay with us during one of the Company's long seasons. Freda was about my own age, perhaps a little younger. She had a London smartness which I much admired, and I made up my mind to buy a hat with a small veil like hers at the earliest possible opportunity.

She was a nice child, though, and not nearly as sophisticated as she looked. I well remember the shock she gave me on the first afternoon of her visit, when she asked me please to take her to a grocer's shop. I waited on the pavement, and she came out clutching a large bottle. 'It's for Daddy,' she explained naïvely; 'he simply can't sing Iago without his Wincarnis.'

My obsession with the Beecham Opera Company lasted for several years, during which I must have been exceedingly exhausting to live with. I don't propose to dwell on it, since it had no more to do with the shaping of a critic than had my passionate attempt at novel-writing: but each, in its way, was a sort of education, a part of the inexorable process of growing up.

Meanwhile, my formal education had taken a fresh turn. After a year as secretary to the Registrar it was suggested—I don't remember now by whom—that I should join the University as a student and read for a degree in English.

Since responsions did not qualify as an entrance examination for the northern universities, only for Oxford, I had to take a paper in an extra subject. It should have been geometry, only I had been cast out of the geometry class at the age of twelve as a hopeless dullard, and French was permitted as a substitute.

I prepared myself lightheartedly for this paper by reading Merimée's *Carmen*, Pierre Loti's *Madame Chrysanthème*, *La Vie de Bohème* for a second time, and the libretto of Charpentier's *Louise*, which was currently shocking the good citizens of Manchester.

> '*Depuis le jour ou je me suis donnée,*
> *Toute fleurie semble ma destinée.*
> *Je crois rêver dans un ciel de féerie,*
> *Mon âme encore grisée de ton premier baiser.*'

Not at all the thing for a city which would not countenance Sunday concerts.

To brush up my grammar, I went through a pile of old matriculation papers until I found an exercise that took my fancy. It was based on Beaumarchais' *Barbière de Seville*, and required the candidate to turn such sentences as the following into French:

'(1) The Count had merely to show himself in order to win the day.
   (Use "*afin de*" with infinitive.)
 (2) The Count is not at all handsome, he might almost be called ugly.
   (Use impersonal construction with "*on*".)
 (3) It would be better to stay quietly at home, instead of running after the Count.
   (Use "*il vaut mieux*".)'

These sentences I found considerably more stimulating than questions designed to test my knowledge of the Use of the Auxiliary Verb, or Conjunctions which take the Subjunctive Mood.

I passed the French examination without trouble, and it was only after I had enrolled as a first-year student in the English School that I began to have misgivings.

'I wonder,' I wrote to Jean during the first week of term, 'why the blank blank I threw up a good job which made me happy, just because I imagined that I had a brain which was made for higher things than earning twenty-five shillings a week as a secretary? I think I must be mad.'

These misgivings turned out to be largely justified. Other people speak with warmth and affection of their years at Manchester University; but I was a misfit from the start.

The maladjustment was partly my own fault, partly the effect of circumstances. I came into the lecture theatre from the wrong side of the footlights. I had few illusions about the members of the Faculty, because I knew so much about them.

Many of them were familiar figures of my childhood, fathers of my school-friends, judged long ago and found to be either satisfactory or wanting. Others were colleagues of the Registrar's, to whom or about whom I was accustomed to Take a Letter.

I knew just which of them were wartime substitutes, keeping the job warm for someone in the Forces; which were likely to be promoted and which likely to retire; who had, and who had not, a voice in the inner councils of the college. The Registrar himself was irreproachably discreet, but some of his associates were less so; and there is very little that escapes the notice of a normally observant private secretary.

If my attitude towards the lectures was unfortunate, so were my relations with the students. It was the autumn of 1918 and I was over twenty-one. The other members of my class were fresh from school. I was too old and sophisticated for them: they were too young and earnest for me.

None of them had grown up in the world of Manchester that I knew. Some of them came from places as remote as Hull, Keighley and Chester. They lived in one or other of the Halls of Residence, where they had their own communal affairs and interests. Most of them intended to be teachers.

I found it difficult to make new friends. Of my old friends, Margaret Tout was in her final year in the History School; Sylvia, in her second or third year as a medical student, spent most of her time in hospitals or attending classes in a building separate from the main university block. We saw very little of each other.

Stupidly perhaps, but ineluctably, I began to adopt a Garbo attitude towards university life. I wanted to be alone. Quite deliberately I cut myself off from the social activities of the college. There were dances, but I didn't go to them. There were lectures by distinguished visitors, which I rarely took the trouble to attend.

There was a lively and progressive Women's Union, which tried hard for a time to get me interested in its debates, its pet causes (the W.E.A. was one of them) and its internal politics. I found the pressure difficult to dodge, for there are few people in the world as tough as a band of thoroughly determined, administrative women.

However, I escaped them in the end, and continued all through my college career to regard the Union less as a body than a building; a highly superior sort of Ladies' Toilet and Rest Room, also useful as an accommodation address.

At lunchtime I avoided the busy, clamorous canteen, and slipped away to a confectioner's shop where I was certain I should meet nobody I knew. Its name was Weigenthaler's; in the old days Mother had a regular order there for the Othellos, Desdemonas and other creamy delights which she used to give her visitors for Sunday tea.

Of course such luxuries had vanished long ago. We were in the fourth year of the war by this time. But though the choice was small, everything that Weigenthaler's sold was good. I would take a book, find a corner table, and lunch on a brioche and a cup of chocolate in blessed peace.

Perhaps the ugliest part of college life to me was the importunity of the Student Rags; when gangs of large young men, often dressed in women's clothes, would hold up the traffic, board the trams and menace the timid passers-by, shaking collecting boxes.

I think it was in those days that I conceived a loathing for the sight of men made up and dressed as women which has never left me. (I get much the same feeling of revulsion when forced to look at those bloated heads which people wear in carnival processions, or limp guys carted round the streets at the beginning of November.)

Thirty-five years later I found it physically impossible to sit through a Hollywood comedy called *Some Like It Hot*, which was much praised by the critics. The sight of Tony Curtis and Jack Lemmon, thinly disguised as girls, pressing their painted faces against the cheeks of Marilyn Monroe, and batting their beastly beaded eyelashes, filled me with nausea and sent me rushing to the cloakroom.

I believe that any honourable critic, if pressed, would admit to some such idiosyncrasy. It may take the form of a horror of heights, or a shrinking from displays of mental abnormality.

It is a weakness which must be recognized, fought and conquered; an exercise which is possible, but far from easy. It is one of the reasons why criticism can never become an exact science; so long as it is practised not by automata but by human beings such as you and me.

My years at college would most likely have been wasted, and certainly remained a gloomy memory, had it not been for one remarkable character: our English tutor, H. B. Charlton. It was the greatest stroke of luck for me that I fell into this man's hands at that particular moment. His ruthless treatment was exactly what I needed. Nothing less drastic would have served.

He was a Yorkshireman, with all the tough attributes of his county, who had recently come to Manchester as assistant to the veteran Professor Herford. His caustic tongue, abrupt manner and newfangled ideas of teaching made him by no means uniformly popular, and the Faculty had not found him easy to assimilate.

From my point of vantage in the Registrar's office I had heard a good deal of loose talk about Charlton. He was tubercular and wouldn't stay the course. He was a Bolshevik and would destroy the University. He was only kept on as a wartime substitute, and would find himself out on his ear, you'd see, the instant that the war was over.

Mr. Fiddes, the wise Registrar, would listen patiently to these outbursts; pass a diplomatic hand over his small, Macmillan moustache, and achieve a masterpiece of saying nothing. In due course Charlton was to succeed Herford in the Chair of English Literature, and occupy it with distinction until he retired.

That was after my time, however. I shall always think of him as I first knew him: a dark, dramatic person in the early thirties, with violent movements and a mocking voice, an academic Heathfield. Browning, Shakespeare and Dante were his specialities; his Browning was magnificent. His entrances to a seminar *were* entrances. He would swing suddenly into the room, shabby gown flapping; pause for a moment; then fling himself into a chair, one leg hooked over the arm; put his fingertips together and bark out something addressed apparently to a corner of the ceiling, but clearly designed for the discomfiture of one of us.

I was the one who seemed elected to get most of the rough edge of his tongue. I can see why now, although I couldn't then. He thought me snobbish, self-centred and opinionated; which indeed I was. He thought me old enough to stand it; which the others weren't. And I think he saw I had the makings of a creditable First, if only I could be bullied into working.

His methods were drastic, but they got results. He made me so angry that I worked like a devil just to *show* him. He was a brilliant tutor, and my debt to him is boundless. In spite of our constant brushes, we understood each other very well.

Charlton was not a man to encourage familiarity between staff and students, yet in some way he seemed able to divine exactly what was passing in our minds. When the time came for doling out the subjects for our final thesis he showed a knowledge of his class that was quite uncanny.

Our special period was the eighteenth century, and precisely the right students were allotted Pope, Swift, the novel, the periodicals, the political writers. When it came to my turn he fixed his gaze on that favourite corner of the ceiling, and remarked in a very dry voice indeed, 'Miss Lejeune, I propose that you should try your hand at opera in the eighteenth century.'

The clever devil, what a cunning choice that was! It allowed for my preoccupations; it offered a challenge which he knew I would not be able to resist; it involved a great deal of hard and specialized research; and in the last instance it presented the examiners with a recondite subject in which they were less likely to be informed than I was.

That thesis was the first really stiff piece of work that I had ever done, and it was impossible not to grow absorbed in it. So far, my approach to opera had been emotional; now it had to become factual and critical.

The background must be wide enough to cover the whole field of sung drama from Peri to Wagner and Verdi. The foreground was busy with eighteenth-century scenes; the Handel operas, which were the rage of the town in the days of Addison and Steele; the fruity battles between supporters of rival singers; the emergence of the ballad opera, and the history of its rise and fall in the sixty-odd years between Gay and Dibdin.

It was an exclusive story and I revelled in it. University life no longer worried me; I was far too much absorbed to notice. Nobody, I found, had done much work on the ballad opera, apart from a few sketchy histories of *The Beggar's Opera* (which Nigel Playfair was reviving at that time in London, with a score by my old friend Frederic Austin) and its short-lived successor *Polly*.

By a great stroke of luck, I found a hoard of forgotten ballad operas in the basement of a second-hand bookshop. I bought the lot for a few shillings, which is about all that they were worth, artistically. But with their long esses, their staves of contemporary folksong and their lively topical allusions, they were undoubtedly collector's pieces, and added the needed touch of novelty to my thesis.

The end product must have been reasonably impressive, since it bamboozled the authorities into giving me a first-class degree and a graduate scholarship. As things turned out, I was never to make use of either; but I couldn't know that at the time.

7

FIRST VENTURES INTO PRINT

DURING my first year at college I surreptitiously became a journalist. I can't for the life of me remember how this happened, but I do know that it was something rather hush-hush, which must on no account reach the ears of the university authorities.

My first venture into print was an anonymous little piece in the *Guardian*'s Woman's Page about books for children. It was followed, a few weeks later, by a review of a National Sunday League Concert, with Desirée Ellinger and our old friend Frank Bridge among the soloists.

I was critical, I find, of Miss Ellinger's choice of songs ('She is essentially a lyrical, not a dramatic singer, although her voice is gaining in argumentative power and weight'), but I gave Mr. Bridge a big hand ('He played an Andantino of Martini, and a Preludium of Bach, and showed in both that he is a musical colourist of the first rank'). Flown by the sound of my own words, I went on to discover that 'one could not but be struck by the similarity in quality between the highest notes of his violin and those of Miss Ellinger's voice when it is most pure and delicate'.

This piece of arrant nonsense appears over the initials L.C. I was rather pleased, not only with the review, but with my choice of signature. Subtle enough, I thought, to hide my true identity, but not entirely barefaced lying, since they *were* my initials in reverse. Besides, there was another advantage. Samuel Langford, the *Guardian*'s music critic, invariably signed his articles S.L. My own L.C., I thought, sufficiently approached the classic pattern; and if any reader happened to glance through the paper carelessly . . . well, I was not too proud

63

to be mistaken for the master. I *was* writing about music, after all.

For some reason which I can't determine, except that Sammy Langford was elderly, probably overworked and may have been thankful to let anybody take the worst chores off his hands, I was allowed to go on writing occasional pieces about music.

There were several midday concerts, mostly chamber music, for which I fell back shamelessly on programme notes. There were a few minor musical comedies, of which the only one that stays in my memory is *The Lilac Domino*. The circumstances of the first night were unusual. The unhappy company arrived bedraggled in a pea-soup fog; the curtain rose forty minutes late; and 'the indulgence of the audience' (all twenty of us) was 'craved for any inadequacies in the presentation'. It turned out that all the scenery and most of the costumes, including the essential domino, had been left behind at Crewe.

In the spring of 1921 came the first big excitement. The black-and-red posters of the D'Oyly Carte Company made their annual appearance on the hoardings, and unbelievably L.C. was asked to cover the first three nights of the season.

At the time I fondly imagined that someone in the *Guardian* office recognized me as a Gilbert and Sullivan specialist. A far more plausible explanation was suggested to me quite recently by Derek Oldham at a Savoyard dinner. 'Sammy Langford hated our guts,' he said. 'He told our manager that he would never review the operas again if he could possibly avoid it. The audiences in Manchester were wonderful, but reading the *Guardian* notice next morning in Sammy's days was agony.'

This accords with my own memories of Sam Langford. He was a musical perfectionist and a great local character. His hobby was the cultivation of delphiniums, and I'm told he kept a splendid market garden. His Lancashire accent was as rich as a fine, fruity Eccles cake. His formal clothes were very dark, and his aggressive beard was very white.

He couldn't stand fools gladly, but for some reason he was always temperate with me. Sometimes we would share a cab back to Withington from the *Guardian* office in Cross Street. I would chatter nervously and artlessly, but never once did he make fun of my naïve enthusiasms.

However, during this D'Oyly Carte season of March 1921 he gave me my first sharp lesson in the art of journalism. I had written what seemed to me a beautiful and profound notice of *The Yeomen of the*

Guard, which appeared duly in the *Guardian*. The next night, sent to review *The Gondoliers*, I caught sight of Sammy Langford leaning against a pillar in the stalls.

He had obviously dropped in for a few minutes to make his own check, and was preparing to slip away in the interval when I rashly accosted him.

'Oh, Mr. Langford,' I said breathlessly, 'I do hope my notice was all right last night?'

Swivelling on his heel and speaking in his broadest Lancashire he told me: 'It doozn't matter what tha writes, lass. If they doan't see my initials at the bottom, they woan't read it anyway.'

When Samuel Langford said 'they' he meant the regular readers of the *Guardian*, the central core of educated Manchester opinion. This remark was no rebuke, but a plain statement of fact. It has taken me half a lifetime to recognize how true it was. The fidelity of newspaper readers to their favourite columnists is something that must be experienced to be believed.

How often you hear people say, 'We took the Such-and-Such for So-and-So's column, and now he's gone we've given it up and changed to the other paper.' Or, discussing a new book or play or film: 'What does X say about it?' 'It isn't X this week, he's gone on holiday. It's somebody called Y.' 'Oh, is that all? Then I shan't bother to read it.'

Even today, two years after my retirement, I get Christmas cards and letters from unknown correspondents, with touching messages, 'We still miss you every Sunday', or The *Observer* isn't the same without you'. Of course, every gap can be filled, and every journalist is forgotten in time, but so long as he reigns supreme over a column he commands amazing loyalty from his readers.

For all newspaper reports, however, there is another kind of 'They', who react in quite a different way from the habitual reader. These are the people directly concerned with the success or failure of the subject under review; in the case of entertainment the producer, the publicists and the performers themselves. Especially the performers.

It is of small consequence to them whose signature appears at the top or bottom of the column, so long as their names are printed squarely in the middle. They have their own simple standards. If their work is praised it's a good notice. If their work is damned, or worse still ignored, it's a bad notice. If some subtlety which they have struggled to perfect is picked out for special mention it's a wonderful notice.

These subtleties are things that often catch a fresh reporter's eye but tend to be neglected by the regular reviewer. Alexander Korda always used to say that the people who understood his films best were the substitute writers who took over the column while the first-string critics were on holiday. There may have been some grain of truth in this, for an accustomed viewer tends to see what he expects to see, whereas a novice is on the watch for anything.

I remember being greatly struck once by a remark of Michael Redgrave's. 'You ought to look at every performance as if you were seeing the performer for the first time,' he said. This approach, to a veteran critic, is just as proper as it is difficult.

My ingenuous reviews of the Gilbert and Sullivan operas may have been ignored by readers of the *Manchester Guardian*, but they caused a small stir in the company. There was, as I learnt later, a good deal of speculation about the identity of this man L.C., who discovered subtleties in the performance where S.L. had only suffered boredom.

The Pirates of Penzance, I pointed out, can succeed only if it is consciously performed in mock-heroic style. 'Mabel's valse song, "Poor Wandering One", has become so familiar out of its dramatic setting as a concert number that one is apt to forget its intrinsic connection with the previous bit of chorus work. In its own context the song is sheer mock heroism, and no soprano, however gifted, should attempt to sing it if she lacks a sense of humour.'

This was hot stuff by the customary standards of provincial D'Oyly Carte reviewing, but my comments on *The Yeomen of the Guard* surprised them even more.

'Jack Point,' I wrote, with what amounted almost to *lèse-majesté*, 'is the acknowledged central figure, but he has his niche chiselled out for him by some very heavy concerted work on the part of the other principals, in whose hands lies the ultimate unity of the opera.

'Colonel Fairfax is generally regarded as a foolproof tenor part, with all the advantages of his sentimental aria "Is Life a Boon?" In fact, he is one of the least lovable of Gilbert's heroes. He has a tendency, with inexpert handling, to appear a fool in the first act and a knave in the second; but Mr. Oldham has the genius to accept the character with all its flaws, and raise it to something approaching lovableness by a perplexed consciousness of its own deficiency.'

To round off this startling review, I praised Mr. Darrell Fancourt for his performance as Sergeant Meryll, 'a somewhat thankless part'.

'Mr. Fancourt has already proved himself to be a singer of unusual dramatic power, and to this he now adds a subtlety of interpretation which transforms a minor character into a chronicler of events, and invests with new life a pivotal, but usually neglected, figure of the drama.'

I quote these pompous extracts just to show that if I wasn't very fluent as a critic I was at least beginning to rely on my own judgement. Also I was in a fair way to making friends, as I was soon to learn.

Since childhood it had been my amiable habit to walk up to anybody that I liked the look of and say hollo. This tactic had worked with a concert-party comedian, a Wimbledon tennis-player, the driver of a steam-roller (though this proved more difficult, since he was a proud man with a sense of protocol) and a pretty chorus girl called Ruby, with whom I was soon drinking stout out of a tooth-mug and eating salad from a cracked washbasin.

So it seemed quite natural to me to waylay Darrell Fancourt, as he was walking up Quay Street to the tram-stop, after a matinée of *Ruddigore*.

'Hallo, Mr. Fancourt,' I told him in my artless fashion, 'I'm Caroline Lejeune and I've been reviewing some of the operas for the *Manchester Guardian*. I wish I could have reviewed *Ruddigore*, because I haven't seen it before, and I like the way you sing "The Ghosts' High Noon".'

He looked me up and down and said, 'Don't tell me you're the mysterious L.C.?'

'I *sign* myself L.C.,' I replied with gravity, 'but that's a pseudonym, because I'm still at the University and they mustn't know about it.'

He threw back his head and roared with laughter. I couldn't quite see why, because I hadn't said anything particularly funny. When he had finished laughing he shook hands with me and said: 'I'm sorry, but you took me by surprise. Are you busy, or will you come back to tea and tell my wife about it? I know she'd love to meet you.'

So I went back to tea and that was the beginning of thirty years of friendship with the Fancourts. Through them I got to know Derek Oldham, and found, to my amazement, that the D'Oyly Carte's star tenor had a sister who sang in the choir of what we still called 'Grandfather's Chapel'.

Of all my remembrances of these Savoyard friends perhaps the most vivid is the night when they smuggled me up into the flies to watch a performance of *H.M.S. Pinafore*. It was Easter Monday and the house was packed. There wasn't a seat to be had for love or money.

From my exalted perch—although perch is hardly the word, since I had nothing to perch on and stood throughout the show—I could see the tiny stage below; like a kitchen rug, I thought, crawling with human beetles; the players waiting to make their entrances from the prompt side; and to my right, tier upon tier, the banked multitude of the Bank Holiday crowd.

Many years later I would tell this story in a programme of *Desert Island Discs*, and to this day I have never forgotten the experience.

To the reader who gets this book out of the library because somebody told her it was written by a film critic, and has been impatiently turning over the pages to find where films come into it, I can now bring words of comfort. Take heart, good reader, you are getting warm.

A young person has the capacity to live in a great many worlds at once; and at about the same time that L.C. was reviewing Gilbert and Sullivan operas in the *Manchester Guardian*, and Miss Lejeune, English Honours student at the University, was exploring the mysteries of ballad opera in the eighteenth century, a 'back-pager' appeared in the *Guardian* over the initials C.L., entitled 'The Undiscovered Aesthetic'.

This was an impassioned plea, running to a full column, for recognition by 'discriminating persons' of the new art form, the kinematograph.

'That it remains undiscovered as yet is no shame, for kinematography has barely grown beyond childhood, and her powers are not fully developed. Shame however it is, and black shame, that the finer intelligences, the more perceptive critics, should ignore the need for discovery and allow the young art to mature unworthily for lack of sympathetic guidance. . . .

'What realms of experience can the new materials of kinematography most perfectly express? The instruments of the scenario-maker are borrowed on the one hand from drama and on the other from painting; here is the one art which can represent actions successive through time and objects adjacent in space; thereby confusing, more completely than the rhythmic school in painting or the descriptive school in music, Lessing's famous distinctions of the arts.'

I shall never know why C. P. Scott agreed to print this article, whether as an act of mercy or out of the liberality of his views on current attitudes. But I know exactly how I came to write it. I was in my last term at college and the problem of my future had become acute. Somehow or other I should have to earn a living. I was no true scholar and had no aptitude for teaching. There didn't seem much future in a secretarial job at twenty-five shillings a week. I knew by now that writing, the setting down of words on paper, was my one small talent. But my mind was not inventive. The stories I made up were stories without an end; I found it difficult to create original plots and characters.

It was a hot summer afternoon, and I had been to see Douglas Fairbanks in *The Mark of Zorro*, when my goal in life suddenly dawned on me. 'I won't say there was a blinding flash,' as Jean Kerr writes in *Please Don't Eat the Daisies*, 'just a poignance, a suspension of time, a sweet recognition of the moment of truth not unlike that memorable instant in which Johnny Weismuller first noticed that he was Tarzan and *not* Jane.'

I was going to be a film critic. Why not? I had to be *something*, and preferably something which would combine writing with the entertainment world. I was not enchanted by the cinema as I had always been enchanted by the theatre, but I enjoyed it. Why shouldn't I turn this enjoyment into profit, and earn my living by reviewing films?

Such an idea would seem not in the least remarkable to a young woman nowadays. But at that time, soon after the First World War, it was a very strange and bold idea indeed.

Moving pictures were still regarded as 'not quite the thing'. Not more than three or four national newspapers recognized the 'kinematograph' as anything but a minor novelty.

The profession of film criticism had not yet come into being, if one excepts the reviews in the trade papers, the best of which was still subtitled *The Magic Lantern Weekly*. A filmed version of a well-known book or play, with a London actor in the leading part, might earn a couple of paragraphs from the local theatre critic. 'Mr. Cecil Humphreys appears in a kinematograph version of Mme Marie Corelli's novel *The Sorrows of Satan*. Unfortunately . . .'

An extra deterrent was the fact that women had very little standing yet as journalists. They were relegated, nameless, to the back pastures of the paper's 'Woman's Page'. The Press was still materially a man's world in 1921.

But I was at the optimistic age when nothing that one knows dismays one. I had been seized by this brilliant idea and was determined to pursue it.

The next time C. P. Scott parked his bicycle in our hall I took my courage in both hands and told him that the *Manchester Guardian* ought to have a regular film column; not occasional reviews of films that were appearing in Manchester that week, but serious criticism of new films as soon as they were shown publicly in this country.

He thanked me gravely for the suggestion, and said he would consider it, adding the momentous words, 'But I think that would have to be done from the London end.' I don't know whether this was meant as a hint or a dissuasion, but I do know that in that instant my mind was quite made up. I must get to London somehow, by fair means or by foul.

8

AND SO TO LONDON

IRONICALLY enough, it was the University which furnished me with the means to go to London. I was to be given a graduate scholarship. The idea was that I would read for a few months at the British Museum; write a bigger and better thesis as the result of my researches; go back to Manchester and take a Ph.D. degree next summer. As I say, that was the *idea*.

Mother and I left Manchester and came south in the early autumn of 1921. For me it was a final leave-taking. In forty years I have been back only three times, for overnight visits with my friend Sylvia. Mother, I feel sure, had no notion of the finality of the break. She hoped, though she never said so, that I would presently grow tired of this London escapade, give up the wild idea of journalism and come home sensibly with a splendid thesis.

That was why we travelled light, with only a few personal belongings in suitcases. For the first few weeks in London we lived in a temperance hotel in Bloomsbury (so handy for the British Museum, if only I had *wanted* the British Museum) and looked round for a furnished flat. This was my first experience of London flats—presumably of flats in most big cities forty years ago—and I was horrified by what I found.

Each 'order to view' by an estate agent brought a fresh dismay. I had no notion human beings lived, and chose to live, like this: in a world of airless semi-darkness, among dustbins, with the overwhelming odours of stale cabbage and carbolic.

In the end we settled for a flat in a new block in Maida Vale. It was featureless but adequate. The front windows looked straight on to the busy Edgware Road, but we were high enough up to miss the worst roar of the traffic. The back windows looked down into a deep dark well. You whistled through a tube and the groceries and milk came up by lift. You whistled again and the refuse was taken down. Still, there was a telephone; and the geyser would provide hot water when it had the whim to.

By some means or other Mother managed to persuade our dear old Lizzie to come down from her home in Huddersfield and help us through our first few months in London.

Lizzie thought poorly of the place and didn't hesitate to say so. By this time she was iron-grey, looking more than ever like a stern Savanarola. But she was still spry, strong and erect; undaunted by her new surroundings; ready to meet any Cockney tongue on equal terms. The things she said down the blower in the kitchen were nobody's business, but they got results.

Errand boys treated her with the deference due to a holy terror. They didn't speak her language, but they knew exactly what she meant. Shopkeepers soon found they couldn't fool her with a wilted cabbage, or get away with yesterday's fresh fish.

About one thing Lizzie was adamant. 'You can't eat the stuff they call bread down here,' she said to Mother. 'All gas and rubbidge, that's what it is. No wonder they look so poorly. You leave it to me, Mrs. Lejeune.' And presently the flat took on a faint semblance of home, with Lizzie asking me if I had washed my hands for dinner, and the smell of loaves and scones and gingerbread baking in the oven.

From my point of view the Maida Vale flat had several distinct advantages. The Fancourts lived just round the corner. The Tyases had a flat only a few minutes away near Baker Street. There was a bus-stop opposite the door, and a red, roaring No. 6 would take you direct to Fleet Street, which had been my objective from the beginning.

Mr. Scott had given me a letter of introduction to James Bone, the London editor of the *Manchester Guardian*, and I lost no time in asking for an interview. Bone was a Scotsman; short, bright-eyed and compact. He guarded the paper's interests like a terrier; a small, Scottish terrier. His bark was much worse than his bite.

My first meeting with him was brief but memorable. He read my letter of introduction, put it down carefully on the desk and observed 'Mphm'. After a pause he asked me what I supposed I could valuably contribute to the *Manchester Guardian*. I said film criticisms, and proceeded to explain why film criticism was becoming vital. He took a typed list out of a drawer and studied it. Then he said quietly: 'No doubt, Miss Lejeune, no doubt. You are the twenty-seventh person who has come to me with the same idea.'

I took this as a dismissal. But Bone hadn't quite finished. As I was picking up my bag and gloves, he shot a sudden question at me.

'Could you write a paragraph about a pew-opener opening a pew?'

I gaped.

'I've never seen a pew-opener opening a pew,' I said.

'That doesn't matter. Could you write the paragraph?'

'Well, I don't know . . .' I began.

'Come back and see me when you do,' he said. 'Leave your address and telephone number with my secretary. Thank you, Miss Lejeune. Goodbye.'

In another instant I was out in Fleet Street; bewildered, furious with myself and challenged. Frustration gave me just the stimulus I needed. One way or another, twenty-six competitors and pew-openers notwithstanding, I *would* be a London film critic I determined, as I rode the red bus back to Maida Vale.

'Of course you might try Cousin George,' said Mother at lunch over the Yorkshire pudding. She sounded doubtful: I felt doubtful; but there could be no harm in trying.

George Morison, a remote connection on the MacLaren side, was the veteran theatre critic of the *Morning Post*. I have no idea how old he was; he looked to me at least a hundred. He lived in King's Bench Walk, and received me in a dark, cluttered study reeking of dust, old books and pipe tobacco.

He was kind, but had no hope to offer. Clearly he thought this young provincial cousin would be better off in Manchester. However, he said, if I wanted to earn a few guineas there was this Devonshire House affair. The periodicals might pay for a bit of advance publicity.

The Devonshire House affair was a charity performance of an old melodrama by Lord Lytton called *Not So Bad As We Seem; or, Many Sides to a Character*. It had originally been played in 1851 by 'a distinguished cast of amateurs', including Charles Dickens, John Tenniel and Wilkie Collins. Dickens had been the centrepiece; 'a dissipated gallant with a heart of gold'; a reformed profligate, 'sober, but affecting inebriety'.

The revival was to take place in the room in Devonshire House where Dickens had once trod the parquet. The proceeds were to go to the Children's Free Library in Dickens' old house in Euston. The performers, who included Mrs. Margot Asquith, were all Top People in contemporary London society.

Obviously the gossip columns would want a nibble at it in advance. Obviously, too, the subject would need quite a bit of tedious research. This was the job that Cousin George handed to me, and I managed to unearth enough material from the records to turn out a piece that was printed (anonymously) in *John o 'London's*, and another that appeared (with a byline) in *The Graphic*.

I don't remember whether I was paid for these two pieces. What I do remember is the fate of a third piece about the Devonshire House play which I submitted, on Cousin George's advice, to one of the London evening papers.

It was a sound bit of research and I knew it. As days passed by, and the manuscript was not returned with a rejection slip, my hopes began to soar. Every day I was waiting on the corner to snatch the paper from the newsboy. At last the great moment came. Opening the paper, I caught a glimpse of headlines. 'Devonshire House Play . . . Victorian Melodrama for Charity. Charles Dickens Sober but Affecting Inebriety. . . .'

I tore into the flats to read it at my leisure. They had printed everything, exactly as I wrote it. A full column and no cuts. With an enormous byline—'By Lady ——, a leading member of the sparkling social cast.'

That was the last I heard of the Devonshire House play. There was no credit and no remuneration. I was told later by his junior, L'Estrange Fawcett, that 'your Uncle George was rather cross about it'. I have no evidence of this, but to the best of my knowledge I never heard from nor set eyes on Cousin George again.

It was my first bitter experience of the jungle of London journalism, but I was too young to be more than momentarily shocked by this betrayal. Things would come all right in time, I knew. Meanwhile, there was the whole of London to be explored; a London which, apart from a few schoolgirl visits, with tea at Lyons' Corner House,

AND SO TO LONDON

I only knew from books. The London of Chesterton, Galsworthy, Edgar Wallace, Conan Doyle; of Bulldog Drummond and the Bastables.

I wanted to see with my own eyes the places I had read about. Blackheath and Notting Hill; Green Street and Half Moon Street; the heights of Hampstead and the suburban villas of Lower Norwood; the City and the Inner Temple; Paddington Station and St. Paul's.

All this involved a deal of travelling, but travelling was cheap in those days. For a few pence you could sit on the open top deck of an omnibus and ride all the way to the London docks or to the green quiet of Kew. The leaping omnibuses thrilled me after the staid trams of Manchester. The Tubes were exciting, too, with their clanging, iron lifts and curious *yellow* smell. (How odd it may seem to future generations to read that their grandparents spoke glibly of 'going home by Tube').

Most of all I liked discovery on foot. It was my joy to wander down the gracious curve of Regent Street; gazing at the silks and velvets in Liberty's window; glancing a little covertly at the naughty Café Royal; buying a ribbon or some other trifle of haberdashery at Swan and Edgar's, which was still an old-fashioned draper's full of delightful ups-and-downs, smelling of calico and faintly reminiscent of *Cranford* and Jane Austen.

From Piccadilly I would walk to the Embankment Gardens, to pay my tribute to the Sullivan memorial, and watch the barges passing along the grey Thames; perhaps sit on a bench and share a sandwich with the sparrows. Then up the narrow, climbing passages and along the Strand until I reached the newspaper world.

It was high adventure to walk along Fleet Street, gaping at the homes of famous newspapers, although I had neither part nor lot in them; watching the vans roll out of side streets with their load of evening papers. It was heady to listen to the newsboys' cry of '*Star—News—Standard!*'; well worth a penny to buy a newspaper still damp from the presses; any paper, it didn't matter which.

In Shaftesbury Avenue I found a shop which sold the film trade papers: *The Cinema*, the *Bioscope*, and *The Kinematograph* (and *Magic Lantern*) *Weekly*. I pored over the reviews of the new films in our flat in Maida Vale, often deprecating the style but always relishing the substance.

75

To the best of my recollection I never ventured into any of the cinemas in the West End, where the prices were beyond my reach, but I did drag poor Mother to countless flea-pits in Kilburn and the Edgware Road.

In one of these we saw John Barrymore in *Dr. Jekyll and Mr. Hyde*. The transformation scenes chilled my blood delightfully. They had the splendour of the truly horrid, as admired by Lydia Languish in *The Rivals* and Catherine Morland in *Northanger Abbey*. Since then I have seen four film versions of the Stevenson story, and not one of them was half as horrid.

At the height of one of these appalling scenes, when Barrymore's handsome face was changing into a repellent and putrifying mass, I was filled with a sudden filial compunction. I glanced at Mother to see how she was taking it. She was taking it in the best way possible. She was fast asleep.

One day I had a note from James Bone, enclosing a ticket for a fashion parade by floodlight in a Hampstead garden. 'We might be able to use a London letter par. on this,' he wrote with native caution.

I have often wondered what led this most perspicuous of editors to send a novice off on this assignment. It must have been obvious to anyone who looked at me—as indeed it still is—that the last thing in the world I know or care about is fashion. Did he give me the job with his tongue in his cheek? Was he being gently needled by the Manchester end? Was he offering me an alternative subject to the description of a pew-opener opening a pew? Or did he really think it might be a bright idea to get the provincial view on an extra chi-chi London occasion?

To my regret, I can find no trace of that review today. It would be interesting to find out what sort of fashions top models were modelling in a floodlit London garden in 1921. I can remember that I was startled by the bold display of rouge and lipstick; according to my book of etiquette, a lady's make-up should be confined to a light dusting with a *papier-poudre*. I know that there were glasses of champagne, and plates of crackers spread with some frogspawn of black eggs. There was a chill wind blowing across Hampstead Heath, and I thought the girls should have wrapped up more warmly.

I seem to have cut out very few of the odd bits and pieces that I wrote for Bone during those early days. Perhaps I was ashamed of them, and rightly so.

The art of writing paragraphs is highly skilled, and only attained after long years of practice. It isn't easy to compress a statement of facts, a comment and a shade of colour into the space of a hundred and fifty words. One of the trickiest jobs I ever tried to do in later years was to give readers the gist of a film in a couple of sentences, which would be fair, informative and with luck a little funny.

Bone was a great teaching editor, with an inexhaustible supply of patience. He schooled his cub reporters with the knowing care which a good race-horse trainer gives his two-year-olds. He worked himself as hard as he worked us. He never minced his words, but he was always just. A loose statement was a fault to be corrected. An opinion was an opinion, and he would not tamper with it.

For instance, there was the memorable night when I was sent to the theatre to review *Lilac Time*. For some reason I took an unconscionable dislike to the play. Having been brought up on the Schubert songs, familiar in German, the English theatre version struck me as uncouth, *schwärmisch*, a rather vulgar medley. I said as much in my review, but had not the confidence to claim the judgement as my own.

'Schubert would have said . . .' I wrote, and Bone banged down the copy on his desk.

'If we had wanted Schubert's opinion,' he said, 'we should have asked for it. We're paying you for *your* opinion.'

Half crying with rage and mortification, and panic-stricken because every minute the clock was ticking nearer to the paper's deadline, I rewrote that review of *Lilac Time* and gave the *Guardian* people the opinion they were paying for.

It was a very sour review indeed, and, as I see it now, utterly wrongheaded. I thought the play puerile and said so. Bone, with his sure finger on the public pulse, knew it would turn out to be a vast success.

But he sent the amended version over the wire to Manchester without a word of comment. I had withdrawn Schubert's opinion; I had said my say; for the moment I was his appointed critic, and he was not the sort of editor who lets down his staff. The vocal score of *Lilac Time* is on my piano now, and whenever I play through the charming, treacly tunes, I realize where I was half right, and he was wholly wise, and appreciate the lesson that I learnt on that soul-searing night in Fleet Street.

As the autumn of 1921 wore on, I found that Bone was sending me to see a lot of films. There were trade shows of *General John Regan* with Milton Rosmer; *The Old Wives' Tale* with Fay Compton; D. W. Griffith's *Dream Street* with Carol Dempster; *The Three Musketeers* with Douglas Fairbanks. These seemed to me assignments just like any others: fashion shows, conferences, London letter pars. on this and that. I wanted only to write well for Bone. In my eagerness to become a journalist I had no notion of the pattern that was forming.

Suddenly, at the end of the year, I learnt that the *Manchester Guardian* had decided to give me a regular film column. It was to start with the new year of 1922. It was to be called 'The Week on the Screen' and signed with the initials C.A.L. To the best of my remembrance, I was to be paid five pounds a week.

One of the first things I did, on hearing this astounding news, was to sit down and write to Charlton, returning the money for the graduate scholarship, and explaining there would be no thesis, because I had just been made film critic of the *Manchester Guardian*. He replied with congratulations; said he was sorry but not at all surprised. 'I only hope,' he added, with characteristic Charlton dryness, 'that you will not adopt the noxious attitude of the *Manchester Guardian* toward the arts.'

9

A COLUMN OF MY OWN

THE years I spent as film correspondent of the *Manchester Guardian* were so busy, so crowded, so full, like the world, of a number of things, that it is hard to realize there were only six of them.

Every week was the beginning of a fresh adventure, glowing with hope and promise. I loved London and I loved my job. Romance lurked in the most unlikely places. In those days I even found Wardour Street alluring.

The curious all-pervading smell of acetone went to my head like wine. The musty, dark, private theatres, sometimes in the basement, sometimes high up beneath the roof, where we sat on dirty velvet chairs with broken springs and listened to the whirr of the projector showing silent films, had the magic of a cave in the Arabian Nights. The garish posters, windows full of advertising stills, were a continuous delight. It was my first experience of organized vulgarity, and I *liked* it.

Reviewing films in those days was a very different business from reviewing films today. There were no official 'press shows'. The small band of us, perhaps six or seven, who wrote about films for the national newspapers, as distinct from the trade papers, were known as 'lay critics' and invited to see films on sufferance.

Some of the invitations were extremely odd. My favourite, which I have kept as a curio for forty years, comes from Warner Brothers Pictures Ltd. It invites me to the 'Premier Presentation of *The First Auto*, the Romance of the Last Horse and the First Horseless Carriage, with Barney Oldfield and Patsy Ruth Miller.'

It ends, in italics, with the civil caution: '*The tickets will be nontransferable and we would ask your co-operation to avoid our having to refuse admission to any person other than yourself.*

These were the last years of the silent screen. All the pictures I reviewed for the *Manchester Guardian* were wordless, with subtitles or 'art-titles' to explain them.

Art-titles were the fashion of the moment. Sometimes, though not often, an artist who could really draw was hired to draw them. The most skilful and ingenious art-titler in this country was a plump, unknown young man called Alfred Hitchcock. His amusing sketches brought him no fame, but provided him with a modest income. Most of the designs for titles came ready made from Hollywood.

A film called *Experience* had sketches of torches guttering down into their sockets. *Singed Wings* had moths blundering into a candle-flame. The seduction of a pure girl was suggested by a cartoon of tilted champagne glasses and the simple caption: 'Oh, What One Little Glass of Wine Can Do!'

In desert films (and there were a great many desert films, once Valentino set the fashion with *The Sheik*) no bald addresses such as 'Thou son of a dog!' or 'Thou whitewashed filthiness!' were complete without a camel or a minaret. *Came the Dawn* was bound to have its sunrise, and Love would seldom Bloom without a rose.

In the last period of the silent films there was a forlorn attempt to dispense with titles altogether and let the pictures tell the story. To the best of my remembrance, the only time this antic really worked was in *The Last Laugh*, which Murnau directed with Emil Jannings. But then Jannings, like Chaplin, was a natural mime; and could get his meaning over to the audience without a word.

The most painful and painstaking picture without titles that I ever saw was a British film, in which the leading characters had to inform the audience that they were planning to pick hops. Believe me, they did really stand on one leg and hop across the screen. Sometimes I recall this incident while watching *What's My Line?* ('And now for a little bit of mime') on B.B.C. television.

To make up for the absence of dialogue, silent films were provided with non-stop musical accompaniment. This became so much of a fetish that presently the order came to London from New York, 'No film to be shown to critics without music.' Any old music.

A COLUMN OF MY OWN

In the larger halls mighty Wurlitzers were springing up like mushrooms, and a live orchestra was engaged for most of the main feature films. The smaller houses still clung to the support of the hardworking pianist, who held his tea-cup in one hand and attacked the keyboard with the other. He kept his eyes glued on the screen for 'action cues', which would direct him to play hurry music, storm music, 'Hearts and Flowers', Mendelssohn's 'Spring Song' or one or other of the Wedding Marches. When the climax was signalled he would put down his tea-cup and plunge two-handed into something vibrant; with plenty of loud pedal and a slight tremolo in the bass.

At the same time there broke out a rash of colour pictures; a few of them laboriously hand-tinted, but most of them the hopeful products of some new, scientific, wonder process.

In January 1922 we had a British film in 'natural colour' (Prima) called *The Glorious Adventure*, with Victor MacLaglen as the heavy villain and Lady Diana Manners as a hapless victim of the Great Fire of London. The first night was a glittering occasion, when every woman who could sport a mink coat and a tiara turned up at Covent Garden in full panoply. The film was less distinguished than the audience. Lady Diana, shown in 'natural colour' among the embers, had all the significance of a sugar fondant dropped into the blazing centre of a barbecue.

Nevertheless, the die was cast. The cinema had come out of the shadows of the flea-pit and was beginning to be accepted as a social institution. Smart people, as well as commoners like us, were now going to the pictures; even if they sometimes did so with an air of slumming.

Palaces now took the place of picture houses. Neon lights blazed over canopies, and organs rose from subterranean depths in a pink shaft of limelight.

An orgy of affluence pervaded the Hollywood scene. Cecil B. de Mille indulged in bath-tub epics. Eleanor Glyn endorsed *It*; recumbent, sensual, on a tiger-skin. A young dancer from the Argentine called Rudolf Valentino snaked his slim hips, smiled his inscrutable smile and half opened velvet eyes upon a world which had suddenly discovered its Dream Lover.

This was the heyday of stunts and presentations. Tom Mix came to London and rode his horse up the steps of the Guildhall. A military band was hired to play the print of an absurd Hollywood film from the docks of Southampton to the vaults of Wardour Street.

Douglas Fairbanks stopped the traffic in Piccadilly by performing Tarzan antics on the balcony of his suite at the Ritz Hotel. The Talmadge sisters, Norma and Constance, sponsored a film beauty contest, in which a hundred hopeful girls were brought to London from all parts of the country and touched up for the cameras by the hallowed Talmadge hand.

Madame Kirby Lunn, in black sequins, consecrated the new Tivoli in the Strand with the National Anthem. The film was *Where the Pavement Ends*, and Little Tich topped the variety bill in the supporting programme.

The lobbies of West End picture palaces exuded 'atmosphere'. Usherettes and veterans of the Corps of Commissionaires were forced into fancy dress, vaguely suggestive of the subject of the picture. Theatrical costumiers must have done a roaring business. The usherettes, most of whom wanted to look like film stars anyway, found plenty of admirers, but I've often wondered what the old soldiers said to one another when the trappings were cast off and they forgathered at the local for their pint of mild-and-bitter.

Lobbies were the shop-windows of the cinema. Lingering in lobbies was encouraged by every conceivable device of showmanship. The walls were hung with portraits of film-players. Flora proliferated and fauna was abundant. It might be monkeys or tropical fish; a golden eagle or a hooded falcon; every smart lobby in those days provided *something*.

White roses were supplied to patrons of one theatre; red roses to patrons of another. An enterprising hall set up a free handkerchief bar, with the superscription. 'You will need this handkerchief for the tears you will shed when watching . . .' whatever was the title of the feature.

(Quite recently, when horror pictures were the vogue, some film company offered an immense insurance policy on the life of the first person who died of fright while watching the atrocity within. To the best of my knowledge this benefit was never claimed. A pity; the case, which would certainly have been disputed, would have made good reading in the law reports of *The Times*.)

I remember being invited to attend a trade-show at which two hundred clergymen were to be the main attraction. This was closely followed by another with two hundred politicians. Then there was something with the lure of two hundred mothers-in-law (I may be wrong about the figure, but two hundred is a good round number), and a less emotional one with two hundred Royal Academicians.

To a British film called *Comin' Thro' the Rye* trooped two hundred grandmothers, whose total age, we were told with pride, would 'aggregate more than ten thousand years'. The dear old ladies were provided with fifty Chelsea Pensioners as a guard of honour.

Two hundred authors were requisitioned for one trade-show; two hundred 'Alsatian Wolf Hounds' for another. The dogs were much more entertaining than the authors; also, taken by and large, more handsome. Unfortunately their remarks could not be quoted, whereas too many of the authors' were.

By the summer of 1922 film companies were thinking hard in terms of press publicity. That June I paid my one and only visit to the Derby, as the guest of a Hollywood producer who was shooting the Big Scene of Hall Caine's *The Christian*.

If you have read that powerful work you will remember that the Big Scene requires the hero, the Reverend John Storm, to step out and harangue the Derby crowd about the wages of sin, and their certain doom, as gamblers, of eternal damnation.

Our Rev. John Storm was the Hollywood star Richard Dix, renowned for his prowess in Westerns and other robust films. Seldom have I seen a more frightened person. He gave one look at the crowds he was expected to harangue, and turned a wilting shade of lettuce green. The sweat poured down his face and he began to quiver like an aspen. For at least half an hour he walked up and down in frenzy, rehearsing the words he would have to speak; for although *The Christian* was a silent film, you can't get the full effect of a harangue without *some* sort of haranguing. In the end, I thought, he got off very lightly. The punters in the Silver Ring good-humouredly ignored his threats of fire and brimstone. 'Nuts!' I heard one of them say to another, 'he's only just a loony, one of them there Mormonists from Yutah.'

In the meantime the heroine of *The Christian*, Glory Quayle, had driven up to Epsom Downs in an antique four-in-hand, with a party of binoculared ladies and gentlemen dressed up to the nines for

Royal Ascot. They threw pennies to the gipsy children. They backed winners in each race and embraced one another fervently. They represented Worldly Sin, of course, and the crowd accepted them as affably as they would accept any extraneous sideshow on Derby Day. One woman did remark that the four-in-hand looked 'a bit old-fashioned like', but apart from that there was no noticeable criticism.

The Derby was won that day by Captain Cuttle, trained by the great Fred Darling and ridden by Steve Donoghue, at a starting price of 10 to 1. This was the second in a hat-trick of Steve Donoghue Derby successes that was to make racing history. I wish I could say that I had backed the winner, but it would not be true. I didn't back a horse at all. I didn't even watch the race. While the crowd was roaring 'Come on, Steve!' I was smugly sitting with my back turned to the race-track, involved in an argument with a young man from the *Morning Post* about the aesthetics of criticism.

My necessarily scant account of Captain Cuttle's Derby appears in a *Guardian* article headed 'Riding to Win'. It seems that the industry had gone all out to show horse-racing films that week. Apparently they were a big draw at the time ('A good race is the one event on the screen which will infallibly bring its round of applause'), although in later days they were dismissed as 'poison at the box-office'.

I find an enthusiastic but somewhat ambiguous review of something called *Stable Companions*, in which 'The Big Race', when it comes, is both ambitious and successful. The hero has entered two horses, the pride and joy of his stable. 'Here is an opportunity for a double event; two races, two thrills, two hairbreadth successes, and as pretty a bit of running, with the stable dog to set the pace, as one can remember in films of the turf.' All very nice and cosy, but which horse won what? Or did the stable dog beat the pair of them?

In the same week we were shown a picture called *Long Odds*, based, I wrote, 'on a little-known National Hunt rule which says that if a jockey is disabled on the course any qualified rider of the right weight may take his place. So the hero,' I went on, 'knowing his horse's weakness, is ready at the open ditch when the jockey is thrown and disabled, and by some very fine riding against incredible odds he comes home a winner.'

When I was preparing a rough draft of the present book I came across this passage and found it so peculiar that I decided to learn more about it. I applied to the current sports editor of the *Daily Express*, and asked him: 'Was there ever such a rule? Does it still exist and was it ever implemented?'

For those who are interested, here is his reply. 'The rule has since been rescinded, but there was such a rule. Clive Graham recalls a case at Haydock Park in the middle thirties when a rider was knocked unconscious and a bystander mounted the horse and completed the course. By coincidence the bystander happened to be the right weight and the horse was officially placed third. I take it that only two had completed the course up to that point.'

Valid corroboration, if not quite the spectacular triumph of *Long Odds*.

That same summer I enjoyed an odd experience in the Highlands. A British film company was making a picture about 'gipsy life and feud, the story of a Romany king who falls in love with a white girl and is cursed and deserted by his people'.

Actors and crew, with fifteen caravans of 'real Romanies', including their horses, their children and their dogs, were to spend August on location near Blair Atholl, and I was invited to join them as a guest.

I jumped at the offer, although I was a little puzzled by it. To be sure, I had met the husky hero several times at a London film club, and made no effort to conceal my admiration. But I hadn't realized quite what power he wielded.

All was made clear on the first night in camp, when he marched into my tent (we all slept under canvas, except the stars) and took it for granted that he would share my bed. I told him to get out or I would scream. He was genuinely affronted and surprised. He said in bewilderment: 'I've had all the cows in this camp already. If you don't want me, what in God's name did you come here for?'

During the rest of my stay at Blair Atholl I shared a tent with a young married woman, Margaret Greenwood, whom I trusted at first sight. How Margaret ever got into the film racket I don't know. She wasn't cut out for the life at all, and soon abandoned it. She was a dark, sallow girl, with a thin, clever face. No glamour; no allure; and hardly any make-up. Her father had been editor of a provincial newspaper, and she was what old-fashioned people would have called a lady.

I had met her at supper for the first time that evening and taken an instant liking for her. When I came over to her tent in the middle of the night, dragging my blankets and my mattress with me, she asked only one question, 'I suppose *he* bothered you?' Then she brewed tea, brought out a tin of biscuits and moved her bed over to make room for me at the other side of the tent.

Had it not been for Margaret I should have caught the first train back to Euston in the morning. But she was my sort of person. We understood each other, and I felt safe there in her leaky tent. Nothing was said to the authorities about the reasons for this change in billeting, but I fancy any explanation would have been redundant.

I stayed out my full time with the company at Blair Atholl, and found it a memorable experience. It rained almost continuously, although the natives preferred to describe the weather as 'a wee bit mist'. The actors wore their heavy screen make-up all day long, ready to rush in front of the cameras at the first gleam of sunshine. This nearly always seemed to happen when the kettles were on the boil for tea.

We did have a fine day, though, for my own Big Scene. The script included a gipsy fair; with wrestling, fortune-telling and all the appropriate side-shows. I was picked to be a moron watching a thimble-rigging act, registering bucolic astonishment and mouthing 'Oo-er!' when the pea turned up under the unexpected thimble.

Most nights we sat in a big ring round a campfire, singing community songs and listening to that wrinkled walnut of a comedian, Hugh E. Wright, telling his spine-chilling ghost stories. But every now and then there was the call, 'Who's for Blair Atholl and a bath?'

Then we piled into cars and trucks and drove down to the hotel at Blair Atholl through miles of dense, dark woods, crowded with little furtive creatures whose eyes glowed in the night, and whom I prayed would never cross our path. By this time it was late August, and the burns ran full and brown. The rowans were ripening; the bracken was turning; bell heather had given place to ling; the highest mountains were already capped with snow. It was very cold and very beautiful.

In my routine report to the *Manchester Guardian* I wrote: 'The film, with its virile action and fine Scottish scenery, will undoubtedly provide a rich two-and-fourpence worth to the man in the stalls. But if only it could show him as well what it will recall to the people who lived with it and made it! It will never be a pure gipsy story to them. It will be a queer mixture of memories and sensations, with a background of bare mountainside and rain, a foreground of caravans by a river, and a running accompaniment of gipsy horses, gipsy curs, gipsy babies, all restless and all dirty.

'They may forget the days of work round the caravans,' I went on, 'but they will never forget the day when the snakes escaped, the day when the Romany women fell upon each other tooth and nail, the day of the mock trial, the day when we laid a dancing-floor in the dining-tent.'

To my intense regret I've forgotten all these things. I am particularly annoyed about the snakes. Which snakes? Whose snakes? What were snakes doing in the film at all?

One ought to be positive about snakes, I feel, but they have left no impression on my mind. Whenever I think of Blair Atholl I remember rain, Margaret, the smell of pinewoods, paraffin and canvas, the utter disillusion about film stars, dense woods, the eyes of animals at night and the luxury of hot baths at the hotel.

The company spent two months on location in Scotland. When I saw the finished film a few months later the two months had been reduced to four minutes on the screen. This was my first practical experience of the waste of time and money that goes into the production of most moving pictures. It was also a very useful piece of education; a sharp lesson in the toilsome art of growing up.

10

'CHARMANTE SOIREE!'

AFTER a year of camping out in furnished flats, Mother and I found a place of our own in Chelsea. It was a flat, too, but sunny and pleasant, in a quiet cross-street between Flood and Manor Streets, close to the river. It had the makings of a home, and by this time Mother was no longer in any doubt that I, at least, was going to make my home in London.

Looking back on it now, I can just begin to imagine what a wrench it must have been for her to break her final ties with Manchester; the place where she had been born, grown up and raised a family; the place where all her friends were and all her memories lay. There must have been a multitude of them, for by now she was well over sixty.

At the time I was much too young and self-centred to see the thing at all from Mother's point of view. Nor did she give me any chance to do so. She made the decisions about practical affairs, while my mind ranged romantically between Fleet Street and Wardour Street.

To me the move was no more than a casual happening. Satisfactory, of course, but simple. One week we were living in a horrid furnished flat in Coram Street, Bloomsbury, opposite a noisy public house; raucous with the eternal newsvendors' cries of '*Star—News—Standard!*' The next week we were living in a pleasant flat in St. Loo Mansions, Chelsea, with our own familiar furniture, sent down from Manchester.

Mother shopped in the King's Road. I caught a No. 19 bus to film shows. Every Thursday I would rattle off 'The Week on the Screen' on an old Corona, at a table in the large light kitchen comfortably filled with the smells of Lizzie's cooking.

'CHARMANTE SOIRÉE!'

A woman on the *Guardian* staff told me that I ought to join a club. I couldn't see the need myself, but she put me up for membership of the Lyceum, and it would have seemed churlish to refuse.

The Lyceum was a highly respectable woman's club in Piccadilly, not far from Hyde Park Corner. It daunted me from the beginning. The size and price of meals there were prohibitive to someone accustomed to lunching on a Welsh rarebit at an A.B.C. The rooms were high, dark, Victorian and leathery.

The members all seemed very old to me. The committee women were indomitable organizers. They seized avidly upon newcomers and rounded them up to attend formal dinners with celebrity guest speakers. I was much too frightened of the organizing women not to go. But I found the speeches soporific, and grudged the money that I had to spend. Even in those days a salary of five guineas a week would not buy much in the way of food, travelling expenses and clothes. As it happened, this extravagant adventure proved worth while, for it was at the Lyceum that I met Velona Pilcher.

Velona was about my own age, the middle twenties. She was an American and, like me, a prentice journalist, reviewing films and plays for the *Christian Science Monitor*. I don't know what had brought her to live in England, and through all the years that we were friends I never asked nor discovered anything about her family; except that she appeared to have none, and had been left a considerable sum of money by her godmother.

She had short, straight, straw-coloured hair, light blue eyes full of humour and intelligence, and was very pale, with a deep, matt pallor like a piece of parchment. Her hands were long and thin and beautifully shaped, and she gave the impression of being built on birds' bones. She had a boyish, rather than a girlish, look, and her mind was as vigorous and unsentimental as a man's.

I had never met anyone quite like her before. Indeed, I have never met anyone quite like her since. She disturbed and fascinated me at the same time, just as an unfamiliar object in his natural surroundings disturbs and fascinates a dog.

But because I was as anxious to listen as she was eager to talk we quickly drew together. At first it was in the staid lounge of the Lyceum, where we would find a corner to ourselves for after-dinner coffee; Velona in a black corduroy jacket, smoking a cigarette in a long ebony holder; myself puffing away inexpertly at a gold-tipped Ariston.

Before long we gave up going to the club, which was too formal for her and too expensive for me. She lived in a row of horrid little houses in Earls Court, in a quarter that was quickly turning into a slum.

Her bit of slum was next door to a fish-and-chip shop. There was no electric light, no indoor sanitation, no hot-water system, and cold running water only in the kitchen; where she kept the sink piled up for days with dirty dishes. The chimney smoked; little light came in through the crusted windows; the place was indescribably squalid.

Velona didn't seem to notice. For all her fastidiousness of mind, there was something of the slattern in her make-up. The only time I saw her really angry was the day when I arrived early and started washing up the dishes. She made it plain that this was an intrusion on her privacy, a disturbance of the pattern of her life. I never meddled with the kitchen sink again.

When I had supper with her at Earls Court, which was often, Velona would go next door and bring back fish-and-chips wrapped in a greasy sheet of newspaper. She would light a couple of candles stuck in old wine bottles. We would drink Chianti with our fish, and she would brew a great deal of black aromatic coffee. Sometimes, after supper, she would bring out her guitar, and sing folksongs, negro spirituals and ballads like 'Frankie and Johnny' in her husky, confidential voice. This, I felt with a sigh of satisfaction (although I would have loathed to share it), is the veritable *vie de Bohème*.

Velona's conversation was more heady than the wine we drank. She was utterly possessed by 'theatre'. If we spoke of other things it was mostly in parenthesis. She thought in terms of theatre all the time, with the concentration of a fanatic.

It was less the content of the play that excited her than the manner of its presentation. She was an avid reader of *Theatre Arts Monthly*, and well versed in all the contemporary theatre jargon.

She made my head spin with talk about skeleton stages, the importance of stairs and levels, the possibilities of theatre in the square and in the round. She talked about Gordon Craig and Stanislavsky; Norman Bel-Geddes and the Capeks; the Moscow Arts Theatre and the Stürm Group in Germany. Michelangelo was freely mentioned, and so was the French architect Le Corbusier. As far as I could make out, the bond between these people was something called expressionism. And an expressionist was the smart thing to be.

I never quite discovered what expressionism *meant*, but it was a fascinating word, like Piccadilly, and I used it freely in my articles. Another word I overworked was *avant-garde*, which meant just about as much or little as the expression 'new wave' means today.

Each successive generation is inclined to think of its contemporary idiom as an advance on what has gone before, the first tide to sweep over virgin sands. In fact, it is thousands of years since the sands were virgin. They have been embraced by wave after wave in the longest and most fertile courtship in history. Everything that is created by this embrace has been created before in the same image, and will continue to be created.

Today we talk as if the cinema had suddenly sprung to life in the late 1950s, with films such as *Hiroshima, Mon Amour*. But we were talking in just the same way about the cinema in the early 1920s, with the arrival of the first post-war films from Germany and France, and with as much justification. Something exhilarating had happened. A fresh wind was blowing from the continent, and we relished the vigour in the air.

Up to this time the Swedish films had been the best in Europe. We didn't see them very often, for the Swedish export has never been abundant and the British market never markedly responsive.

But the few films from Sweden that were shown have become collectors' pieces. The people who hunt down the Ingmar Bergman films today are sons and grandsons of the people who once hunted down the Victor Sjöstrom pictures of the early twenties: *Thy Soul Shall Bear Witness*, *A Lover in Pawn*, *Love's Crucible*, *The Dawn of Love*, *The Secret of the Monastery*; and, perhaps the most prized collectors' piece of all, Stiller's film *The Atonement of Gosta Berling*, which introduced a new girl by the name of Greta Garbo. The critics considered she was immature but promised well.

The Swedish films borrowed a great deal from literature, but went for their expression to a technique clear of literary idiom, in which the eye and curiously the sense of touch were equally involved.

Watching those old silent pictures, we almost felt under our fingers the texture of velvet and satin and lace. Our feet used to sense the roughness of the cobblestones in the courtyard. The old wood of the beams was warm to the touch and grained.

The candlelight, too, the thin sunlight, the deep, strong shadows, had an almost tangible quality. We felt the light as a physical experience, caught the chill of dark entries. Inanimate objects, as well as growing things, were invested with a secret life. They were characters in every drama.

With the Scandinavians, as with few other creative people, we get a vivid sense of private life in every stick and stone. Much of it, in films, is due to a masterly trick of photography and lighting. We get it in all the Ingmar Bergman pictures; morning light slanting through spring woods; evening mists along the harbour front. We got it in the opening sequence of Arne Sücksdorf's *The Great Adventure*, showing the beginning of a new day on the fringes of a forest.

The old personification of the elements has never left the Scandinavian mind entirely. Wind, wood and water are still alive and intimate; often more articulate than the human characters. We find a touch of this in the writing of Selma Lägerlof and Sigrid Undset. We find it in the craftsmanship of Swedish textiles. It is something indigenous, out of time and indestructible.

The Swedish cinema has always been a thing apart. It seems to be wholly uninfluenced by, and unconcerned to influence, the work of other countries. Sjöstrom, Stiller and Garbo left home for Hollywood in the early 1920s, and for more than a quarter of a century we were to hear practically nothing about Swedish pictures. The loss, however, made no perceptible impression on the course of cinema history.

Potent forces were at work in Europe. Both Germany and France were suddenly awake to the opportunities of the film medium. It was an uprush as irresistible as the thrust of spring, and an exciting time to be a critic. There was something fascinating to write about almost every week, something stimulating to look at almost any day.

Germany in particular, turning hungrily to art for refreshment and rebirth after the First World War, was making film after film that teased and captured the imagination.

My first intimation of the German riches came on a day when I was invited to an underground theatre in Wardour Street to watch 135 reels of *Dr. Mabuse*, and advise whether they could be cut in such a way as to make a single feature film for British exhibition.

'CHARMANTE SOIRÉE!'

I realize now that the little man who showed them to me had no interest in my advice at all. He was simply interested in getting a gullible young woman to himself for something like nine hours in a dark, private theatre. He made a number of half-hearted passes which I was too much engrossed by Fritz Lang's startling film to notice. When they became a nuisance I got up and moved into a seat directly in the shaft of light from the projector. By this time I had learnt something of the art of self-defence in Wardour Street. It must have been a disappointment to the little man, who was not, I learnt later, accustomed to rebuff by unattached young females. At all events, he went away and left me with the picture, which struck me as one of the most exciting things I'd ever seen. I suppose I am one of the very few people in this country who had the chance to watch the original, uncut version of *Dr. Mabuse*.

The German films were not shown widely, but they created a stir wherever they *were* shown. For the first time we heard the names of Lang and Lubitsch, Emil Jannings and Conrad Veidt. This was the golden age of myth and legend; of *Siegfried*, *The Golem*, *Destiny*, *The Student of Prague*, *The Street* and *Warning Shadows*.

Nothing could have been farther removed from the demands of modern fashion, which call for an anti-hero, anti-spectacle and no plot.

If one film only could be picked to represent the German movement of the period I suppose it would be *The Cabinet of Dr. Caligari*, which had been made by Robert Wiene and a number of theatre people—writers, painters, architects, photographers—who called themselves the Stürm Group. These people, Velona explained to me over the Chianti and fish-and-chips, were avowed disciples of *expressionismus*, and *Caligari* was their testament.

I almost understood what the word meant as I watched the picture. In fact, it seemed so obvious that I felt I must have missed some subtlety.

Caligari was the expression of a world seen through the eyes of a madman. When he walked down a street the houses tilted together above his head, the roofs nudged one another and conspired to crush him. Everyone he met looked mad and menacing. Light was blinding. Darkness was sinister.

Eventually he took these symptoms to a doctor—the first psychiatrist, to the best of my knowledge, to make an appearance in screen fiction. I can't remember now what ailed the victim, nor whether it was ever clearly stated, but I do know that the doctor's treatment proved successful, and by the end his patient was able to see the world just as straight as you and I do, who are presumably sane.

Wiene's film was produced in 1919, but failed to reach either England or America for several years. When at last it did arrive it caused no particular commotion in the theatres. By that time the public was licking its lips over a spectacular item from Hollywood called *Foolish Wives*, directed and played by a certain Erich von Stroheim, who was credited with drinking ox-blood as an appetizer for breakfast and billed on all the sandwich boards as 'The Man You Love To Hate'.

Caligari, however, was to have a marked effect on studio techniques. It suggested a new line in camera work. Its huddled roofs were the forerunners of Orson Welles' ceilings in *Citizen Kane*.

Psychiatry was sweeping into fashion. Before long it would seem abnormal to be normal. A tilted camera shot, with walls askew, roofs narrowing to form a funnel, could mean something solemnly significant; return to the womb, pre-natal experience, mother fixation and all that. Even if it meant nothing it *looked* suggestive; it made an impression on the audience. Wiene's film, so precisely wrought for its own purpose, was the innocent cause of some of the most vexatious tricks in movies. Even today directors are inclined to tilt their shots to draw attention to them when they haven't the wit to think of anything more sensible to do.

While the film-makers of Germany were busy with expressionism, the livelier spirits of the French cinema were also stirring. Gance, l'Herbier, Poirier and, above all, Jacques Feyder were responsible for some exciting pictures in the twenties. Feyder (the husband of Françoise Rosay) was a Belgian by birth, but all his finest work was done in France. From those early years I still recall a touching film called *Crainquebille*, the only really satisfactory film version of Pierre Benoit's romantic *L'Atlantide*, and a *Thérèse Raquin* that has never been surpassed. Almost impossible to realize that in this classic tragedy of small-town life not a word was spoken.

The *avant-garde* movement in the Paris studios had a brilliant advocate in the critic Louis Delluc. Why has no eager student of the cinema written a thesis on this remarkable young man? There is an award named after Delluc today; a feature of the annual film festival

'CHARMANTE SOIRÉE!'

at Cannes. Sometimes I wonder how many people, if indeed any at all, know much about the man whose memory the award perpetuates.

Louis Delluc died in 1924, when he was only in his early thirties. He was one of those ardent, undecided beings who spill their enthusiasms into every form of words. He was a critic, poet, novelist and playwright *manqué*. He produced some films, ardently though not very well: but his flair for criticism was remarkable.

He preferred the cinema to all other forms of entertainment, and his judgement of films was an extraordinary mixture of idolatry and reason. He could be deceived by precocity and often was, but could also be astonishingly perceptive.

His constant plea was for more *affection* for the cinema in French studios. 'The great secret of our inferiority', he wrote, 'lies in lack of love. We have despised the cinema. How can we understand after that? . . . Ah, if only we had loved it enough!'

Delluc loved the cinema enough for ten. His books *Cinéma et Cie*, *Photogénie* and *Charlot* are blazing with ardour. They are also perceptive and amusing, and I am astonished that in all these years nobody has thought it worth while to make and publish an English translation of them.

I have all the books in yellowing French paper-backs, and like to refresh myself with them every now and then. They strike one as curiously free and modern for film criticism written soon after the First World War, when most of us who bothered with the cinema at all were labouring after apologies for an Undiscovered Aesthetic. I don't know of anyone but Delluc, for instance, who could at that time have written, or been allowed to print, the running commentary on a popular serial called *La Nouvelle Mission de Judex*. It appears regularly between other film reviews, and I can't resist the chance to quote some of the extracts.

'*Charmante Soirée!* Des amis m'ont mené voir *La Nouvelle Mission de Judex*. Je me suis brouillé avec eux.'

'*Charmante Soiré!* Des amis m'ont mené voir *La Nouvelle Mission de Judex*. J'ai somnolé, comme si je cedais à une digestion monumentale. J'avais pourtant diné d'un legume, d'un fruit et d'un verre d'eau de Vals.'

'*Charmante Soiré!* Des amis m'ont mené voir *La Nouvelle Mission de Judex*. C'est un très joli film, sans doute. La petite X etait assise devant moi. Elle avait sa robe en lainage bleu-de-roi, avec un grand chapeau de satin noir qui d'ailleurs masquait entierèment l'ecran.'

'*Charmante Soiré!* Des amis m'ont mené voir *La Nouvelle Mission de Judex*. Je n'irai plus dans une salle de cinéma. jamais, jamais, jamais.'

'*Charmante Soiré!* Des amis m'ont mené voir *La Nouvelle Mission de Judex*. Des amis?'

This is criticism that everyone can understand. We have had our own experiences with friends, charming soireés and egregious hats.

Delluc died too soon to see his dreams of a new French cinema fulfilled. He saw only the budding, not the blossoming.

One day in the spring of 1925 there came to London a strange film by a young and unknown French director, René Clair. The film was originally called *Paris Qui Dort*. Then the title was changed to *Le Rayon Invisible*. In England it was put out as *The Crazy Ray*, a cheapjack title almost guaranteed to keep away the people who would like the film and understand it.

Under any name it told the story of a night watchman on the Eiffel Tower, who comes down from his lofty post one morning to find the whole of Paris struck into a trance. Or so it seems at first, but presently he discovers four other animate beings: the pilot and passengers of an aeroplane just arrived from Marseilles. This is the beginning of a series of adventures in a spellbound city which are freely and fantastically imaginative, often funny, sometimes touching, always close to human nature, told with an individual and distinctive charm.

I was fascinated by this film, and later, when René Clair had become a family friend, even more fascinated by his story of the way he made it.

We were talking in the half-dusk after dinner, by our living-room fire. René was speaking English, as he always did in courtesy to his English friends, although with equal courtesy he always wrote to them in French.

It was not hard in the dusk to make inconspicuous notes of what he said, and I have just dug them up from an old file. The pencilwriting is faded, but still decipherable. The phrases are so typical o Clair that I should like to quote them verbatim.

'Always the trouble with a young man is no money,' he said.f 'With an old man too. With me the trouble will always be no money. I cannot keep it. And always the people I meet who are nice, who would have me work with them, are just the same. They have no money too. That was how I got my first real job as a director.

'I wrote a story, *Paris Qui Dort*, and found a producer who wanted to use it. He had no money, so he was willing to take me, because I was cheap and wanted to make my own films. So we started and I was very happy. But presently he said, "We can't go on." The salaries stopped. I asked one day to pay a taxi at the office, going on location, and this man told me, "Can't, no cash".'

There was a long pause of bitter memory as he gazed into the fire. I think he had no knowledge of my flying pencil.

'Then I found out. In the office was no one but creditors. The producer had an arrangement with the bank by which he got so many francs' credit for every film he started. So of course he started them. Dozens of them. He was always starting, never finishing.' A shrug of the thin shoulders. 'It was natural, yes?'

I said yes with all my heart and added, 'So what did you do next?' to keep the story going.

'So we went on with the film for nothing,' he said. 'I was young and a little romantic and I suppose I believed in it. And there was Albert Préjean too, who was just starting as an actor. We used to wander about Paris together, dreaming and planning and talking about our ideals.

'Some days we ate and some days we did not eat.

'When my family were in Paris we ate often, but in the summer when they were in the country we were very hungry. They were not quite pleased with me, you see, for going into the cinema. So I could not ask for money. You understand that, yes? You have a son. You would not like for him to go into the cinema?'

I agreed that I would not like for my son (who was at that time of a very tender age) to go into the cinema, and René went on, with seeming illogic:

'But we were very happy. I think those were the happiest days. We worked when we could afford it. But although we were on the picture eight months there were only twenty working days.

'There was one thing that was very difficult. We had to shoot from the platform of the Eiffel Tower, and to go up there cost four francs a head. Sometimes Préjean had the money, sometimes I had. But seldom both together. When we did have it we were so happy that we wanted to stay up there all day, looking over the roofs of Paris and eating nothing at all, or perhaps all day only a *madeleine*.'

It would be nice to be able to say that *Paris Qui Dort* brought riches and réclâme to its young director. It brought neither. Only a few mad foreigners, such as Velona and myself, rejoiced in its felicity. In its own country it passed almost unnoticed.

Clair was never to have much honour in his own country, nor to achieve the highest honours anywhere. He must have made something like forty films by now. His name is one to gabble off when talking about the cinema. His record is on file in all newspaper offices. He is recognized as having been one of the big names in the cinema, but not one of the giants: Griffith, Eisenstein, Chaplin, De Mille, Hitchcock.

'My films,' he said to me when he was in England directing *The Ghost Goes West* for Korda, 'have always lost money and I suppose they always will. When I make them in order to make money,' and he shuddered at the memory, 'they lose always more than ever.'

I believe him. It would surprise me very much to learn that Clair was ever a rich man. He has never been happy working outside his own country, but even at home he has missed the common touch. His nearest success was built on an accordion tune. And even that has since been outclassed by a success built on a zither tune. He has failed either to be the rage of cocktail parties or the favourites of the boulevards.

Perhaps the secret is that his work has never been contemporary. In the beginning he made collectors' items before there were collectors ready to collect. His later films have been collectors' items too, but the collectors have passed on to other more competitive markets.

Clair has always been a gentleman in an industry largely operated by vulgarians. A few years ago I found myself reluctantly locked in conversation with a sharp, successful little showman who had thriven on the belief that the cinema should be violent, sexual, neo-realist or even neo-decadent.

'Who is *your* favourite director?' he asked me, and before I had time to answer added, 'I know; René Clair.' He made the name sound like a dirty word, and the allegation a smear on both our characters.

Up to that time I had never played the game of picking my favourite director, or choosing which films of his I would take with me to a welcome desert island. After a night's consideration I decided that this shrewd and sneering little person was quite right. René Clair *is* my favourite film director, and the pictures I would choose to take are *Paris Qui Dort, Un Chapeau de Paille d'Italie, Sous les Toits de Paris, Le Million, Les Grandes Manœuvres* and *Porte de Lilas*.

There have been greater directors than René Clair, but none of whom I have been quite so fond. I have liked him in his green spring, his golden summer and his mellow autumn. His nonsense is my kind of nonsense, his melancholy my kind of melancholy. There has never been another film director with quite his gift to offer; this special, rather private, mingling of compassion, gaiety and grace.

HOME AND ABROAD

READERS who are primarily concerned to learn about the old-time cinema can well afford to skip this chapter, which is almost entirely personal and will teach them nothing at all.

In the middle of my spell as film critic to the *Manchester Guardian* I met my husband, Roffe Thompson, and we were married at Chelsea Register Office, which was just round the corner from Mother's flat.

My husband is a Yorkshireman, as he would be the first to tell you. (Yorkshire people, in my experience, always tell you, though it often seems an act of supererogation.) He was also a journalist, writing film reviews for *The Kinematograph (and Magic Lantern) Weekly*. Later on he was to rise to higher things; for a while he was one of the successors to the notorious Horatio Bottomley as editor of *John Bull*, and later still acted as public-relations officer to various unpredictable characters in the film industry, with whom I was well acquainted.

Married life introduced me to a couple of novelties, both of which I held in deep distrust: the wireless and the motor-bicycle.

My husband was the first person I knew who owned a crystal set. It was his latest toy and he would play with it for hours. Ear-phones clamped across his head, a slightly besotted look of rapture on his face, he would listen to any mortal thing that was broadcast by 2LO; even the jolly uncles and aunties on *Children's Hour* ('Hallo, Twins!') inviting some unknown Pip and Emma to look behind the piano for their birthday presents.

Sometimes, in a fit of generosity, he would offer me the headphones, and for the sake of domestic peace I would take them, very briefly.

But I was always thankful to hand the harness back again, babbling something like: 'Wonderful, isn't it? Sounds almost *real*.'

The fact was that the feeling of constriction, of claustrophobia, induced by the pressure of my head, took away all sense of pleasure from the sounds emitted. Time has in no way changed this idiosyncrasy. If anything, it has enhanced it. Once upon a time I went regularly to the hairdresser's for a shampoo and set. Now I wash my hair at home, because I refuse to be shut up in anybody's beehive dryer. And I doubt if I could be induced today to clamp on earphones, even if it were to listen to the voice of God.

All the same, there was a great deal to be said for the old crystal set and head-harness form of broadcasting. You had a plain choice: you could take it or leave it alone. True, it was an ungregarious form of entertainment, but in its own fashion it was thoroughly unselfish. Wireless, before the days when we learnt to call it radio, was not in any way a public nuisance. Today it has become a fact of life from which it is difficult for an individual to flee.

Perhaps it is just that I'm old-fashioned, but I abominate artificially disseminated sound. I don't want to walk along a suburban street and hear the plum-pudding voices of the B.B.C. from every window. I don't want to listen to radio transistors at the seaside; I want to pay attention to the rhythm of the water.

I like, above all things, to enjoy the kind of private silence which is crowded with an infinity of sound in depth.

At almost any moment of our being, if we allow the inner ear to take control, we can discern at least a dozen layers of sound; from the uppermost call of a blackbird or the patter of rain on leaves, to the innermost snatch of song half remembered from childhood.

Once on a June morning, just for the fun of it, I tried to strip the layers off, as silkily as you would peel the skins off an onion. I had counted eleven layers before the telephone bell rang, and my delicate experiment was done for.

This is the sort of private listening that delights me, but the opportunities to indulge in it today are few; you have to seek far afield to find the place, or get up very early in the morning.

The sort of listening I abominate is public listening; compulsory exposure to noise, the battery against your eardrums of irresponsible sound, almost always ugly and often incomprehensible.

Among my pet abominations: loudspeakers on railway platforms, in theatres, at public meetings, in hotel lounges and bedroom corridors. 'Piped music' in the smartest elevators. Piped music while you eat and drink. Piped music everywhere you go.

This artificially disseminated sound has almost put an end to the art of clear speaking and singing; the art of the projected voice, so well understood by a former generation of singers, actors (Sir Ralph Richardson has it to perfection), music-hall entertainers and public speakers.

In my grandfather's day no minister could count upon preferment until he had convinced the elders of the chapel not only that he could preach with eloquence but that every syllable of his preaching would be clearly heard by every member of the congregation.

Today things are done differently, and by no means for the better. The loss of clear, unaided speech and song marks the death of a skill that was achieved with difficulty and practised with honour.

A little while ago I read a piece in an American small-town newspaper which really shocked me. The gist of it was that nobody need bother to go to church on Sunday, as the whole service would be tape-recorded and played back on Monday morning—while the housewife was busy with her domestic duties. This was advocated as a tremendous time-saver, but left me wondering what was the housewife supposed to do with the time she saved.

My husband owned a motor-cycle as well as a crystal set. It was another of his proud possessions. He loved everything about it, even the persistent smell of carbide and its habit of breaking down in the most inaccessible places.

One of the first advances that he ever made to me was after a morning trade show of a film at the old Shaftesbury Pavilion (now part of the rubble under the lordly foundations of the Columbia Theatre). He said: 'I've got to go and collect my motor-bicycle from somewhere down in Kent. Care to come with me for the ride back? We could have some coffee and sandwiches at Victoria.'

I did not care for the ride back, nor for any other rides taken on that bumpy pillion seat. But since it seemed inevitable that if I were to marry at all it must be to a motor-bicycle, I set my teeth and made the best of it. Before long, mercifully, the old pillion model was replaced by a motor-cycle with sidecar; then by a real car with three whole wheels; and after a time by a second-hand, serviceable four-wheeler.

Some people, unlike myself, actively enjoy the experience of travelling by car. To Mother, for instance, it was always an immense treat. A faint pink colour would come into her cheeks, and she would be as alert and noticing as a child. Her chief merits, as a passenger, in my husband's eyes were that she made no attempt to drive the car from the back seat, was always punctual and never kept him waiting.

One of my happiest remembrances of Mother is the day when we drove her to Southampton to meet the boat that was bringing my brother Russell back from Australia for his first visit in nearly twenty years.

It was some time in late spring, in the year of the Wembley Exhibition. We picked Mother up at Chelsea soon after daybreak on a fine, misty morning. Nothing was on the roads at that early hour except a number of scurrying rabbits and a few wild ponies in the New Forest. I dozed all the way down, but Mother (who almost certainly hadn't slept a wink the night before, for Russell was her favourite child) was wide awake in the back seat, and ready to eat a hearty breakfast at Southampton.

I have just asked my husband what he remembers of that journey. He says: 'Nothing. I was so sleepy that I nearly ran into a telegraph post. I couldn't think what it was doing there in the middle of the road.' To this he adds: 'What I really remember about your Mother and the car is the time she asked me to go down to the shops and buy her three-quarters of a pound of tomatoes, no more and no less.'

Motoring in those days was still comparatively peaceful. There was no great amount of traffic on the roads, and such traffic as there was proceeded at a pace almost as decorous as if a man with a red flag were walking in front of the car. It was possible to drive down to the coast and back at weekends, by the main Brighton and Worthing roads, with no more discomfort than a slight hold-up in the shopping centres of Richmond and Kingston.

We made the weekend journey fairly often, for Franziska and her husband, Laurence Meade, were attempting to run a small poultry farm in the little village of Ashington, between Horsham and Worthing. It was not a successful venture, as too many small poultry-farmers have discovered to their cost. But Ashington was a charming place, the banks and woods starred with primroses in spring, the steep lanes wild with honeysuckle and hedge roses in the summer. And anywhere that Cis and Laurence had a home has always been a second home to me.

I was very fond of my brother-in-law, whom I had known since I was six years old. He was considerably younger than Franziska; a sweet-tempered, companionable person whom everybody liked. Except Miss Herford, who had disapproved of the match from the beginning. It would be more appropriate, she told Mother, for Laurence to wait until I grew up and marry *me*.

In spite of his sweet nature, perhaps because of it, he was easily discouraged and infirm of purpose. Somehow he never made a real success in any of the jobs he tackled.

For the first years of their marriage he worked as an engineer on the old London, Brighton and South Coast Railway. I have pleasant recollections of that period. It was before the days when ice-cream was considered food for ladies, but many were the glasses of iced milk I drank at Laurence's expense in the refreshment room of Brighton station.

When engineering palled he decided to become an actor. He had always enjoyed playing comic parts in the charades we did at Christmas parties in Manchester. We children thought him deliriously funny, but the Profession didn't seem to have the same opinion. He did get an engagement, though, as Third Walking Gentleman with the Compton Comedy Company, and kept it for some time; chiefly, I think, because he proved to be an obliging assistant to the assistant stage manager, and could be relied upon, when necessary, to arrive promptly at the station and meet the young Fay Compton on her way back from boarding school.

I never saw Laurence in his role of Third Walking Gentleman, although his dress sword is still in our hall stand amongst the umbrellas. I did see him in his next part, which ran to a whole 'side' in the touring production of George Birmingham's Irish play *General John Regan*.

In this one Franziska also had a part; a very small one, without lines. She appeared briefly as an Irish colleen; barefoot, black hair on her shoulders, leading a donkey. She looked extremely decorative and entirely out of place. Also harassed. You never quite know what will happen with a donkey on a stage—or elsewhere, for that matter.

When acting proved to be unremunerative Laurence turned to poultry-farming. He liked living in the country. He was devoted to dogs and cats, of whom the house was full. But he never seemed to get along with poultry. In a fit of despondency he took off for Canada one day with the dim idea of earning his living as a waiter.

Franziska, who had far more resolution than he had, promptly went and fetched him back; and it was a good thing she did, for by that time he was nearly starving. With Mother's help they bought a plot of land at Bexhill-on-Sea, and built a small house in which they lived frugally but happily for the rest of their lives. That house at Bexhill was to become very dear and familiar to me, but its right place is later in the story.

It was at Ashington that Laurence saw the ghost. At least, he always said so, and I liked to believe it true. A few nights before Christmas he was walking home from the bus-stop at Washington, after spending the day at Worthing poultry market.

Few people were about, for it was late and bitter cold. But he did meet one fellow, muffled up in a long cloak, with a hood drawn closely over his face. As they passed, my brother-in-law called out a cheery good night. He got no answer. When he turned to look after the stranger he had vanished.

The Shop, the Milk and the Blacksmith, told about it, nodded their heads wisely and said: 'Ar, you've seen Our Monk. He always walks Christmas time down along Washington way.'

My sister resolutely pooh-poohed this story. Her comment, as she got on with her baking, 'There must have been a fancy-dress party somewhere.' She was always set against anything that smacked of superstition. She had a vivid enough imagination, as I know from reading her early attempts at fiction, but she liked to have matters of fact corroborated by the evidence of her own senses.

Mother once told me a story about her which delights me. When she was a small child she had listened attentively to a bible lesson (we all had bible lessons on Sunday afternoons) about faith moving mountains.

That evening Mother went up to say good night to her in bed and found her singularly thoughtful. 'What's the matter, Franziska?' Mother asked. 'I've been believing and *believing*,' she replied, 'that

that lamp would jump off the mantelpiece on to the table. And it hasn't and I knew it wouldn't.'

Before my marriage I had never been abroad. This seems odd when you consider that of all my father's people not one was English or had lived in England. My elder sisters had often told me about the holidays they spent in Switzerland with Father. I have an account of one of these holidays beside me now, in Marion's handwriting. It is headed: 'Trip to Switzerland, Summer Holidays 1898', and begins: 'Bank holiday Monday. Father, F. and I left Fallowfield for King's X.' At that time Marion would have been about to go to Newnham; Franziska was already at Somerville, pertly pretty, highly flirtatious, surrounded by clusters of admirers; I was fifteen months old and in the nursery under Lizzie's charge, completely indifferent to the comings and goings of my elders.

Marion was a dutiful observer rather than a revealing diarist. Her travel brochure is freely illustrated with picture-postcard views of 'Chillon et Le Dent du Midi', 'Lac Leman—Barque', 'Zürich—Blick von Mühlesteg', but the text is generally bleak.

'We also from the distance saw the castle of *Chillon*, famed by Byron, we wanted to go to see it, but had not time.' 'In Zürich, Father and I went to Aunt Juliet's and were just in time for coffee. The Schloss is on the lake next the Tonhalle and the Bindschedlers' (our cousins) 'live on the 2nd storey. The rooms all open out of one another and are lovely. Everything is lit by electric light, and worked by electricity.'

This must have seemed a tremendous novelty to a girl accustomed to the dim yellow gaslight of the tall house in Manchester. But Marion adds no comment to the bald statement. 'A Trip to Switzerland' is not that kind of diary. I have searched the pages in vain, for instance, for any phrase that might throw light on Father's character: I hoped to have some living image to lend warmth to that cold photograph of the man in the billycock hat which was all I really knew of the individual who was to be addressed as *'lieber Vater'*. But I couldn't find a thing.

Only once does Marion's diary spring to life, in her shocked description of the stopover in Paris, where they were to change trains for Switzerland.

'At Paris', she writes, 'they insisted on looking at our luggage before we went into the town. We drove in an open carriage from the

Gare du Nord to the Gare de Lyons, it was very interesting. The Paris cab-drivers drive very strangely; they never look where they are going to, but drive straight on until they nearly run into something and then have to draw up suddenly with a jerk. In the Gare de Lyons we had dinner (8 o'clock) in a buffet literally *without* windows; the atmosphere was indescribable. I suppose the French like warmth. It was very full and very hot and everyone in a tremendous hurry; the French people all seemed as if they were having a race to see who could eat most in the shortest possible time.'

Paris was naturally the first 'abroad' place which Roffe and I visited after our marriage. For some odd reason I never fell violently in love with Paris, as I did later with the Black Forest and the Landes and Pyrenees. The mistake was mine, I'm sure. Except for a trip to Passy, to discover the place where Peter Ibbetson spent his boyhood, we saw only, by and large, the tourists' face of Paris.

The Grands Boulevardes, the Louvre, the Madeleine, the Opéra (and how horrified I was by the standards of French opera with its intromissions of vapid ballet!). And there was, of course, the ritual visit to the heights of Montparnasse, to find the small restaurant with its superb view and inflated prices, where Charpentier is supposed to have written 'Louise'.

We went to Paris several times, however, and there are many things about those visits that I recall with pleasure. Hot chocolate and croissants in bed for breakfast. The gay flower-stalls in the Place de l'Opéra. Empty early-morning hours when pavements were washed down and swept, and no trippers were abroad except ourselves. Slivers of crisp fried onion or melting vol-au-vents served while a violinist played the 'pop' song of the moment, 'Millions of Harlequin'. Cognac with a lump of sugar outside a café. Wild strawberries. A rakish white beret which I bought for twopence somewhere. The enormous crabs and lobsters in the windows of Prunier's, which we passed each night to reach our small hotel.

The visit to Paris that I remember most vividly took place at Christmas. Mother came with us on that occasion, and I remember it chiefly for the ungodly horrors of the journey home. When we reached Calais it was blowing half a gale. Seas were enormous, and travellers were advised not to attempt the Channel crossing until next morning. Most of them accepted this advice. But Roffe had to get back to his desk at

John Bull, and we were among the few who decided to take the risk.

They shipped us in an old minesweeper and battened down the hatches. The route was changed from Calais–Dover to Calais–Southampton. The journey took something like fourteen hours, for it was too rough, when we neared the English coast, to put into Southampton Water.

I never was so sick in all my life. I was also terrified as the ship shuddered, and pitched and rolled. I felt certain that one way or another I was going to die.

When eventually we dropped anchor in Southampton Water we had to make our way through three anchored ships before we could land. My husband and I were pretty shaky specimens by that time. I had been a good deal worried about Mother. But when we crawled out of our cabins, feeling and looking like bits of wilted lettuce, there she was on deck, composedly talking to an officer, as fresh and blooming as a child.

It must have been the summer after this Christmas ordeal that we took our longest foreign tour. James Bone had decided that it would be a nice idea to run a series of articles in the *Manchester Guardian* about film production on the continent; specifically in France, Germany and Italy.

It was fixed to coincide with my husband's annual leave, and this time my sister Marion came with us. Her wide experience of travel and her fluent German were a boon, as we were quickly to discover.

I can remember as if it were yesterday one scene of her resourcefulness. We had found some excuse to spend a night in Prague. Strange night. Strange food and wine. Strange music everywhere. Strange feeling of the borders of the East. Absurdly I found it all a little frightening, and was relieved to get away.

We took the train to Vienna in the morning and found a compartment to ourselves. Marion and I were sitting on one side of the carriage. There was a curious little cubby-hole on the other side, where Roffe sat, with a table in front of him. He was writing something for *John Bull,* and had all his papers spread out on the table when we reached the Austrian frontier. Two Customs officers, dressed in gorgeous cloaks and light blue uniforms, came in, looking like fugitives from *The Merry Widow.*

They looked at Marion's passport and mine, then surveyed Roffe with deep suspicion. Once of them turned to Marion and asked in German, 'Who is this gentleman, and what is it he writes?'

Quick as a flash she answered in the same language, 'He is Herr Diplomat; he is taking documents to your Minister.' Without another word the pair clicked their heels, saluted and withdrew, looking more than ever like something out of *The Merry Widow*.

The *Guardian* had put me in touch with their correspondents in Berlin, Vienna and in Rome. (By this time I could find my way round Paris for myself.) The kindest and most charming of all was Herr Fodor, their man in Vienna. He was a gentle soul, a passionate lover of his city and its ways, and nothing was too much trouble for him.

He showed us not only where to find Vienna's art treasures and jewels of architectural baroque, but where to find the best 'schalgobers' (hot chocolate with whipped cream on top) and Wiener schnitzel. He introduced us to out-of-the-way restaurants which served out-of-the-way food and wine. He directed us to a shop where we bought wallets and purses and blotters in the most beautifully tooled and coloured leather. Nearly forty years later some of those wallets are still in use, and *The Radio Times* is modestly encased in a blotter from Vienna.

There was no film industry that we could find in Austria, but there was plenty in Berlin. At that time Ufa was almost certainly the most important film-producing organization in Europe, including Britain. The Ufa people were not the sort to shun publicity. From the moment of our arrival they took complete charge of us, and before we had time to unpack our bags we were whirled off to the studios at Neubabelsburg, where Fritz Lang was directing *Metropolis*.

It was impossible not to be impressed by 'Babelsburg', as its intimates called it. The sheer size and bulk and feverish activity might not have surprised a visitor from Hollywood, but I had never seen a studio to compare with it. Later one was to get something of the same impression at Denham, but the heyday of Denham was more than ten years ahead.

We were shown over the lots—on one of them a solid castle had been built for *The Chronicle of the Grieshuis* and looked as if it were to stand for all eternity—by a strange old man whose provenance I never quite discovered. He gave the impression of having worked at Neubabelsburg as man and boy, mostly on the consumption of liquor in the canteen. He was a friendly native, but his English had its limitations.

Indeed, it was mainly restricted to the beautiful words 'More schnapps'.

After Neubabelsburg the Berlin studios at Tempelhof seemed puny and unimpressive. We didn't stay there long. There was only one film on the floor, a comedy of some sort, starring the Hungarian actress Maria Corda. We watched for a few minutes while the lady was directed in a small scene in a doorway by her husband, Alexander Corda.

I had not heard of this man Corda (the name was spelt with a C then) and thought, if I thought about it at all, that his personality was colourless and his work would never amount to anything of significance. In both of which assumptions I was wholly wrong.

There was plenty of news to send home about film production in Berlin, but an article had still to be written about the film industry in Italy. This article turned out to be a brief report of utter inactivity. Only one film was being made in the whole of Italy, as far as I could discover. This was a stereotyped affair of pageantry, with hundreds of extras dressed up as ancient Romans or early Christians, on location along the Appian Way. Nobody that I spoke to seemed particularly concerned about it. Indeed, few people were to be seriously concerned about the cinema in Italy for another twenty years.

Still, if I had only a negative report to send back to London I did get a free holiday in Rome at the *Guardian*'s expense. A few days of it were quite enough for me. It was mid-August, and very, very hot in Rome. The sky was full of swallows, wheeling and calling, and I wondered where in the world (you couldn't say 'on earth') they found their energy.

I remember dragging aching feet along white, relentless streets, looking at innumerable churches and 'doing' the Colosseum and St. Peter's. The Colosseum was a disappointment in merciless sunshine. I felt I had seen it more comfortably before in the big photograph which hung in the hall at Lady Barn House. St. Peter's was cool, at least, and I was fascinated by the multitude of visiting priests from various countries in robes of many colours.

Marion and I saw the Pope at quite close quarters. We bought tickets from the reception clerk at our hotel, borrowed black headscarves from the chambermaid and went to the Vatican to watch the Pope pass in ceremony from room to room.

Roffe, who had been brought up a Quaker, refused to come, but

I had no scruples about kneeling for the Pope's blessing. I did, though, have a guilty and foolish feeling that the Papal eye was on me and the Papal voice was saying, 'Out, you heretic!'

I sometimes have that feeling still, when I go into Westminster Cathedral for a few minutes to sit and think, and light another candle at a shrine where the flames seem to be guttering low. In spite of my nonconformist ancestry, my Church of England upbringing, I *prefer* Catholic churches for quiet and meditation. Perhaps it is the sense of drama, but I find great solace there.

Rome was the last place on my official *Guardian* schedule; but, perhaps with memories of *The Gondoliers* in mind, I insisted on spending a couple of days, at our own expense, in Venice. Very few things come up to one's expectations in life, but Venice transcended mine.

I fell in love with it at first sight, as we stepped out of the train late one night more or less straight into a canal. Nothing had led me to understand that the streets of Venice are really waterways, and that the taxicabs are really gondolas. That first discovery of Venice was like something out of a fairy-book, and indeed, in spite of the mosquitoes, it never quite lost the sense of magic.

In those days there were comparatively few tourists. There was room to move at ease and gaze into the little enchanting shops in the *calles* round St. Mark's Square, although the whole thing had the charm of the perfect miniature. A miniature in rose with pigeons. Fairy palaces flowering like iris on the banks of the canals.

The single disappointment of Venice was the Lido, which seemed to me an ostentatiously dull place, as vulgar as Blackpool and far less human. We spent a couple of hours there, ate an outrageously expensive lunch at some snob hotel, walked a few hundred yards along the unexciting beach and went back with relief to the canals and *calles*, the mosquitoes and the pigeons.

That one experience of the Lido has been enough to keep me resolutely away from the Venice Film Festival, although I have been invited to attend it many times, once indeed to act as British representative on the panel of judges. Venice, apart from the Lido, is one of the memories I cherish, and I prefer to keep the charm unbroken, the mystery unresolved.

All holidays, even working holidays, are difficult to get over, and this one seemed more difficult than most. I went back to London with no great enthusiasm for the Hollywood films which I was regularly required to criticize; the weekly fare that was fed into our picture palaces. For palaces, no less, they had become, with marble halls and clinging plush and mighty Wurlitzers. With very few exceptions, the pictures themselves were crudely unimaginative or ostentatious.

But in Berlin we had seen a film which made this gilded Hollywood stuff look puny. It was called *Der Panzerkreuser Potemkin*. It came from Soviet Russia, and was directed by a man named Eisenstein. We caught it by accident one afternoon in some flea-pit in the workers' quarter.

In my report from Berlin I had hailed it with enthusiasm. Many months were to pass before *The Battleship Potemkin* reached England, bringing with it the last and greatest configuration of pictures ever made for the silent cinema. It was nice to know that one had at least recognized its quality and heralded the news.

12

A HOUSE OF OUR OWN

It is hard, in any book of reminiscences, to balance the account between public and private life, but I am inclined to give the preference to personal impressions and intimations, since these are things that the writer alone possesses. For the critical records the most important thing about the middle 1920s is the glory of the Russian cinema, and the giant stature of Eisenstein, Pudowkin, Dovjhenko and their fellows. In my own private record the most important thing is that we built a house.

Neither my husband nor I had taken very kindly to life in London flats. Nor had Mother, although unlike me she never grumbled. We were all North Country people, and to us this sort of existence was alien. We wanted a real home with an upstairs, a downstairs and a garden of our own. We wanted a place within reach of London, but away from the rush and tumult; a place where one could breathe fresh air. Some place, as my Swiss cousin Ella aptly described it, 'green and cal-ming'.

We found the somewhere green and calming in the spring of 1925, at Pinner Hill, in the north-west tip of Middlesex. They were developing a new private estate, and at Easter we drove out there with Mother, and immediately fell in love with it.

Mother saw a small house that had just been finished, with about half an acre for a garden. It was a pretty house, with four bedrooms and two sitting-rooms, enough to accommodate any of the family who happened to be at home. But I think it was really the garden space that took her fancy.

She loved flowers dearly, and had always missed, as I now realize, our grubby old gardens in Manchester, with their few azaleas (the old-fashioned orange ones, with their sweet, penetrating scent), the hardy annuals, the tulip tree and the masses of pale anemone japonica.

She liked to pore over plant catalogues and poke little things into rockeries. She filled diaries with botany notes and names and descriptions of wildflowers. Whenever I see a cherry tree in blossom I think of Mother quietly saying, 'Loveliest of trees, the cherry now. . . .' As a child, I used to tease her about her favourite quotation, but now I find it haunts me every spring. Pinner Hill is prettily pink today with ornamental cherries, but give me for choice a mass of branches of the old bird cherry, the wild white one, banked against an April sky.

Mother bought her little house and moved into it that summer. Meanwhile Roffe and I had bought a plot of land almost opposite, and our house was busy building. We had wanted a plot much farther up the Hill, with a view on clear days to the North Downs and the Hog's Back, but there was some problem over the drainage, and the land wasn't available. As I grow older, and become increasingly conscious of the gradients, I am thankful that we had to settle lower down. Our Hill is a real hill, approached by other hills. To walk home from anywhere, particularly with a loaded shopping basket, is quite an ordeal for the woman who is no longer an Atalanta.

That was a wonderful summer, coming over to visit Mother and watching our own house grow. At first there was nothing to see except a rough pegged-out plot on the side of a sloping field. Yellow squelch from the excavations. (We live on heavy clay.) Then the foundations, the flat pattern of a house. So very small they looked; I never thought a house could be so small.

Next the walls began to rise, and every time I came to visit, the two little girls from across the road were skipping and clambering over the bricks. By autumn it was nearly finished, for the summer had been dry and warm, and there was hope of moving in by Christmas. Never mind that the garden was rough field grass, bounded by bare posts and single strands of wire. It was something of our own at last; the beginning of a new life, the fabric of a home.

I don't believe I gave much thought to films that summer, though I did my best to be a conscientious critic. But the private mind behind the reviewer's mind was filled with measurements of curtains, with puzzlement over the right shade of tiles for bedroom fireplaces, with problems of the respective merits of sliding or folding doors, with pride in the parquet flooring which was to set off the rose-red Persian rug that C. P. Scott had given us for a wedding present.

Of course we made the most stupid mistakes, as most people do when they set up housekeeping. If I were to plan the house over again it would be a very different thing. We were over-persuaded by the architect to have what he called a 'loggia' and I call a veranda, the idea being that we could sit there and bask in sunshine almost all the year round. A nice theory, but it didn't work in practice. The long, sloping roof cuts off all but a small patch of sunshine, and blocks the light from the sitting-room windows. However, all our dogs have liked it as an observation post, and it certainly is picturesque.

We did manage to defeat the architect's intention of putting a lavatory in the kitchen exactly opposite the larder, but we had many fights with the builders about windows. Their idea of a proper bedroom window was three lights, and only two of each set of windows to open. We got our way in the end, more or less, but it was quite a tussle, and the foreman obviously thought very poorly of people who wanted to poison their bedrooms with deadly night air.

However, with all its faults, ours is a homey house and I am fond of it. People often ask us why we called it Lane End, since it is clearly nothing of the kind. But once upon a time it was. When we first moved here from London we felt we were living in the heart of the country. Our house was at the end of a quiet lane, hedged with hawthorn, honeysuckle and wild roses. On each side of the lane were fields, a few of them under the plough, but most of them pasture land, with cattle grazing.

It was wonderfully peaceful, with larks and nightingales in summer, and often on winter mornings we would find tracks of hare or fox across the snow. When you got out of the train from Baker Street the air was like wine.

All that is changed today. Ribbon development has brought London to our threshold. The fields and cattle have gone. So have the nightingales and all but a few brave larks. Between the Hill and the new station and shopping centre in the valley there is a packed mosaic of bungalows and houses, each with its television aerial; a labyrinth of roads and 'closes' with hideous concrete lamp standards, uglifying the night with that cold light which makes your dearest friend look like something that has been too long on the butcher's slab.

The noise of traffic beats and roars outside the white gates of the estate (which is supposed to be private and regrettably is not). At rush hours I am quite frightened to take the dog across the road. But inside the gates there is mercifully little change so far, except for the scattered tins, cigarette packs and broken bottles left by triumphant trespassers.

All the land hereabouts, wood, pasture and arable, used to belong to a rambling old mansion, which was described by one Dr. Pell in 1820 in vivid terms.

'We lived on the borders of a great wood on the northern boundary of Middlesex, with no neighbours within a mile, save of doubtful character. So the family blunderbuss was fired at night about once a fortnight to announce that the household was armed, and a few mantraps and spring guns were set in the coverts.'

There are no longer any coverts on Pinner Hill. The mansion has been turned into a clubhouse for golfers. The great wood is reduced to a thin strip of trees between the first fairway and the new housing estate down at Oxhey, just across the border into Hertfordshire.

My own private name for the new housing estate is Sodom-and-Gomorrah. When I see its brave young citizens hacking at the trees, setting fire to bracken, tearing up the bluebells only to drop them a moment later in white and wilting bundles, shooting at the birds with slings and air rifles, and sneaking into the road to smash the gas lamps, I grow atavistic in my fury. I long for the return of Dr. Pell and his family blunderbuss, to announce that the households are still armed.

Even without benefit of blunderbuss, Pinner Hill is still comparatively unspoilt. Our boast is that we are four hundred and fifty feet above sea-level. I never can decide whether the views are more satisfying by day, where you can see clear to the heights of Hampstead in one direction and the North Downs in the other, or by night when the huge bowl of Middlesex seems carpeted with candles, and the sky is pierced by the lighted spire at the top of Harrow Hill.

These parts are mentioned in Domesday Book as 'a park of wild beasts of the forest'. There were few wild beasts left when we pegged out our plot for building, except for the odd hare and rabbit, fox and squirrel. The slopes were open meadow land with hardly any trees, except for a fringe of old pines round the boundaries and an occasional monarch oak or chestnut.

Naturally the first thing that people did was to plant trees in their gardens. 'It looks so *bare* without trees,' we said. So we all planted far too many trees, without considering the way that trees will grow. Silver birches have shot up like weeds; so have maples, rowans and the everlasting sycamore. The long, groping toes of poplars hump the lawns a hundred yards away from the parent tree. The catkins of our scented poplar sprawl across the lawn in spring like fat, red caterpillars, and the top of what was such a small tree when we planted it now seems to touch the sky.

The trees play havoc with the gardens, but it is hard to regret them, both for their own beauty and because they bring the birds. For a home so close to a big city, this is the most *birdy* place I have ever known. Of course, they devour the yellow crocuses, the polyanthus and the rowan berries. They line their nests most impudently and elegantly with stripped petals of the purple primrose. They leave their droppings with no sense of discrimination on garden furniture. But who would be without them? I know I would not.

The dawn chorus in May is something to expect with rapture. First a single voice, tentative, in the half-dark; then another, and another; and by a few minutes after four o'clock the full, jubilant unison.

Only in August is there any pause in birdsong. As I write now, in October, a pair of robins in the silver birches are shrilly singing at each other. This is their autumn song, fierce and penetrating, so different from the sweetness of the spring mating song.

At mating time the robins are quite fearless. They fly in and out of my bedroom windows and conduct their courtship freely on the carpet. Apart from robins, sparrows, tits, blackbirds, thrushes, starlings, cuckoos, and all the more domestic finches, we have a host of owls, woodpeckers and wood pigeons, and are assailed at the moment by the rough cries of at least two pairs of hawfinches.

One day last summer I heard our dog barking in a curiously perplexed way on the veranda. I hurried out to find a fledgling hawfinch perched on the wall, as still as an owl. It let me pick it up—so soft its feathers were in one's hands—then fluttered in a blundering way to a silver birch, where it clung for a few seconds to the slender strands, and then fell of its own weight on to the grass. It wasn't hurt. It was only a silly baby bent on exploring. The parents soon came and scolded it away, shepherding it into the safe underwood with a flap of burnished wings.

We did move into our house in time for Christmas, just as the snow began to fall. Almost the first thing we did, to celebrate our freedom from flat life, was to get a dog. He was an Aberdeen terrier called Jock; not a very good Aberdeen, obviously some kennel's discard; but I saw him in the window of a pet shop in High Holborn, and he looked so wistful that I had to buy him.

Jock was the first of a series of Scots dogs. After him came Mickey, a white West Highland; followed by Jamie, a wheaten Cairn, whom we found as a pathetic little object in a farmyard amongst cocks and hens, infested with worms and fleas, and in such bad condition that the night we brought him home he had a fit, and we thought we were going to lose him. With care, though, he recovered and lived to the ripe old age of fifteen, a darling dog, with a sensibility that was almost human. The present incumbent of the dog-bowl is Christie, so-called because his birthday is at Christmas; another Cairn, with a lion's mane and a coat red as a fox's.

We always say apologetically, when an apology seems called for, 'The Hill is such a lonely place; you couldn't live up here without a dog.' But this is merely an excuse for sentiment. We happen to be very fond of dogs. We *enjoy* keeping a family dog, just as I'm sure the good Dr. Pell enjoyed firing the family blunderbuss, and not only to announce to persons of doubtful character that the household of Lane End is armed.

During that first year at Pinner Hill we were faced with the problem of making a garden out of rough meadow. Neither Roffe nor I had any experience of gardening, and hardly knew a Michaelmas daisy from a lupin. It was simple enough to tell the difference when the things were in flower, but a green clump of something or other given us by friends out of their own gardens meant absolutely nothing.

Of course we made disastrous and costly mistakes. The first and worst mistake was to plant hedges of *Cupressus macrocarpa*. We were told that macrocarpa trees grew fast and would make the bare, open garden private in no time. This was quite true, for ten years or so. They shot up valiantly and were pleasant and evergreen in winter. But after a time most of them began to die. Snow piled up and broke the branches. Cutting seemed fatal to them; so did the touch of wire netting. A few individual trees grew to monstrous size, providing shade where we least wanted shade. The others perished one by one. Solemnly I warn any novice gardener against putting his faith in macrocarpa. It may shoot up in the night like Jack's beanstalk, but in the end it will betray him.

In making any garden one must plant for tomorrow. To try to hurry nature is expensive and improvident. To fight against nature is importunate and ridiculous. Reluctantly, over the years, I have learnt to confine myself to growing plants that do grow and indeed revel in our heavy clay soil. I have abandoned, one after the other, the herbaceous borders, the struggling rockeries, the azaleas and rhododendrons, and more or less given up the garden to grass and roses.

My ignorance of roses when I first met them was complete. They didn't grow in any of our Manchester gardens, except for one scrubby little bush, sticky with greenfly, which seemed to enjoy the shelter of the Presbyterian church. I used to pick a bunch of small, mis-shapen flowers and present them to some embarrassed schoolmistress or Sixth Former, who would be seen surreptitiously removing the greenfly.

I always tore my hands in doing so. The memory still haunts me, and every time I see an actress on the screen arranging, with pale, elegant hands, the roses she has 'plucked', I feel like screaming out, 'You can't do that, you idiot!' No, you can't 'pluck' roses, even wearing gloves, if you have any regard either for your skin or for your plants. Cutting roses is an art that requires a careful eye and sharp secateurs. 'Cut roses as if you were stealing them,' advises an old gardening book, and there is a great deal to be said for that idea.

I learnt how to handle roses from a master gardener. His name was George Herring, and he had looked after the grounds of the big house on Pinner Hill for as long as anybody could remember. He was a majestic old man with a sweeping grey moustache, who could still dig like a navvy, but handled flowers as tenderly as if they were children.

At that time Dr. Pell's house was empty and the gardens were about to be turned into a golf-course. Herring, who lived in the lodge, was kept on to tend the peaches and grapes in the glasshouses for the new owners of the estate. I think he must have grieved a good deal over departed splendours; the walled garden turned to wilderness, the untended rose garden soon to be destroyed, the fine trees which would inevitably be cut down for building.

At all events, he seemed glad when I turned up to see him and ask him naïve questions about gardens. He made a rather special favourite of me, perhaps because I was so eager and so frankly ignorant. He cut me great bunches of the doomed roses, brought down a number of old standards and planted them in our garden.

He taught me how to prune, hard and fearlessly. He showed me how to curl the outer petals of a rose for exhibition; how to breathe gently into a flower that seemed indisposed to open; a version of the human mouth-to-mouth emergency treatment, known grandiloquently as the 'kiss of life'.

In time I learnt to develop my own skills with roses, and today I have something like a thousand bushes. Of the few things that I know really well, including films, opera and detective stories, I think I know roses best.

All this talk of homes and gardens has led me away from the main track of the story, which is about the development of a century as well as the concerns of an individual.

The year was 1926. The Charleston was all the rage, and it was reported that the Prince of Wales was taking lessons. *Thés dansants* were the smart engagements for the afternoon. The top people were wearing hair like birds' nests, hats like inverted coal-scuttles, waists around their hips, strap shoes with Cuban heels, huge ribbon bows attached at random to any and every part of their physical geography, and all the beads that they could muster.

The Derby was won by Coronach in a downpour, but we had enjoyed, according to the newspapers, a wonderful spring. One fine morning towards the end of April (the 21st, to be exact, a Wednesday), those who were up and about the West End very early observed unusual activity outside No. 17, Bruton Street, the town house of the Earl and Countess of Strathmore.

The young Duchess of York had come to be with her own mother for the birth of her first baby. It was not yet daylight when the Home Secretary, Sir William Joynson Hicks, was called to assist, in the French sense, at the birth of the royal infant 'on behalf of Parliament and the people'; according to the curious and embarrassing old custom, now discontinued, which demanded proof of identity, in case some small pretender had been smuggled into the bedroom in the doctor's bag or in a warming-pan.

Everyone was very pleased about the little girl in Bruton Street. It was nice, people said in all parts of the country, in pubs and clubs and shops and omnibuses and over the garden fence, that King George and Queen Mary should have a grandchild. It was nice that the popular young Duchess should have had her baby, like any London housewife, in a plain house with a number. It was nice that they were going to call the child Elizabeth Alexandra Mary, after her mother, great-grandmother and grandmother.

There hadn't been an Elizabeth in the royal family for a long time. Queen Victoria had disliked the name, and said so. It was not in common usage in the 1920s. But it struck the imagination. 'Elizabeth of York', one columnist was moved to write, 'is a name that conjures up the pageant of English history like the blast of a trumpet. May its wearer carry it far, and with the fairest fortunes!'

Few people at that time could have guessed how far its wearer was destined to carry it. The little Princess, it's true, was the fourth lady in the land, but she seemed likely to grow up on the fringe of court life, the daughter of a king's second son, and in due time a king's niece. For her Uncle David, the Prince of Wales, was only thirty-two, one of the most eligible bachelors in the world, and certainly the darling of the people.

In any case, there were more immediate things to think about than the future of the baby in Bruton Street. A couple of weeks later the nation was plunged into a General Strike. For a short time there was utter chaos in all departments of life. How long can it last? we asked one another desperately. How shall we get to work? What work can we do if we manage to get there? Who is going to maintain essential services? Will there be enough food? Any coal? When will there be proper newspapers again? And, of course, the eternal question, What is the Government doing, and why?

Several of our neighbours went out to drive omnibuses and Underground trains. I was talking about the strike lately to a number of journalist friends. 'All I can remember,' said the *Motion Picture Herald*, 'is driving a pirate bus, being knocked out by half a brick and waking up in hospital.'

'I was a theological student then,' said the *Catholic Film Institute*. 'A number of us had been to some meeting or other in a bus, and at the end of the journey we were held up by armed police at midnight in the depot. We were wearing our blacks, and they insisted we were saboteurs in disguise. It was very difficult to disillusion them.'

Some time ago I was asked to write an article for *Good Housekeeping* about the year the Queen was born. I have just dug it out of my files, and find some amusing things that I should like to quote.

When I asked them what they could remember of the year 1926 a number of people foxed me straight away by saying, 'Darling, but I wasn't *born*, or, 'My dear soul, I was only in my *pram*.' But some celebrities were more forthcoming.

Anna Neagle laughed and said she remembered the year only too well. She was in the chorus of *Rose Marie* at Drury Lane, one of the original Totem Tom-Tom girls. 'I was living at Holland Park,' she said, 'and I used to walk to the theatre every night. After the show I walked on to the Trocadero for the Cochran Cabaret, and after that I had to get home as best I could. Sometimes I was lucky enough to get a lift on the back of an electrician's motor-bike; otherwise I used my own two feet. It meant a lot of walking, but I was young and didn't mind.' Today Anna Neagle is not so young, but she likes to put on a raincoat and sensible shoes and take a brisk constitutional before she goes to bed. She is still an indefatigable walker.

Jack Hawkins has a special reason for remembering the year. He was sixteen, and had just made his fourth stage appearance, as Bernardo in *The Cenci*. The play was no great hit, but Hawkins was. 'It is possible', wrote James Agate in his first-night review, 'that in Master J. Hawkins we have a very fine actor in the making. I have never seen a boy actor with so much promise.'

Alec Guinness has his own romantic memories of the year. He was twelve years old, and on the way back to his Hampshire preparatory school after the Christmas holidays. To his immense delight, snow fell so heavily that the line and roads were blocked, and he had to spend the night alone in a small country pub. 'It made me feel grown-up and adventurous,' he said. 'It was like something out of Dickens.'

I asked the ageless and enchanting Fay Compton what she could remember of the year. She is one of the few outstanding actresses who can, or will, admit that by that time she was already a veteran on the stage. She says it was a busy year, interrupted by an operation for a perforated appendix, and her dates are a little muddled.

'But what I do remember,' she said, 'is fairly late in the year appearing with dear Ivor Novello in *Liliom*, which he produced with his own money. It was a terrible flop, but he never stopped laughing about it, bless him. That was the beginning of a long association between us in the theatre. Oh, and there *is* another thing. When we were rehearsing there was a certain character called Ficsur which somehow couldn't be cast. I noticed a young actor wandering about in the crowd who seemed to me just right for the part. I mentioned it to the producer and the suggestion was adopted.' The young actor proved to be the hit of this short-lived play. His name was Charles Laughton.

In the world of film everything seemed prosperous enough. We were dazzled with publicity about stars, their wardrobes, their marble swimming pools, their stupendous salaries and the prospects of a fabulously spectacular *Ben Hur*.

But as 1926 slipped into 1927 and the year rolled on, there were increasing rumours that all was not well with Hollywood. Producing companies had involved themselves too deep with theatre-owning. They were robbing Peter to pay Paul. The only star who brought steady money into the box-office was a handsome Alsatian wolfhound named Rin-Tin-Tin. Two of the major studios were experimenting with synchronized music-tracks, and every now and then a short new item with recorded dialogue gave rise to the dread (yes, it was dread for the whole industry) that sound films must be just round the corner.

About this time a curious thing happened in my private life. For some months my husband had been worried about his position on *John Bull* and, whether on my suggestion or Mother's I can't remember, he went to Manchester to consult C. P. Scott about another job. When Mr. Scott heard that he had been a reviewer on the *Kinematograph Weekly* he advised him, 'Go to J. L. Garvin and tell him from me that it's time the *Observer* had a film column.'

Roffe duly reported the message to J. L. Garvin and got a characteristic answer. 'Go back to C. P. Scott and tell him from me that there will be no film column in the *Observer* as long as I am editor of the paper.'

But that was by no means the end of the affair. A year or so later, at the beginning of 1928, a letter came to me in Garvin's large, sprawling handwriting. It was a charming letter, and in its way quite shameless. For some time, the writer said, he had been considering the introduction of new features to the *Observer*. The first of these, he felt, should be a film column. He had been watching my work in the *Manchester Guardian* with interest. Would I consider a change of paper?

This put me in a fearful quandary. Looking back on it now, the whole thing strikes me as a piece of slight journalistic skulduggery. No wonder C. P. Scott was hurt and surprised when I wrote to tell him of the offer. What shall I do? I asked. I really didn't know. His answer, though grieved, was affectionate and fair. I should consider it very seriously, he said.

For many harassed days I did so. I was unhappy but severely tempted. By nature I am conservative and shrink from changes. The *Manchester Guardian* had been good to me, and Mr. Scott himself was a close personal friend. It seemed rather like a betrayal to leave him.

But there were points to be argued on the other side. The *Observer* offered better terms; the princely sum of seven guineas a week and my name in a byline at the top of the column instead of mere initials at the bottom. It was a national newspaper, whereas the *Manchester Guardian*, for all its liberality, was still provincially controlled. For some time now 'The Week on the Screen' had not enjoyed the freedom of its early days. In spite of all that Bone could do, the advertising side had taken hold, and it was made clear to us that what was wanted was not so much reviews of new films, as notices of films appearing currently in Manchester.

In addition, I discovered that I was going to have a baby. That meant a break of several weeks in summer, whatever paper I was working for. It seemed a hint that this might be the moment to correlate a change in employment with an interruption of routine.

The baby was due in August. I decided to leave the *Manchester Guardian* in July and join the *Observer* in September. It was a hard decision, and I was lucky in dealing with two great editors who understood the reasons for it.

Mr. Scott wrote to me in May, from his home at The Firs, Fallowfield, where I had so often played tennis in my schooldays. All the sweetness and warmth of the man glows through the letter, and I should like in gratitude to quote it almost in full.

'Dear Caroline,
'Forgive a letter written the other day in haste and unhappiness. I think I wrote it for distraction. But I do want to tell you, now that your writing for the paper is nearly at an end, how very greatly I and all who are intimately concerned for the credit of the paper have valued it. I take some credit to myself for having instantly realized that you would be an incomparable person to handle that new and difficult subject and to raise it to its due level as an art.
'You have richly fulfilled my expectation and among writers for the kinema have achieved an easy supremacy. I am so glad, dear, to think of the great change that is coming to you and its glorious hopes and am quite sure—it is obvious—that you are right, without abandoning the work you do so well, to moderate its calls upon you.
'Ever your affectionate,
C. P. Scott.'

That was Mr. Scott, who had known me for thirty years. This is J. L. Garvin, whom at that time I had never met at all. On blue notepaper from his home at Gregories, Beaconsfield, he wrote a few days later (by hand, of course, for in those days typewriting was considered most uncivil):

'My Dear Miss Lejeune,
'I much hope our excellent friends of the *Manchester Guardian* were not hurt, but can't help being glad on our own account. It was I who picked out your work long since as the best of its kind by far. The *Observer* will of course give you three or four times as many readers belonging to the intelligence of the country irrespective of party.
'About the pause before you come, I entirely understand. Notify Mr. Bell (the literary editor) when you are ready and not before. He will tell me when you can come for a conversation, and we shall then start happily.
'Sincerely yours,
J. L. Garvin.'

THANK YOU FOR HAVING ME

The conversation took place in due course. It was utterly one-sided, formidable and very brief. J. L. Garvin, in customary suit of solemn black, the inevitable cigar clamped cater-cornered in his mouth, his tall figure restless and jerky as he prowled behind the editorial desk, welcomed me into the family party of the *Observer*. He told me three things explicitly. The first was, 'Never be afraid of the pronoun I.' The second, 'You will probably not see me again unless things go wrong.' The third was, 'Above all else remember this: nobody can get at you except over my dead body.'

13

THE *OBSERVER* AND THE TALKIES

THE date was October 1928. I had been on the *Observer* a couple of weeks, and our son was two months old, when the first full-length talking picture came to London.

It was not, as people commonly imagine, either *The Jazz Singer* or *The Singing Fool*. It was a Hollywood version of Edgar Wallace's thriller *The Terror*. The scene was Hollywood's notion of an English country house, inexplicably haunted by ghostly organ music. The characters were Hollywood's idea of well-bred English people.

Nobody in his senses could describe *The Terror* as a good, or even a moderately good, film, but as a novelty it was sensational. Hardly had we settled in our seats before the curtains parted and a masked and cloaked figure advanced upon us from the screen. He pointed a menacing finger at the audience, spoke to each and every one of us directly and dared us to discover the identity of the murderer.

This was startling enough, but there were more shocks to come. It is almost fair to say there was a fresh shock every time a player opened his mouth to speak. The unforgettable moment came as the chords of the ghostly Wurlitzer rolled through the Piccadilly Theatre. The heroine, a flower of English maidenhood, who had long been admired as an *ingénue* in silent films, parted her rosebud lips and uttered memorable words, 'Jus' lissun to that *turrible* oirgan!'

I suppose *The Terror* was chosen to introduce the new 'wonder medium' to London on account of its presumed British atmosphere. The first talkie shown in the United States was *The Lights of New York*, with Dolores and Helene Costello.

This reached us a week later, and was followed in short order by

The Melody of Love, with Walter Pidgeon and Mildred Harris, and the far more celebrated Al Jolson film *The Singing Fool*, immortalized by P. G. Wodehouse in his short story *The Song of Songs*. You will, of course, recall that it was the habit of Bertie Wooster to render 'Sonny Boy' daily in his bath, in a pleasant, light baritone, with special attention to the poignant phrase about the angels being lonely, according to Jeeves.

The early talkies were received in London with passionate argument. Except for a few superior minds who affected indifference, everybody was excited. Indignant letters poured into *The Times*, protesting that these so-called 'talking films' were a menace to the cinema as an international art form. Other people, particularly those in Wardour Street with vast stocks of silent film to sell, pooh-poohed them as a passing phase. This nonsense couldn't last, they declared hopefully. After a few weeks the novelty would wear off and the public would go back and revel in a barkless Rin-Tin-Tin. The talkies had a bad Press on the whole. But the public went on flocking to hear them.

I take no special credit for having backed the talkies from the start. It seemed to me obvious that they had come to stay. It was easier for me to accept them than for many other critics. I am not at all an intellectual person. After my first wide-eyed quest for the undiscovered aesthetic I had made up my mind that there was no aesthetic to be discovered, and settled down to enjoy the cinema in comfort, accepting what seemed good to me and rejecting what seemed bad.

That course I pursued more or less consistently through all the years in which I practised criticism. There have been times when I have allowed an academic judgement to outweight my instinctive responses, but not very many of them; and they always left me with a slight sense of dishonesty. To paraphrase Mr. Edwards' remark to Dr. Johnson, 'I have tried too in my time to be a highbrow, but I don't know how, bourgeoisie was always breaking in.'

The success of the cinema from the beginning has been based on an optical illusion; a trick played on the eye and mind so that we think we see movement where there is no movement, simply a series of still photographs taken and projected at a certain rate.

The effect of this conjuring trick upon the great, willingly credulous public for whom the cinema was designed was to make us believe that the figures up there on the screen were real people, active characters in three dimensions. 'It's all so lifelike,' we used to say. Only one thing about it wasn't lifelike. These characters couldn't speak.

Suddenly, after thirty years of silent films, the conjuror-scientists produced a fresh illusion. By playing a trick upon the ear, as well as on the eye and mind, they persuaded us that the figures were actually talking; organs were pealing, locomotives puffing, motor-horns hooting and even ham-and-eggs sizzling in a frying-pan.

Common sense suggests that if films could have talked from the beginning they would have talked. (It is a wry thought that Edison's early experiments in cinematography were designed to provide adjuncts to his phonograph.) The customers were satisfied with silent films, because for thirty years they were the only films they could get. The conjurors weren't ready yet to open the whole bag of tricks. But when the bag *was* opened it seemed inevitable that the public would want it to stay open. That was why I went along with the talkies from the beginning. It was nonsense to regard them as a passing phase. They were here to stay, and no amount of argument could cast them out.

From where we stand now it is easy to think of the talkie revolution as something that happened overnight. In fact, the change from silent films to sound took months and even years to be accomplished. One after the other, in Europe as well as in America, studios were converted and soundproofed, theatres were wired for sound. Schedules for prospective films were turned topsy-turvy. Thousands of feet of exposed celluloid were scrapped. In a desperate attempt to save what could be snatched from the disaster, silent films already finished, or almost finished, were shot again as talkies, or furbished with 'talking sequences'.

Going to the pictures in those days was a hazardous adventure. You never quite knew what was likely to happen. The sound might break down altogether, so that the players were left to mouth at one another dumbly. It might go 'out of synch.', so that hero and heroine were resolutely speaking each other's lines. Or it might stick in the groove, like a disabled gramophone, and repeat with the croaking obstinacy of despair, 'I love you (croak) I love you (croak) I love you (croak, blank screen and merciful silence).'

It was fun to be a critic in those days. We were never gravelled for lack of matter. Each day brought its fresh experiences and comicalities. We were exposed to constant misadventure, but sustained by hope. We hadn't very long to wait before hope was rewarded.

Out of the chaos of the first all-talking, all-singing and all-dancing films came the disciplined *Broadway Melody*. London fell in love with it, and before long everyone who could whistle, and many more who couldn't, were experimenting with 'The Wedding of the Painted Doll'.

Before long everyone was whistling the tunes from *The Love Parade* and its successor, *Monte Carlo*. I still consider 'Beyond the Blue Horizon' as one of the most brilliant numbers ever composed and directed to illustrate the resources of the cinema with sound. I would bracket with it 'Sous les Toits de Paris' and the Harry Lime tune from *The Third Man*. Perhaps 'Over the Rainbow' and 'The Trolley Song', but these were Judy Garland's specials, belonging rather to the singer than to the film she played in.

Meanwhile a series of short cartoons about a mouse and his barnyard friends had made their way into the theatre programmes. Unheralded by publicity and unmarked at first, the Mickey Mouse films and the Silly Symphonies were not long in making their presence felt. Like strawberries and kippers, they appealed to every class of taste. The high brows (the term was spelt in two words in those days) discovered in their antics a fresh art form. The low brows enjoyed them for their engaging artlessness.

The young Walt Disney showed, in many ways, a genius comparable to Chaplin's. Like Chaplin he used very simple figures in familiar, everyday surroundings. His world was a less urban world than Chaplin's, but it was understandable to everyone who has kept white mice, rabbits, a guinea-pig or a tortoise in his childhood, or used his eyes on any country walk.

Like Chaplin too, Disney worked with scarcely any 'props'. His little figures moved in front of static, drawn backgrounds. Such accessories as the story needed were spun one out of another, transformed into a fluent rhythm with the barest economy of line.

In a Silly Symphony the starfish range themselves in rank and sway together, while their five points resolve into the head and limbs of little people. In an early Mickey Mouse, Mickey dances along a railway platform, turning the planks into the keys of a xylophone. He pulls spaghetti out of a can and plays on it with a 'cello bow.

Every line in these films is pregnant with the next; every movement is resolved; every gesture has its architectural function. And matched with the burlesque tripping measure that runs through the cartoons is a burlesque patter of tiny music; a kind of music-box jingle with sharp notes and thin, tingling silences; a nursery joy.

Disney had a wonderfully observant eye for the anatomy of nature: the pattern of a bird's flight, the shape of a young animal at play, an old one watchful. He saw the movement in the stillness, as a sculptor sees the figure in the stone. He felt the texture of fur and fin and feather. There was quick life running through all his animal sketches.

It was only in the long, later films, when he came to deal with the anatomy of human beings, that the talent faltered. Even so, he was successful with Pinocchio, the boy who was not flesh and blood, but a boy of wood. And his dwarfs were splendid. I doubt if he ever did anything better or more touching than the scene in *Snow White*, where the old men tiptoed up, bareheaded, to the glass coffin where the princess lay.

Sometimes I think we may not yet have understood the real charm of the best of Disney. He and Chaplin both raised a still, small voice against the artifice, the vainglory of the screen. But while Chaplin spoke for the common man, the little man who was Everyman, Disney spoke for the individual. 'This is my song, my very own song'; when he put *that* into the mouth of one of his cartoon characters he was revealing his own secret.

Disney has always felt deeply for private enterprise and private affections. This quality has shone through all his work, from Mickey Mouse to the *Hundred and One Dalmatians*. He knows infallibly that a child—which means perhaps you and certainly me as well—needs something of his own to cherish: a Bambi, a Dumbo, a very own song. Not until he has the joy of owning can he understand the joy of sharing. This is something that is too often forgotten by the higher intelligence today.

The pattern of life on the *Observer* was in one way not at all what Garvin had predicted: I saw him regularly each week at 'office lunch', which was the paper's equivalent of an editorial conference.

Lunch was held in the library at the top of the grey, wafer-thin building in Tudor Street: 'Twenty-two Tudor Street, just under the clock'; how often have I given that address to taxi-drivers! The library was reached by a small, bronchial lift, which had a habit of stopping inches below floor-level, so that most people preferred to toil up half a dozen flights of stairs.

There were usually about twenty people present, specialists in each department of the paper. Viola Garvin, who was in charge of our book pages, was always there, among a huddle of reviewers. She was a tall, cool, elegant creature, with black hair, creamy skin, and astonishing violet eyes, a soft Irish voice and a low, delightful laugh. She once told me that she admired Joan Crawford for the way she walked, something I had never studied for myself. I made a point of watching Miss Crawford's walk in the next film she made, and found it much inferior to Miss Garvin's.

There was Ivor Brown to represent the theatre, looking like a kind but sad St. Bernard dog. Sometimes St. John Ervine, the critic and playwright, came up from Devonshire to join us, and in the most polite way managed to convey that he wished he were at home in Devon. Once or twice we were honoured by the presence of Sir William Beach Thomas, a charming and courtly old gentleman who for many years provided the *Observer* with the finest nature column in journalism.

There was a jolly, red-faced little fellow known as Captain Robinson, who was ostensibly our 'ballistics expert', but was presently to blossom out as one of the first television reviewers. There was a Mrs. Pearl Adam, our fashion expert in the days before Alison Settle; an abundant person with a purplish complexion, mobled in a cloud of purplish-pink chiffon. She mothered me, and I was glad to hide under her capacious wing. (She tried unsuccessfully to persuade me to use a dictaphone, but I have always remained true to my 3B pencil.)

Presently there came a tall, new girl, as nervous as myself and a good many years younger. Her name was Joyce Grenfell, and they told me she was Nancy Astor's niece. At that time she had never been heard of in the entertainment world. Garvin was teaching her to become a journalist, to write simple reviews of wireless programmes in words of one syllable. The experiment was not of long duration. Joyce soon had it figured out that the things she could write best were stage lines for one-woman shows: her own.

We sat down to lunch at a long table, with Garvin strategically placed in the middle of the window side; Lord Astor, the proprietor, directly opposite on the other. The food was plain, but good. We drank a pleasant hock, although Garvin stuck to Malvern water. The far ends of the table enjoyed themselves immensely, like schoolboys when the master is out of hearing.

Things were tenser in the middle. It was Garvin's habit to discourse over the soup and cold chicken in resounding phrases, on subjects such as Dickens, Meredith and Goethe. *'Mehr licht!'* his voice would boom across the library, with an echo of the phrase he loved to use in leading articles, 'It is sun clear!'

To this day I have to stop and think whether it was Goethe who demanded more light, or Garvin. He brooked no interruption, although he appreciated a modest ripple of applause, agreement or the odd word from what would be described as a 'feed' in theatre circles. It was an extraordinary star performance. I have often fancied that Angela Thirkell, who was a close friend of the Garvins, based the character of Mr. Middleton in *Before Lunch* on J.L.G.

Over coffee and a cigar, but not before, Garvin would get down to business. One of the big questions every week was the subject of the 'turnover', the column on the extreme right of the page facing the leader page. To be given the turnover was a tremendous honour, and anyone who found himself placed next to J.L.G. at luncheon could guess that he was the chosen writer for that week.

I came in for the turnover several times, for Garvin, with his shrewd editor's sense, was well aware of the hold that films were taking on the popular imagination. I wrote about 'The Film Star as the Modern Hero'. And about 'The Place of Colour in the Cinema'. And about 'Shakespeare on the Screen', of course. Sound had turned this into a lively topic.

We had seen Mary Pickford and Douglas Fairbanks in an 'original' screen version of *The Taming of the Shrew*, with 'additional dialogue by William Shakespeare'. This was followed by Max Rhinehardt's voluptuous production of *A Midsummer Night's Dream*, with Hollywood's wonder-boy Mickey Rooney in the role of Puck, and James Cagney, the favourite tough guy of the moment, as Bottom. The purists were in a state of shock, and lost no opportunity of saying so. The *Observer* was careful not to take sides, but determined to get a thousand words in too.

It was gratifying to be asked to sit at the editor's right hand at lunch, but the invitation brought with it what Bertie Wooster would have called a Nameless Dread. The sense of an impending doom hung over the meal, and one merely toyed with food in expectation of the moment when Garvin would tilt his big cigar in your direction, and harangue you on the article he had in mind.

I never felt wholly at my ease with Garvin, although I'm certain he intended to be kind, and had no notion that his eye was dragonish. Much happier were the Tuesday lunches when I was invited to sit at the opposite side of the table, next to the gentle, courteous Viscount Astor.

Nobody could have been more considerate to a raw, provincial journalist, who came from a world so utterly unlike his own. He hardly ever mentioned films, about which I don't believe he greatly cared, but talked in his soft voice about his horses and his little dogs, his model milk farm and his plans for growing asparagus in a new way for the market. In later years, after the war, I came to know Lord Astor better, and understood more of the things he cared about. But I shall always cherish the memory of his kindness at those first *Observer* lunches. He was a very great gentleman indeed.

Two of the Astor sons were sometimes at the lunches. David, the present editor of the *Observer*, was a golden-eagle version of his dark, handsome father. He was learning the newspaper business in the provinces and in New York, so his appearances were infrequent. The chief things I remember about him from those days are that he was very young and gay, his eyes had the true blue of periwinkles and he taught me the meaning of the word 'kibitzer'.

Bill, the present Lord Astor, was a fairly constant member of the party. He was very easy company, more interested in films than in Goethe, and one could have a good deal of fun with him at the far end of the table, out of earshot of the dominie.

He drove a sharp little car which he parked rakishly outside the office, oblivious of newspaper vans and traffic restrictions, and sometimes gave me a lift to my afternoon trade show on the way back to his bachelor flat in Mayfair. In looks and manner he reminded me a good deal of my eldest brother Alick, the clergyman, who liked to have lots of people near him because he so easily grew lonely. Bill Astor had the same sort of defensive gregariousness; the same trick of turning his head sharply in a startled way, like a bird who keeps a bright eye open for the safety of the nearest twig.

He had, and has, a peculiarly dry sense of humour, which is not always recognized, because it is rarely overt, but hidden and unaccented. When I gave up my film column on the *Observer* at the end of 1960, David arranged a little dinner party, and various people said friendly things about me. It was Bill who took me entirely by surprise by reading out a supposed cablegram from Hollywood, signed by all the big names in the industry. 'Congratulations on Lejeune retirement movie critic the Observer stop best news we had in years.'

The 1930s, from *Broadway Melody* and *The Love Parade*, almost to the time of Munich, when Hollywood began to turn its attention to violent anti-Nazi propaganda, were boom years in the cinema and also happy years. The public took the pictures to their hearts, just as their children and grandchildren were later to embrace the 'telly'.

Films had no serious message in those days. They neither argued nor exhorted. They were equally uninterested in world politics and in social problems. Their whole intent was all for our delight. Most of them were gay, and they slipped easily into song and dance. *It Happened One Night*, *Theodora Goes Wild*, *My Man Godfrey*, *Bringing Up Baby*, *Top Hat*, *The Gay Divorce*, *Three Smart Girls*, *Maytime*, *The Thin Man*—what charmers they all were!

We went to the cinema to enjoy ourselves, and quite frequently we did. Today it is very rare indeed to find a simple, happy, entertaining film, with comedy that can amuse a mind not utterly moronic. The cinema in almost every country has taken upon itself the burden of propaganda. It exhorts us to face life 'realistically', by which it too often seems to mean, 'Look for the worst in everything.'

Contentment, to the modern scriptwriter, as to many other playwrights, is like a red rag to a bull. They just can't bear to find, or leave, a satisfied community. I should like to quote, without comment, part of a *Times* report on the subjects shown at the London Film Festival of 1961. The film under discussion is Chris Marker's *Description of a Struggle*.

'It is about Israel, an Israel in which the struggle is to find a struggle, some focus for national energies and aspirations which will prevent the national home so long looked for from turning into a complacent, commercial society just like anywhere else.'

'Find out what they're enjoying and tell them not to' is what the modern writer seems to say.

Star worship was rampant in the 1930s. Today a Hollywood celebrity can pass in and out of London without attracting more than the most cursory attention, a brief interview on the television screen and a paragraph in the gossip columns. But in those days when any of the adored ones visited England all hell broke loose among the screaming fans. They swarmed like locusts over the idols' cars. They tore their clothes to shreds for souvenirs. Hotels were picketed by relays of cyclists, watching the hotel doors day and night, reporting to their fan clubs on every star movement.

The worst case of hysteria I remember was the day when Spencer Tracy came to London. Long before the boat train was due to arrive at Waterloo the platform had become a seething mass of frenzied girls, most of them absent without leave from school or shops or offices.

The train pulled in. There was a wild stampede towards the doors. Innocent passengers were trampled underfoot. Among them I saw Toscanini go down. Baggage was smashed and scattered everywhere. Porters pushed and cursed to no avail. The startled face of Spencer Tracy appeared for a moment at a carriage window. The furies bore down on the coach with wild cries, hair streaming down their shoulders and stockings torn to ribbons.

They didn't reach their prey. Somebody in authority thought quickly, and the train, having deposited its other passengers, backed out of Waterloo. Tracy was secretly disgorged at Vauxhall Bridge, whence a car rushed him inconspicuously to Claridge's.

There, half an hour later, a few favoured reporters found him white and shaken in his room. He was rocking to and fro on a large sofa, hugging a cushion to his stomach, and groaning: 'My God, Toscanini! To think *I've* done that to Toscanini!' He was as shattered as a man can be. The freckles stood out against his ashen skin like blotches.

A little later, after the tremors had died down, and whisky had brought relief to all, Tracy surprisingly asked the press agent if a girl called Lejeune was present. It seems I had written a review of one of his films which particularly pleased him, and he wanted to meet me and say thank you in person. We met. We shook hands. He took one look at my homely mug, with its weatherbeaten skin and unadorned high Scottish colouring, and made an opening remark unique in my experience. 'Thank heavens,' he said. 'Thank heavens you've got no doodads on your face.' To this day I don't quite know whether this was a simple compliment or the quick imagination of an even greater horror.

Claridge's ('The Claridge', as Alexander Korda always used to call it) was the scene of many quaint encounters. There was the time when I was sent to interview Fred Astaire, then at the height of his popularity with Ginger Rogers. He had just made the pages of the *Encyclopaedia Britannica*, and had little time to spare for casual journalists. However, he agreed to give me ten minutes, and did give me ten minutes precisely in the lobby, carefully saying nothing that could be used for copy (although, in point of fact, nothing is something that *can* be used for copy), his feet dancing as he talked, his eyes fixed on the clock.

Then there was a strange session with a Hollywood actress who was very much kept at the moment by a man of property. I found her in the sitting-room of her suite with a jeweller kneeling at her feet, trying on an anklet. Beside him, an open leather case sparkled with precious stones on their velvet beds. She was turning her lovely neck this way and that, trying the effect of a diamond collar. Her fingers shimmered as she held them to the light, catching the glint of fire from rubies.

'Oh, hallo, darling,' she called out as she saw me in the doorway, 'such a bore, but I'm flying back to the Coast tomorrow. Do come in and help me choose, and then we'll settle down and have a nice cosy chat about things that really matter.'

There was the time I went to Claridge's to interview Grace Moore, the Metropolitan Opera star, who had made such a hit in the film *One Night of Love*. She had come to London to sing Mimi in *La Bohème* at Covent Garden, and was the town's most fashionable stage-door attraction.

She received me in a suite banked high with flowers. The central heating was full on. The whole place felt and smelt like a conservatory.

Miss Moore, all pink and gold, was very charming, very friendly. Teasing at a tiny pink chiffon handkerchief, she warned me never, never to give anyone my autograph on a loose sheet of paper.

'Honey,' she said earnestly, 'you can't be too careful about that. Only sign your name in albums, with another signature on the page if possible.' Fascinated, I listened spellbound to her grave account of the way in which dishonest persons can manipulate a signature. Since then I have always made a point of writing my name in autograph albums on the pink, blue or peach page which already bears the legend: 'To Janice, with love from Uncle Jack', or something of the kind.

When I took my leave she drew out of a bouquet in a tall vase a lily with a stem about six foot long. 'Take this, honey,' she said, 'as a little souvenir.'

I slunk down the back stairs of the hotel, helplessly clutching this monstrous, lovely thing. What in the world was I to do with it? I thought of the Underground in the rush hour. I thought of Bunthorne, walking down Piccadilly with a poppy or a lily. Past Fortnum and Mason's. Past Hatchard's and St. James's Church. Past Swan and Edgar's and down into the bowels of the Circus. No, I said to myself, it simply will not do. A shabby handbag in one hand and a six-foot hothouse lily in the other. On the second floor at Claridge's I found a potted palm on the landing. I stuck the lily down inside the pot, hoping that someone would discover it before it wilted, and that Miss Moore would never have occasion to use the back stairs.

My other sharp remembrance of Claridge's comes from a much later date. It was wartime, and the winter of the first big blitz. It was also the winter of a hard, black frost. At home the pipes were frozen. We had no hot water, no coke and very little coal. The sirens and the bombs were busy all night long. We did get some coal eventually from the council depot half a mile away, by collecting a sack or two and pushing it back in an old perambulator.

For some reason or other I had to go and interview Robert Montgomery at Claridge's. Although he was one of the top stars of the moment, I had never met him. When I arrived at the door of his suite, I must have looked a forlorn and draggled object. He opened the door, gave me one quick glance and said, 'Come to the fire, you're frozen.'

Encouraged by the sympathetic voice, I must have poured out all my woes at once. The next thing I remember is his saying, 'Would you like to take a bath?'

Would I like to take a bath? There was nothing I would have liked better. He went through into the *de luxe* bathroom and filled a steaming tub. He poured in bath salts with a lavish hand, added a sponge the size of a young sofa cushion, gave me a warm, fleecy bathsheet and a huge bathrobe made of Turkish towelling. 'Take all the time you want,' he said. 'I'll call room service and have them send up tea.'

After ten minutes or so of soaking, scented bliss (Bing Crosby has gone on record as saying that he likes the baths at Claridge's because you can lie down in them), I came back to the sitting-room almost a human being. My host was sitting by the fire with tea and sandwiches, mounds of hot buttered toast and a compulsory glass of brandy. I suppose we had an interview of sorts. I can't remember what we talked about. All I remember is a man's instinctive kindness to an utter stranger, his quick sense in grasping the order of priorities.

I never met Montgomery again. But the following year he sent me a Christmas card. It is signed, 'Robert, Knight of the Bath', and is one of my most cherished bits of nonsense to this day.

14

'C. A. LEJEUNE IS ON HOLIDAY'

ALTHOUGH I could have taken my holidays from the *Observer* at any time of year I chose, I always took them in late summer. London is at its least enchanting then. The air feels used up. The trees in the parks look tired, and the grass is turning brown. Gawping strangers string out in family parties across the pavements. Pedestrian speed is sluggish and the traffic seems to crawl in sympathy. In the gardens the first flush of summer flowers is over, and there is nothing much to do but hoe, water, trim the edges and cut the grass.

A heavy slump descends upon the cinema. The long, light evenings keep young people out of doors. Even the most glamorous film star can't compete with the charms of tennis, cricket, swimming, strolling, lazy boating on the river. Year after year the trade, the industry, shrugs fatalistic shoulders and prepares to cut its losses for another season. The new films in the show windows would be described as 'slightly imperfect' if they were vests or stockings. Old films are reissued, frequently in double bills. *Doctor in the House* and *Genevieve* turn up year after year as a double-feature programme.

From mid-June until mid-September is a good time for conscientious critics to go on holiday. I was a very conscientious critic in the thirties. I didn't want to miss a thing, so I chose the reasonable, the slackest time to go away. In later years I was severely tempted to save up my leave until late September, when Hollywood was about to unleash one of its mammoth, stupendous, immortal and intolerable epics.

Accounts of other people's holidays are apt to be a bore. Nobody, except a besotted parent or grandparent, really *wants* to see your snaps, nor to watch the cinefilm you took during that marvellous holiday on the Costa Brava, at Kandersteg, or Skegness, or Rhyl. It is really just to please myself and keep the records straight that I mention two summer trips abroad which stand out clearly in my mind. Please bear with me.

The first was a visit that I paid with Mother to the Basque country. Our hosts, Isabel and Peter Armstrong, were very old friends as well as family connections. My sister Marion had married Peter's brother, Max Enke. The family name was Enke; Peter and Isabel changed theirs to Armstrong during the first war. Isabel herself had been Franziska's and Marion's closest friend in schooldays. All of them had been at Lady Barn House together.[1]

Now the Armstrongs had bought a big place called La Roque in the Landes, a few miles south of Bayonne, and they wanted Mother to come and see it. She was over seventy by this time, and presumably I was invited as a travelling companion, someone to look after her on the journey. But she brooked no looking after. Indeed, as always, she looked after me. Nothing at all worried her: the Channel crossing, the Customs, the change of stations and long wait in Paris, the long night in a sleeper. She took the whole journey as blithely as a bird.

To travel hopefully is better than to arrive, they say; and a remarkably silly saying it is too. I never travel hopefully myself. I feel certain I have left something behind: hot-water bottle? matches? that slip of paper with the times of trains? Did I remember to post those letters? What on earth have I done with the return half of my ticket? Have I got enough small change for tips? How much, really, should I tip the porter? Oh dear, I wish I hadn't come at all. When I was at home I was in a better place.

Travelling without hope can have its compensations. Sometimes it leads to delightful surprises. I had no hopes at all about that long journey to La Roque, but the surprises began before we left Victoria.

Mother and I had found our seats in the Golden Arrow, and the train was almost due to pull out when we noticed a certain muted flurry on the platform. I stuck my head out of the window and saw

[1]. My brother-in-law Max has attained distinction as the original of Lord Uffenham in P. G. Wodehouse's *Money in the Bank*. He was in a concentration camp with Wodehouse, and is frequently referred to in the latter's diary *The Performing Flea* as 'our linguist', or 'Enke, the stoutest man in the place'.

a tall, thin young man and a short, dark young woman passing by, escorted to their coach by station master and minions. They were obviously Somebodies, what would be described today as V.I.P.'s. I turned to Mother and said, 'I *think* it's the Duke and Duchess of York.'

It was. They were travelling to Paris to open something, perhaps the British Pavilion at the Grand Esposition, the French Wembley. When we pulled into the Gare du Nord we found the station hung with Union Jacks and Tricolors. A frock-coated reception committee was waiting on the platform, and porters and police were in a high Gallic state of frenzy.

On the Golden Arrow all was calm. The Yorks might have been any quiet young couple travelling first-class to Paris. I doubt if many people knew they were on the train. No hedge of royalty surrounded them. The doors of their compartment were closed, it's true, but anybody passing along the corridor to the dining-car could peep through the glass with impunity.

I peeped in without shame and was rewarded by the sight of the Duchess asleep in a corner. Her head was propped up on her hand, and on one finger she wore a single, square-cut emerald. Whenever I see a picture of the Queen Mother nowadays I remember that journey to Paris on a hot summer morning, the sleeping Duchess who never thought to be a Majesty, and that glorious stone, gleaming with green fire.

Even without our royal interlude this would have been a fascinating journey. It is one thing to read about the Côte d'Azur in books; quite another to board an express bearing those rich, romantic words.

I had never spent a night in a train before. On our holidays to Scotland, when I was a little girl, we had always broken the journey for a night in some railway hotel. ('Can I go out and watch the trains?' 'Just for ten minutes, if you wrap up well.') When Roffe and I were first married, and made our exploratory trips abroad, we always travelled in the daytime, spending a night or two in each new town.

But the journey to La Roque was different. Mother and I were to leave Paris in the hot summer dusk, arriving at Bayonne in time for breakfast. We had a sleeping compartment to ourselves, and I can remember my excitement when we groped our way back along the swaying corridors from the dining-car, to find our luggage piled up on the racks, a washbasin with towels and soap conjured from nowhere, the upholstered seats transformed into snowy, newly turned-down beds.

This confession will sound artless to experienced travellers. But I think it would be dishonest to suppress it if I am to write sensibly about myself at all. It was a fresh thrill, an entirely new experience, and experience is what our lives are built from.

I can still see in my mind's eye every detail of that small compartment; can sleepily remember Mother combing and plaiting her long hair before she went to bed; can hear in my mind's ear the hollow clank of trucks and the shouts of French railwaymen at some big junction in the darkness.

I can remember as if it were yesterday the waking at first light; pushing the window-blind a chink aside; watching the pine trees of the Landes flow past us, each tree with its cup to collect the resin as it oozed from blood-orange gashes in the trunks.

That wonderful journey was the beginning of a wonderful holiday, as near perfection as anyone can hope for in an imperfect world. Not a thing occurred to spoil it. The sun shone, and sea and skies stayed resolutely blue. The Armstrongs' house, perched on a hill among acres of flowering gardens, with the white Landes villages at its feet and the Atlantic in the distance, was a storybook place.

Isabel and Peter were the best of hosts. She was one of those staunch, North Country women who make a home around them wherever they may be. She had, I think, no selfconsciousness at all. She loved to chatter over the telephone in her busy English-French; *'Oui, oui, c'est Madame Armstrong qui parle'*. She clucked over her guests and sheltered them like a soft, heavenly hen. Peter, who had spent most of his adult life in Belgium, was a natural cosmopolitan, who had patterned himself on correct English lines. He was never a great talker, although he could speak at least five languages fluently, but his reticence concealed a nature that was all kindness and generosity.

They were comfortably off, and used their money to make other people comfortable. Mother and I were taken everywhere at ease in the big Armstrong car. We drove in to sleepy, sunbaked Bayonne for shopping; to the coast at Biarritz and St. Jean de Luz; over the foothills of the Pyrenees to Spain, through the dense, dark woods of Roland Roncesvalles.

We had lunch out-of-doors at jolly little inns, with a stream tumbling at the bottom of the garden, and women kneeling to do the family washing by the edge of the water, rubbing the grime out with stones, spreading it on the hot stones to dry. We stopped at wayside villages to watch games of pelota. We ate brook trout with cool, pale wine, and learnt to take armagnac with our coffee. We saw the strange green glow that fills the sky at sunset in those parts.

Peter and I went bathing in the Atlantic rollers. We climbed a small mountain, a baby Pyrenee, up slopes murmurous with sheep bells. He taught me how to fish, after a fashion, in the deep pools of the stream at the foot of the La Roque gardens. To my horror I was fascinated by the technique of this exercise, though I always threw the fish back when I could.

One night we all went out in a boat to try to catch eels in the darkness, but this trip could not be counted a success. It was cold, with mist rising from the river. The eels refused to take the bunches of squirming, slippery bait, which didn't in the least surprise me. We soon gave up and drove home to warm ourselves by the fire and drink lots of hot, black, filtered coffee.

Apart from the episode of the eels, which was exciting in its horrid fashion, that Basque holiday was sheer delight. I came home with a golden suntan, bringing as trophies a Basque beret and a couple of maquilas.

The beret has long since disappeared, but the maquilas are still in our umbrella stand, along with Laurence's sword from the Compton Comedy Company. We don't goad oxen much in Pinner, and the carrying of swordsticks is not a practice advocated by the Metropolitan Police. But I have found them, along with our singing bird from the Black Forest, a great success with sticky visitors. You produce them casually; allow the guests to unscrew the handle, and unsheath the fine steel blade; explain how the pattern on the shaft is carved into the young medlar shoot and grows with it. Your guests may not be listening, but they are busy fingering. A maquila is compulsive handling, and has passed many an awkward pause away.

The other holiday abroad, at Wernigerode in the Harz Mountains, was disturbing. At the time I could make nothing of the shadow that lay across it. The sun shone all day long. The scenery was glorious.

The woods wore their full panoply of midsummer green, the larches tender against the olive spruce. The people that I met were hospitable. Yet there remained a chill, and I had bad dreams, in which I struggled through a fog to get back to home and England.

The year before, my husband had been to Wernigerode with a film cameraman, who was commissioned to take pictures of the Harz Mountains, particularly the Brocken, with the co-operation of the German railways. He came back full of enthusiasm for the little market town, the small hotel where they had stayed, the kindness of the railway people. I decided to see it next holidays for myself, and persuaded my sister Marion to come with me.

At first glance everything seemed delightful. Wernigerode was even more picturesque than I had been led to believe, with its red-roofed houses from another century, the old Rathaus above the beer-cellar which does not, but seems to, stand up high on spindle legs. The journey to what the natives called 'the Brockentop' was fascinating, with an absurd toy train puffing and twisting its way to the summit through dense woods of pine and larch and beeches. The small hotel made us comfortable in a homespun way, and it was pleasant to laze in a hammock in the tiny *liege-wiese*, which was hot with the July sun and smelt of ripe red currants.

On the surface everything was calm, everyone was anxious to be helpful. But we hadn't been there a couple of days before we felt that something was amiss. The young people were too exhilarated, the old people too wary. Chesterton once wrote a Father Brown story called *The Wrong Shape*. There was a wrong shape at that time in Wernigerode.

Somehow we got caught up in a group of English schoolteachers who had booked for a personally conducted tour of the Harz Mountains. Our guide was a gentle, grey-haired man who spoke English fluently, and was married to a gentle English wife. Marion and I were invited to their home for dinner and had a charming evening, up to a point. But it was noticeable that they would say nothing about politics. When either of us touched on the subject, or sought for information on affairs in modern Germany, the talk, which had been so frank before, withered and died.

We found the same caution, the same withdrawal, everywhere we went. It is probable that Marion saw things more clearly than I did.

I have always been stupid about politics, and it never occurred to me to connect the general unease with the swastikas that were chalked up everywhere on trees and rocks, the boys and girls with swastika armbands selling papers in the market square.

One morning I walked down into the town to buy a novel, Vicki Baum's *Hell in Frauensee*. The shopkeeper made no comment, but raised his brows slightly at my choice of author. In the next street I found a small crowd outside a shattered shop-window. I noticed the name above the broken glass. It was a Jewish name, but I thought that was just an accident. I had never been taught to think that it was bad to be a Jew.

At the end of a fortnight the schoolteachers departed. Marion went back to Ghent, where she and her husband had a house. I should have gone with her, but was tempted by an invitation from a director of the Brocken railway to stay on for a few days with his wife and family.

It was a strange experience, and ought to have prepared me for what was soon to come in Europe. Parents and children lived in different worlds. The ruling spirit of the house was the elder son, a boy of sixteen or seventeen; a boy with a lean, brown face and a scar, like a duelling scar, across one cheek. His hair was very fair, and he wore blue open-necked shirts to match the bright blue of his eyes.

He both attracted and repelled me. I felt sure that he was ruthless. It was my deligh tto beat him at table tennis, which I could do with reasonable certainty, because he so quickly lost his temper. One evening I found him struggling with his English homework and offered to help him. The set book was *Our Island Story*. He sneered at it as a childish exercise, but, childish or not, the exercise baffled him.

When we had straightened the words out between us he suddenly burst into a flood of German, the gist of which was that England need only wait and see, and there would be a different island story. In the middle of this outburst his father came into the room and stopped him. But by that time I had picked up enough German to catch the meaning. I thought his father looked not only grave but sad.

A few days later the old man asked me if I would come with him up the Brocken. He wanted to test the rails at some point or other. I loved that toy journey up the mountain and agreed with alacrity. When we were far away from habitation he climbed down on to the track, signed the engine on and began to tap the rails perfunctorily. There were thick woods on either side and nobody was within earshot.

Suddenly he straightened, looked fearfully over his shoulder and said he wanted to tell me something. 'We are not all like that,' he said, jerking a thumb towards the town below. 'There is another Germany. It was my Germany, and I pray to God that it may come again.'

All this happened nearly thirty years ago. I lost touch with that family long before the war, but often wonder what became of them. I wonder, too, what has happened to the Brocken railway. Do toy trains still puff up that lonely track? Do they still celebrate *Walpurgisnacht* on the summit? Do Communists believe in witches? I should dearly like to know.

Those were the last holidays I spent abroad, although I find it difficult to persuade people to believe it. There seems to be a common assumption that a film critic is always on the go; between London and Hollywood, for instance, and since the war between London and the various continental festivals.

Of course, a critic can attend these functions if he cares to. He is likely to be invited to half a dozen festivals a year, and he is free to take his choice. I have been pressed to go to Cannes, to Venice, to Berlin, to Brussels, to Eire and as far afield as Mexico and India, but have politely but categorically refused.

I don't enjoy a busman's holiday. When I am away from films I like to be away from them. Late nights and parties aren't my style at all, and it seems to be absurd to spend a great deal of money and travel immense distances to meet the sort of people you meet every day at home, discussing the same topic in a less familiar language.

It was no doubt unenterprising of me not to go abroad after the war was over, but in the last few years before the war I had no opportunity. The time had come, familiar to every mother, when summer holidays meant August, after school broke up, and the seaside was the proper place to go to.

We were wonderfully lucky in our bit of seaside. Franziska and Laurence had given up the poultry farm at Ashington and bought their house at Bexhill. We were welcome any time we chose to go there, and we knew there would be no complaints about spades and buckets and trails of seaweed in the hall, towels and bathing costumes on the clothes-line, and soggy, sandy plimsolls drying on the window-sill.

Laurence's married sister, Lilian Jay, lived a few doors away in a rambling house called Sherwood, where the front door was always on the latch, in pleasant country fashion. You pushed your way through a pack of yelping Pekingese (there were never more than two at a time, but they seemed to me like a pack), and shouted at the top of your voice, 'Anyone at home?' (At Sherwood everybody shouted.)

During August and September the house was crowded with young people: the two Jays, John and Violet; three Meade cousins from Bradford, Ann, Joan and red-headed Eve; sometimes another Meade cousin, Francis, from London. Usually, too, there were a couple of French summer boarders, and a German girl helping in the kitchen.

The first German girl was a good mixer as well as a good cook. Everybody liked her, and she came back the following year. The second, a muscular and strapping wench, was by no means the same success. She muttered under her breath in an alarming way whenever she set eyes on the current French guests, who happened to be rich Jewish cousins from Paris. Since she muttered in German, her words were not widely understood, but she made their meaning clear by decorating the butter-pats with swastikas.

She was a magnificent swimmer, and although she came down to the beach with us, always preferred to swim alone. Whatever the weather or the tide, she would walk purposefully to the water's edge, dive in and cleave her way straight out to sea, until her bobbing cap was out of sight.

'Oh dear,' Lil would sigh, 'I do wonder if it's safe.' The others laughed and told her it was safe enough. She would come back in an hour or so when she had handed the plans of Bexhill's coastal defences to a German submarine.

Every August until the war broke out, Tony (my son) and I spent our holidays at Bexhill. They were happy holidays in every way. Four weeks of the simple life, with a circus on the common, a conjuror on the marine parade, a shallow boating pool in the park, where young oarsmen could learn to use a paddle and boast like anything about their enterprise in repelling the advances of a placid swan; a beach hut of our own; hot doughnuts for 'elevenses' and ice-cream at Forte's; and the cheeriest of company.

'C. A. LEJEUNE IS ON HOLIDAY'

All the big boys and girls from Sherwood came down to our hut to bathe. They were wonderfully patient with the small boy, allowing him to believe he had a part in all their ploys. Amiably they would help him to build sand ramparts against the tide, tug him about rock-pools on a rubber raft or carry him on their backs up the steep cliff path (reputed to be a smugglers' road) and over the railway tracks (strictly illegal and therefore most exciting), which was the shortest way home. But they put up with no nonsense from him either, never allowed him to become a pest. Like most small boys, he flourished on this discipline, and felt himself a member of a big, jolly family.

Bexhill is by no means the liveliest of seaside resorts, and is sometimes referred to with contempt as 'a nice place for old people'. But it can also be a nice place for young people who are satisfied with simple pleasures. The sea is well behaved. It seldom fumes and frets and dashes spray over the esplanade, as it does a few miles east at Hastings. It lacks the majesty of the sea at Eastbourne (so charmingly encountered in *Pride and Prejudice* as East Bourne) a few miles west, which seems to be continually renewing its assault on the bastion of Beachy Head.

Admittedly there is too much shingle, but when the tide does go out it goes out a long way, leaving miles of safe paddling water, enough sand and plenty of rock-pools, where you can gather mussels if you have the energy.

It is a splendid centre, too, for children who are interested in Ancient Monuments. The ruins of Hastings Castle are within easy reach, perched high above the fishing harbour of the Old Town; so is Battle Abbey, with its reminders of William the Conqueror, 1066 and all that; so is the charming, moated Bodiam and our own special favourite, Pevensey.

Not much is left today of Pevensey Castle, which long ago kept watch over the marshes and a busy harbour. Only a few grey ruins with yellow wallflowers growing in the crannies, a crumbling corkscrew stair leading to nothing, some rudimentary traces in the grass-grown courtyard of the outlines of a dining-hall, and a hint of dungeons. No much, but enough to stir the imagination. It reminded me of my favourite E. Nesbit book, *The House of Arden*.

Franziska had a passion for archaeology of all sorts. Tony had a passion, fed on Kipling, for the ancient Romans. The three of us would take the train to Pevensey once or twice every holidays. The old custodian learnt to know us, and it was a great day when he showed us a freshly discovered treasure, the imprint of a Roman legionary's foot on the wall of the moat; authenticated Roman sandal, nails, thongs and everything.

I have never quite been able to determine why the legionary so obligingly left his footprint in the stone. Pevensey Castle isn't the Brown Derby, and he was obviously no star, but an extra. However, it made our day for us, and gave Tony something to boast about for weeks at school.

It was on one of these early trips to Pevensey that he gave away the fact that he could read. So far, he had resolutely refused to spell out the simplest words in large print on a page; every book had to be read aloud to *him*. But on this occasion he forgot his pose.

The train stopped at the first station, familiar to golfers. Tony looked out of the window and announced nonchalantly, 'COO-DEN.' I can only suppose that this tempting disyllable was irresistible, proving too much for the caution of a mind which had already dismissed 'A Cat Sat on a Mat' as juvenile.

By this time my husband had given up journalism for the film world. He worked for a time with John Grierson at the Empire Marketing Board; then at the new Gaumont-British Studios at Shepherd's Bush in charge of the 'shorts' department; later as 'press liaison officer' to Alexander Korda.

These connections helped me a great deal in writing. I don't mean as a critic, but as a journalist. There were offers for articles from newspapers and magazines, both here and in America. For many years I wrote a regular Sunday piece for the *New York Times* about goings-on in English studios. It was useful to have an easy passage behind the scenes. I got to know a number of people whom I might not have met otherwise, and picked up a lot of background information.

When Roffe left *John Bull* his secretary, Constance Redfearn, gave up her job at Odhams and came to live with us as a combination of secretary, housekeeper and baby-minder. She is still with us after more than thirty years, and I don't know what we should have done without her.

With Connie at Lane End and Mother just across the road, I knew

I could go out and leave Tony with impunity. But I was never really happy about doing so. I am a firm believer in a parent's responsibility to children in their early years. If you don't keep close beside them *then*, sharing their changing interests and perplexities, you may well lose them later, become perplexed yourself as they grow up.

This doesn't mean that you should pamper them, or allow them to have things all their own way. In one of Mother's old diaries I find the note: 'Lost my patience with T. today. This is bad. Mustn't do it again.' I have no doubt it was bad for Mother and upset her. But I daresay it was very good for T. Children throve on the tongue-lashings the old-fashioned and devoted nannies used to give them. I reckon that our downright Lizzie Sellers was worth more than a dozen educated faddists to a normal child.

The Lizzies of the nursery are rare today; so indeed are nurseries in the old segregated sense. Most of the middle-class mothers that one knows, with a middling-sized house and a husband earning a middling income, share meals and quarters with their children; put up the play-pen in the living-room; conduct their conversations with friends to a constant accompaniment of chatter, varied with bombardment by soft toys; dispense hospitality and answer the telephone against a hubbub of young voices.

This may be inconvenient, it often proves exhausting, but parents and children can both profit by it in the conditions of the world we live in.

'A child's soul,' says Father Borelli of Naples, 'is like a bank. Whatever you put in you get back ten years later with interest.'

The first things to put into the bank, I believe, are truthfulness and candour; and then, but with the greatest caution, stimulus of thought. It isn't good to feed a child with too much at a time, but it is reckless to deny him information about anything he really wants to know.

You cannot guard children wholly against shock. They are at the mercy of the unexpected. I have known children who hid their faces and burst into tears at the sight of plants growing and buds opening in a slow-motion nature film. A brilliant *New Yorker* cover of a year or so ago showed a child shrinking back in terror as a bee emerged from a lily blossom.

My own most shocking memory of childhood dates from a wintry afternoon when I was seven or eight years old and was helping to wrap

Christmas presents for my brother Russell in Australia. One of the presents was an illustrated magazine, which fell open at a picture in the serial. The picture showed a young woman in the act of lifting her wedding veil to turn a livid face towards the bridegroom. Under it were the fearful words, 'The bride was dying, dying of the plague.'

There is no way of protecting children from these sudden shocks, which are occupational hazards of the world they live in. The only thing one can do is provide a balance of good, positive things; a sense of home with somebody to allay doubts and answer questions seriously; a place where puzzlement is cleared, and the young mind can pass naturally to its next occupation.

A wise mother that I know was talking to her young son in the bath one night. He must have been five or six years old, and had reached the stage when he wanted to find out about the facts of life.

Ignoring the birds and the bees, for he was not a child likely to be impressed by parables from nature, she told him in simple terms how babies were made. He took the news in silence, and appeared to ruminate. Fearful lest she should have gone too far, the mother asked, 'Is there anything else you'd like to know?'

'Yes,' replied the child quite gravely, 'I want to know how they make cotton.'

15

'COMPANY AT LANE END'

'COMPANY at Lane End' is an entry I find again and again in Mother's diaries. She always wrote 'company' in inverted commas. Whether this was an implied comment on her choice of word or our choice of guests I have never been able to determine.

The 'company' was generally film company, stars or directors whom Roffe and I had got to know in the studios. Mother was in no way interested in films or film people. Once she had safely launched me on my peculiar career, she left me to get on with it, and retired to her reading, her garden, the writing of what she called 'mail letters' and the cares of her large and scattered family.

She never asked about the films I saw. To the best of my knowledge she didn't read my criticisms. 'C. in town all day, came back v. depressed' was her way of describing a bad day of press shows. With shame I find how often she felt bound to write 'C. worrying today', 'C. badly rattled.'

The only diary entry I can find which bears even remotely on the cinema is a note for 1935, the year when Korda was planning to produce *The Shape of Things to Come*. C. saw Wells this p.m. Interesting, but v. tiring.'

Our most spectacular guest at Lane End was Paulette Goddard, who was over here making *An Ideal Husband* for Korda. She came to tea one hot Saturday afternoon in summer—when most of the natives were in their gardens in shirt-sleeves and shorts—wearing a rig that would not have disgraced a reception at Claridge's.

Over a scarlet dress she wore a coat of white summer ermine. She carried an immense scarlet handbag of the softest leather. Her shoes were scarlet kid with six-inch stiletto heels. When she teetered up the garden to look at the roses a neighbour who was clipping a privet hedge was so startled that he almost fell off his step-ladder at the sight of her.

Our most unusual guest was Elisabeth Bergner. I was on the point of calling her the shyest, but the word would be misleading. The thing that looked like shyness in Bergner was a deliberate withdrawal, a curtain consciously dropped against scrutiny. Once she gave her confidence to anyone, she was all warmth and generosity. But it was very hard to gain her confidence in the first place. In the studios she had the reputation of being unapproachable. She would run like a deer at the sight of any stranger on the set, lock herself in her dressing-room and refuse to speak to anybody.

I don't remember how I managed to break through the barrier, but somehow I did. The first time I met Bergner was at Elstree when she was playing Rosalind in a film version of *As You Like It*, directed by her husband Dr. Paul Czinner, with the young Laurence Olivier as Orlando. She was an actress very much in the news just then, as the star of *Dreaming Lips*, *Catherine the Great* and *Escape Me Never*, and presently she was to be still more in the news when J. M. Barrie wrote *The Boy David* for her.

I was frightened when I was presented to her, and allowed inside the ivory tower which few could penetrate. But nobody could be frightened of Bergner for long. She was a delightful little creature, sensitive and merry, with an impish face and a voice that seemed all the more attractive for its imperfectly accented English. Perhaps it was unwise of her to have attempted to play Rosalind so soon in an English-peopled Arden. Perhaps she should never have essayed Rosalind at all. James Agate thought so.

'Throughout the entire film', he wrote in his review, 'I was not conscious at any moment of establishing contact with Shakespeare's heroine. That which is substituted is something else—something German, something *gemütlich*, and something nearer to Wagner's Eva than to Molière's Célimène. . . . Miss Bergner gives Rosalind every other quality that is to be found in the part except the wit. She has any amount of tenderness and gaiety. But both of these are artless as they were in *Escape Me Never*, whereas Rosalind does not utter a single word of whose value she is unconscious.'

This is percipient writing from one of the shrewdest of our critics. And Agate has given me the very word I wanted. *Gemütlich* is the perfect word for Bergner, as she always seemed to me.

After that first meeting I was free to go on the set of any Bergner film at will. Sometimes, when all I wanted was a quick newspaper story for the *New York Times*, I had a few words with Czinner, watched a take or two and left. Journalists have no time to wait around in studios, and after a few years in the job they learn to take the temper of a scene and disappear as soon as possible. But it wasn't all that easy to slip away from Bergner. She spotted her friends on the set, even in obscure corners, as quickly as she detected strangers in the house.

Once, I remember, it was wintry weather, and I was wearing a thick wool scarf tied round my head. I didn't think Elisabeth could see me, but she did. She came straight over to me with an anxious face. 'You have something the matter with the jow?' she asked, and it took me a long time to assure her that no, I had nothing the matter with the jaw.

I have found amongst my papers a little scrawl which reads:

'Caroline dear, why did you run away so fast this afternoon? I looked for you and could not find you when the scene was over. I hope I do not hurt you that I must speak to Miss ——' (name illegible). 'It was an affair of business, but I think I make you unhappy and that makes me unhappy too. My love, Elisabeth.'

I have no recollection whatsoever of this incident, nor of the illegible Miss ——, but whatever cloud there may have been passed quickly, and we were soon on happy terms again.

Bergner and her husband came out to see us several times. Both of them were at their most relaxed with children. One night I remember in particular. She went upstairs to say good night to Tony, who was supposed to be in bed. Through the closed door we heard gay voices and much laughter. When at last we broke in to tell her that dinner was ready we found the pair of them squatting on the floor, counting the pennies from a money-box. Elisabeth looked up at us for a moment with her huge brown eyes and put a finger to her lips. 'Sh-sh! We are very beezy,' she said.

The Czinners were extraordinarily kind to our small boy. Among the Christmas presents they sent him (they were delivered on Christmas Eve by a proud Rolls-Royce) was a fly in amber, and a travelling clock, barometer and thermometer in a folding leather case from Asprey's. The timepiece has never divagated by five minutes in almost thirty years. Once, and once only, it had to be taken to a jeweller's for cleaning. The jeweller whistled when he looked at it. 'Where on earth did you get this?' he said, knowing our modest circumstances. 'I reckon it's a beauty. We don't see many like it now. It would cost about eighty or ninety pounds today—if you could get it at all.'

When Bergner was about to play in *The Boy David* she offered Tony the most precious gift she could bestow, a meeting with Sir J. M. Barrie. Barrie, like Elisabeth, was a shy bird to catch. He was reluctant to meet anybody at that time. But he shared her sympathy and natural way with children. We met one Sunday afternoon on a set at Denham. Cordial relations were immediately established when the great man poked a finger into the middle of the small boy's jersey, and said, with a twinkle in his eye, 'Hullo, young man.'

Another star who showed remarkably good sense with children was Valerie Hobson, now Mrs. John Profumo, wife of the ex-Minister for War.

Valerie was at all times the most elegant of creatures. She had a natural good taste not always to be found in film stars, and her tall, long-legged figure carried off good clothes to perfection. She was a gift to press agents who wanted to get fashion pictures into magazines, though some of the photographers found it slightly startling to deal with a film star who was, before all else, a lady. I am no fashion expert myself, but I could see at a glance that she was well dressed in the sense that her clothes were exactly the right clothes for each occasion. I remember her most vividly in a suit of leaf-brown sportswear, playing ludo on our hearthrug on an autumn afternoon.

When we had guests for dinner our daily help was ready to come back for an hour or two and 'oblige'. We have been wonderfully lucky in our dailies. In the older part of Northwood, the unfashionable, Victorian end, there is still a strong village spirit, a quality which in the abominable modern jargon would be termed 'togetherness'.

Every household knows the affairs of every other household, and many families are related. There is an extraordinary loyalty among these people. They never gossip to outsiders. They are well informed about everything that's going on, but will not disclose the sources of their information. If they like you they will do anything for you, get anything you need in some mysterious fashion. But they take a long time before they will accept you as a foreigner deserving of trust.

I think it was through Mr. Herring the gardener, and Mr. Kennerell, who sang in the choir at the Presbyterian church, and called on us every Tuesday with pork pies and delicious acelet straight from Lincolnshire, that we first made acquaintance with the Bell family.

Old Tom Bell (so called for the last thirty years to distinguish him from his eldest son, young Tom) is a retired sheet-metal worker and a tremendous character. Now in the middle eighties, he is still as strong as a horse. He has lost all his teeth but refuses to wear dentures. He says he can bite anything with his gums, and does.

He enjoys his annual holiday at Yarmouth and likes to go sailing in the roughest weather. He is a keen student of racing form and has the reputation of a 'scholard'. That is to say, he gets real books from Boots as well as the public library, and actually reads them.

He also writes a fair hand, and if the language is a trifle flowery there is never any doubt as to the meaning. Not everyone can spell the names of horses, but old Tom Bell makes no mistake when he sends me pencilled slips during the flat season, suggesting each-way bets next Friday at Doncaster or Kempton Park or Ripon.

Mrs. Bell was a massive, outsize woman with kind brown eyes and a very gentle voice. It was difficult for her to climb our hill, but until weight and illness got the better of her she persistently came up and 'did' for Mother. Her daughter Ada 'did' for us. When she married and gave up work to have a baby she bequeathed to us her sister Matilda. 'I think you'll like Till,' she told us. 'She's never had much schooling. But she's a good girl.'

She was marvellous. She may not have had much schooling, but she is a better judge of character than many of us who have. Tilly has been with us now for twenty-seven years. In her own way she is as much a character as Lizzie Sellers. Tall and upright as a dragoon, she still bangs through the work with a tremendous zest and clatter. She can answer back with the best, but there is no ill-will or bitterness in her backchat. Dogs love her, and she loves dogs, which is useful in our household. I don't think she is afraid of anyone; except a mouse.

Unlike 'my father', Tilly is no scholard. With effort she can read the directions on tins and packets, the captions on the pictures in the papers. She dotes on illustrated catalogues, and the fashion sections of 'books', by which she means women's magazines. She cannot write a laundry list, but can add the figures to it (3 for instance, when Towels is already written in).

When she goes on holiday she always sends us picture postcards about having wonderful time, but it is 'my father' who writes the messages. With dogged conscientiousness she chooses her own Christmas cards, very tasteful pictures always, with messages she thinks appropriate to the recipient.

I have her last year's Christmas card beside me now. It is a very jolly one with robins, and the greeting says:

>'Here's a good old-fashioned wish,
>   Christmas joy to YOU,
> The best of health and happiness,
>   Throughout the NEW YEAR too.'

Under this runs the legend, 'The Above Words are the Wishes of Tilly', in 'my father's' scholard hand.

Tilly has never been an ardent film fan, and she only goes to the pictures nowadays when pestered by the children to take them to see Hayley Mills in what is known as 'Pollyarner', or some musical whose tunes she knows from the wireless or long-playing records.

Perhaps familiarity has bred contempt. She certainly has met film people 'by galore' (a favourite term) during her quarter of a century at Lane End. Some of them she likes. Others she can't abide. And she speaks her mind without fear or favour.

She has a peculiarly soft spot for director Anthony Asquith, an unexpected choice. 'A proper gentleman he was, stridin' up and down and talkin', with his muffler round his neck. He come into the kitchen and was still talkin' fit to beat the band, but very nice, you could see he was properly brought up.'

Another talker gets a colder mention. Fay Wray, the screaming victim of King Kong, undoubtedly had a powerful pair of lungs. Her voice has left a sharp impression on our Hebe. 'All the time I was servin',' she declares, 'she kep' on talk, talk, talk till my head was fair openin' and shuttin'.'

From a kitchen's-eye view 'that Pauline Goddard' was unsatisfactory, although every detail of her outfit has been memorized and it is admitted that she was 'made up real posh'.

Anna Neagle, on the other hand, is mentioned with cordiality. Anna has that touch of warmth and tact which is so often found in naturally shy people. She finds it difficult to 'mix', and has studied more than most to overcome the difficulty. She has the gentlewoman's knack of dressing in a way appropriate to her company. Her make-up, when she wears any, is completely unobtrusive. When she and her husband, Herbert Wilcox, came out to spend an evening in outer Metroland they might have been a casual pair of neighbours.

Anna likes very simple food—'a bit of hot rice pudding before I go to bed'—but I discovered that only in recent years. In early days we made a special effort for the Wilcoxes. There was a small delicatessen shop in Pinner called Don's Delicacies, which would cook and send up elegant little meals, with vol-au-vents and lobster mayonnaise, savouries and salads.

One evening we had ordered a very special Don's dinner for the Wilcoxes. Amongst other things I remember a basket scooped out of half a melon, filled with fruit salad and decorated with handles of angelica. Tilly was waiting at table that night, in her best black dress with a very new, tight 'perm'. Before she went home she screwed up courage to ask Anna to 'sign a picture' she had brought with her.

With her warmest smile Anna, experienced in the art of signing pictures, inquired her name and wrote across the corner: 'For Tilly. Thank you for a wonderful dinner.' Tilly blushed to the roots of her perm, while expressions of delight and honesty chased each other across her face.

Honesty won. She opened her mouth to reveal the horrid truth that the dinner was not hers, when my husband gave her a warning look, and she subsided into a murmured 'Thank you'. There are times when deception is a courtesy, and this, I feel sure, was one of them. If Anna ever reads this anecdote she will laugh and understand. At all events, she remains the kitchen's favourite actress.

The kitchen's favourite actor was Robert Donat. 'Ever so nice he was, that Robert Doughnut, really a lovely man. He didn't seem a bit ill then. Dreadful the way he was took. I remember his little girl, she come to one of Tony's parties. Ginger she was, like her mother, with her hair tied up in yellow ribbons. She said they *was* new and come from Woolworth's. Proper old-fashioned she was, pore little thing.'

The Donats, both Robert and his first wife Ella Voysey, were from my home town. I had known Ella very slightly as a girl, when she had lived for a time at Professor Rutherford's house as companion to his wife and daughter Eileen. Robert himself was born and grew up in Withington, only a few streets away from me, but I never came across him in those days. People say, 'But you *must* have known him,' rather as they might say to a native of Western Australia, 'I expect you know my sister-in-law in Sydney.' Manchester, to be sure, is not as big as Australia, but even in the early 1900s it was quite a considerable warren of its kind.

The great advantage of coming from the same place is the ease of conversation it induces with a stranger. Donat and I met for the first time as adults, but we quickly felt like friends, because our young days had so much in common.

He told me how he used to tear round the shops at the corner of Withington village on his tricycle, past the grocer's where there was a sharp slope to whizz down. The grocer's was called Seymour Mead's, and it was there that my parked pram once ran away and overturned, and a wailing Caroline had to be comforted with ginger biscuits at the counter.

He told me about the Presbyterian church where he went with his elocution master to give penny readings. Did I know the church? he asked. I did. I had good reason to, considering the number of tennis balls I had lost through its leaded windows.

He told me how he would walk home from drama classes, night after night, beside the tramlines along Wilmslow Road, declaiming Shakespeare as he went. 'I always saved the purple passages for the points,' he said. 'That was when you got the biggest clang. It was splendid, like hurling your voice in challenge to a great brass band.'

I always remember that story when I think of Robert Donat. I don't know whether the Manchester tramlines had anything to do with it, but his management of voice was Donat's special triumph. He cut a handsome figure on the screen or stage, but was never, in my opinion, a great actor.

As a speaker, however, he was remarkable. Even in the last years, when the voice grew thin and breathy with illness, he conserved and used it with mastery for what it had to do. He could recite Kipling's 'The Way Through the Woods' on the radio as if it were an enchanted poem (which I sometimes think it is). He could pay tribute to lost friends like Leslie Howard with a warmth that gave the tired voice more than volume; it managed in some way to speak for everybody, as if it had picked up our private thoughts.

One of our most welcome and amusing guests was Alfred Hitchcock, who sometimes came out to dinner with his tiny wife Alma, bearing sheaves of flowers.

With a picture in my mind of Alma, almost hidden behind an armful of multi-coloured tulips, I should like to suggest that the giving of flowers is a grace which might well be more encouraged in this country. Almost every woman likes to receive flowers. The older she gets, the more she cherishes them.

They need not be expensive flowers. Not all of us prefer orchids; many of us dislike hothouse roses with wires piercing their tender stems and, as I have told you, a gift like Grace Moore's exotic lily may prove positively embarrassing.

Simple flowers are the safest and comeliest of gifts, and I am grateful for the many I have received. There was an elderly reader who delighted me by sending me wild flowers and sprays of foliage from the Lakelands. There was a country wife who used to work for Franziska at Ashington, and never failed to send spring parcels of early primroses and wild daffodils.

There was a press agent in charge of the Disney films when they first came to this country. His name was Harry Burgess, and because at that time I was almost the only woman critic, he decided of his own accord to send me flowers at Christmas. When he retired, his successor, David Jones, who had looked after our young son at Disney parties, took it upon himself to continue this private practice. Every Christmas Eve I would await with confidence the arrival of cheerful Disney flowers to brighten up the evergreens; chrysanthemums, mimosa, iris; and every year they came.

I shall never forget a wonderful box of flowers that came to me one morning with the compliments of director Jean Renoir after I had written an article about his lovely Indian film *The River*. I can still relive the moment of rapture when I lifted the lid and saw flowers of every kind and size, from tiny grape hyacinths and anemones, through daffodils, freesias and carnations to tall delphiniums, gleaming at me in their jewelled colours, and arranged (for they came from one of the best florists in London) with a loving hand.

Perhaps the flower present that has touched me most was a small Victorian posy of violets and other spring flowers, sent me a dozen years or so ago by an American girl; a shy, quiet Southerner whose name was Laurie. I never knew more than her given name. She was up at Oxford for a time with my son, and he brought her out to lunch one day at Pinner Hill.

A couple of weeks later I was producing a play with a bunch of young local amateurs; I think it was *The Heiress*. Just before the curtain rose, Laurie's posy was delivered by special messenger. She said this was the custom on first nights at home. The play proved to be one of our biggest successes, and I like to think her posy brought me luck.

When I first met Alfred Hitchcock he was a chubby, rosy-cheeked young man with eyes like bright boot-buttons. He spent his time writing and designing subtitles for silent pictures. He used to announce 'Came the Dawn' in black letters on a white ground, or whisper that 'Heart spoke to heart in the hush of the evening'. He liked to embellish these moving words with slightly iconoclastic sketches, for he was a born draughtsman with an impish sense of humour.

By the time the Hitchcocks came out to dinner with that mass of tulips we had been good friends for nearly eleven years. Hitch—the full name is unthinkable to those who know him—was beginning to be famous as a director on both sides of the Atlantic. After the success of *The Man Who Knew Too Much*, *The Thirty-Nine Steps* and *The Secret Agent* even the more sober New York papers were not hesitating to call him 'brilliant'.

He had become a 'must' for visiting journalists, one of the compulsive sights of London. It seems strange now to remember that at that time hardly anybody knew what Hitchcock looked like. His fleeting personal appearance in a picture had not yet become a trademark, and of course there was no television.

My friends from overseas, almost without exception, envisaged this prince of melodrama as a lean, tough, saturnine fellow, a compound of Dashiel Hammett, Sherlock Holmes and Perry Mason. It used to be a constant source of entertainment to me to lead one of them up to the genial, rotund Hitchcock, and watch him as he found his hand engulfed in the vast directorial paw.

There were limits to Hitch's geniality, however. Affectation and stupidity enraged him. He could bellow on the set as well as coo. I have heard him thunder at a leading man who fumbled one entrance after another, 'Come on, So-and-So, you Quota Queen!' I have seen him startle animation into the face of some super-refined leading lady by whispering into her ear words which no refined girl would expect to hear.

He also had his teacup-smashing days. This used to be a great Hitchcock act, which he picked up, he told me, as a result of smashing crockery for sixpence a go at the Wembley Exhibition. I remember one day at Shepherd's Bush when I found him standing, rather like a malevolent kelpie, among a litter of broken china.

'Hullo, kid,' he said. 'You came five minutes too late.'

'What for?' I asked him.

'For the big scene.'

'Murder?' I asked.

'No, temperament. Me breaking china. Makes you feel good. Gets rid of inhibitions. That was a teapot once, executive model. I like to get up on a high rostrum and tip the tray over. Or push cups over the edge of a gantry. Or just open my hand and let the whole thing drop—like this. Wouldn't you?'

He kicked a sugar-bowl across the set and added, pleadingly: 'I got to have *some* fun, kid. I'm on a diet. And I don't do crazy things in my pictures any more. I've turned a technical ascetic, kid, no more luxuries or gimmicks. Surely you don't grudge me a bit of innocent fun?'

Hitchcock was a grandmaster of the art of wheedling. He could coax a performance out of the dumbest blonde in the industry, and make her look ravishing into the bargain. His methods were often cavalier, but his humanity was catholic. He loved to startle and still loves to startle, with the relish of a schoolboy who jumps at you out of a dark corner shouting 'Boo!'

For myself, I dislike Hitchcock in his moods of ghoulish glee. I used to tell him so, and he would sulk for days. We were on what René Clair once described as 'the not-so-speaking terms' (Clair's reference was to his current relations with Alexander Korda) for a long time after Hitch decided, in *Sabotage*, to blow up a schoolboy in a bus with a time-bomb he was carrying. I told him that it wasn't entertaining. He declared it was.

You can't skip the horrors in a moving picture as you can in a written thriller. They take you unawares. Hitchcock in particular has perfected the art of the sudden, unexpected body blow. He sickens you with the shock discovery of the shrivelled human head in *Under Capricorn*, the terrible onrush of murder in *Psycho*, before you can guard yourself against what's coming.

Time and again I could have taken him by the scruff of the neck and shaken him until his boot-button eyes popped out of his head for lending his naturally humane genius to cadenzas of inhumanity.

These touches of jocose, professional sadism aside, he was the gentlest of creatures. He has done more kindly turns to out-of-work actors, writers down on their luck and other friends in trouble than almost anyone I know of in the industry. At heart he is an old-fashioned man, a family character; believing in the importance of small, common courtesies, of promises given and habits formed; the trivial, ordinary events which alone make the big events extraordinary.

Up to the time when Hitchcock went to Hollywood it was an invariable custom for me to lunch with him on the day after the press show of one of his pictures. By that time I had sent in my review, and we were free to mull over his film, as well as to discuss prospects for the future.

Hitchcock was a connoisseur of food and drink; he understood the pleasures of the table. Sometimes increasing girth persuaded him to try a diet, but the diets in those days were of an eclectic kind. He never imposed a fast on guests, nor embarrassed them by an ostentatious abstinence. Perhaps his king-size steaks were rather smaller, perhaps he eschewed French-fried potatoes and cut down the cream on his strawberries. But he still lunched like an epicure, albeit an epicure restrained.

Most of my luncheon dates with Hitch took place in the now vanished Carlton Grill, where he ran an account and was allowed to scribble on the tablecloth to his heart's content. This was important, because he is a man who never can talk freely without scribbling.

He visualizes both by instinct and by training. The script of every film he makes is interspersed with diagrams and sketches, showing exactly how the shot should be taken and what it ought to look like. As he talks to you, his broad, draughtsman's pencil sneaks out and blocks in groups or figures on the napkin or the table-top.

Before me as I write I have his celebrated self-portrait, scribbled on the back of a menu, with four pouting lines, a hint of a down-dropped eyelid and a sharp circumflex for the nose.

I also have a piece of blotting paper, on which my pencilled signature and his copy of it stand indistinguishably back to back. If all other means of livelihood had failed, Hitchcock might have made his fortune as a forger. 'It's only a trick, kid,' he told me; 'you don't think of it as writing, just drawing. It's easier to draw it upside down.'

For many years Hitchcock resisted all attempts to lure him out to Hollywood. He was a Londoner, a solid hunk of British bloodstock, who took a deal of moving. When at last he did agree to go, after the international success of *The Lady Vanishes*, he never broke his ties with friends in England.

After every London press show of a Hitchcock film I would get a telephone call from Hollywood. 'What did you think about it; honest, kid?' It was an echo of our traditional luncheon inquests, and I often wondered what he was scribbling at that instant.

When war broke out he lost no time in sending me a cable. Would Tony and I come out to California as his guests? He was almost certain he could get me a job on an American magazine. I am certain that he could and would have done so.

It was the action of a true friend, and I still remember the heaviness of heart with which I walked the mile to the nearest post office and sent back a refusal. Impossible to explain, in the scant words of a cablegram or even the phrases of a censored letter, exactly why I felt that I and mine were part of wartime Britain; why flight was inconceivable; why, when one's closest things are threatened, one has to stay and guard them. It was something too subtle to be expressed; one had to be on the spot to feel it.

I hope, but have never been quite satisfied, that Hitchcock understood.

THE AMAZING MR. KORDA

ON A bracket in one corner of our living-room stands the carved head of a young African woman, about life-size, in ebony. Her hair is piled high and intricately braided. Her lips, full but demure, are not quite smiling. The delicate ears lie close against the small, neat head.

She comes from the Congo, and was a present from Zoltan Korda, who found her there in some small village when he was making *Sanders of the River*. He had a special fondness for the carving, and was pleased when we put it in a place of honour. The last time I saw him, not long before his death, we were talking about old times and suddenly he asked me, 'The Congo lady, be she still with you?' He was as happy as a sandboy when I said she was.

'Zolly' was the easiest of the three Korda brothers to get to know, although as the years went on he became an infrequent visitor to England. He suffered from tuberculosis, a legacy of war gas, and our climate didn't suit him. His later life was divided between California and Switzerland. Many of his letters are dated from a sanatorium. But, wherever he might be, he remembered his old friends. Always, at Christmas, one might expect a case of wine from some London merchant, with the compliments of Mr. Zoltan Korda.

There was a boyish eagerness and candour about him which endeared him to shy people and to children. He had young sons of his own, and was splendid with small boys. I remember how patient he used to be with Sabu, who was brought from India to play in *Elephant Boy*, knowing only a few words of English.

Zolly had a fellow-feeling for bewildered and uprooted people.

He was shy at heart, I think, a good-natured, uncomplaining fellow, with no very positive habit of self-assertion. He saw himself as the mediocre member of the brilliant Korda family. In that he did himself less than justice. Alexander Korda thought the world of him. 'Everybody in the film industry has brothers,' he once said to me; 'that of course is customary. What is not so customary is to have brothers who can *do*.'

What Zoltan Korda did, as well as directing his own films, was to act as an invaluable *aide* in cutting, editing and doctoring the films of others. It was the trade to which he had been apprenticed as a boy in the old barn studio in Budapest, and the cunning never left him.

What Vincent Korda did was to design sets for almost all the Korda films; sets that were at the same time educated, imaginative, exact to period and practical. He was a 'real' painter, who liked to mess about at peace in his own studio in Paris, happy and free amongst his paints and canvases. He had no love at all for motion pictures. 'Alex,' he once said to his elder brother, 'you are all in a crazy trade. I hate your bloddy industry. I was an honest man, now you try to make me dishonest. I design this one picture for you; then I go.'

He kept his word. But it was not to be the last word. A few months later Alex telephoned to him in Paris. 'Vincent,' he said, 'I make now a new company of my own. I am taking a great risk and I need you as art director. You must come and help me.' And because no Korda ever said no to another Korda after the first hundred times, Vincent came to London; and there he stayed.

He was the silent member of the family. I remember his room as the last resort of peace in all the turbulence of the Korda empire, the calm spot in the centre of the hurricane. He lived apart from the reeling studios in a world of his own philosophy. His corner of the art department was unmistakable, a place peculiar to Vincent.

You would find a coffee percolator dripping beside a glass of paintwater, long oil-brushes soaking in a pot next to a jar of wild flowers, a hat flung on the floor under a plan of ancient Rome, a wall of sketches for his current picture. And somewhere, vaguely, there was Vincent, laconically glad to see you; pleased to talk on any subject except films, without looking up from his drawing; ready with the unexpected comment; hiding a world of wisdom behind his slow, Cheshire Cat smile.

Alexander Korda's 'new company' was called London Film Productions. The trade mark, soon to be known all over the world, was Big Ben. It came into existence in the spring of 1932 with a light comedy known as *Wedding Rehearsal*.

That was when I first made the acquaintance of the amazing Mr. Korda. During the next twenty years I was to see a great deal of him. I came to know him well; or as well as he would allow anyone to know him outside the circle of his family and what he always described (in invisible capitals) as 'My People'.

When he died in the January of 1956 the world seemed a duller place. I missed him, and shall continue to miss him. He still seems more alive to me than many living people.

I miss his stimulating talk, his high enthusiasms, his shrewd anticipations of things to come. I remember how amusing he could be, and how exasperating. I remember the black days when he was 'terribly tired' and the golden days when he was 'wonderfully happy'. I remember our stubborn quarrels, and the soft, purring voice with which he contrived to make them up: 'We are too long friends for this sort of thing.' It was impossible to stay aggrieved with a person who bore so little malice.

The Hungarian land agent's son who became a British knight was a great man in his way. Everything he did was on the grand scale. Even his failures had to be colossal failures. Like all great showmen, he made big mistakes, and frequently spent too much money. But he had the resilience of a rubber ball, and bounced back triumphantly after every tumble.

He was a man of taste and culture, a scholar and a natural spellbinder. A Hollywood executive once said of him, more in puzzlement than chagrin, that Korda could 'make the folks run after him, just like the rats of Hamburg ran after the Pied Piper'.

He drew towards him the best talents, in writing, acting, direction, design and music. The world was his field. He was intensely patriotic about his adoptive country, but his view was never insular. He could speak six languages fluently and inaccurately, with a charming indifference which was all part of the set-up. Even his native Hungarian occasionally appeared to fail him, but the charm never did.

Of all the figures in the British cinema, Korda's is the one around whom legends gather thickest. Alex in his heyday was the best film 'copy' in England. Physically colourless, with pale hair, pale eyes which looked naked when he took off his spectacles, pale skin, pale clothes, he was the most flaming personality in a highly coloured profession. No journalist had to go around hunting for Alexander Korda stories. They fell into his hands each day.

Alex had been a journalist himself, and knew exactly what each paper wanted.

You went to him and said: 'Alex, I need a story for next Sunday. Can you help me?'

He would start prowling up and down his office, with his soft panther tread. 'Darling,' he would throw over his shoulder, 'I am so tired, I cannot think today. We buy the rights of *Jungle Book*' (or *The Four Feathers*, or *Knight Without Armour*). 'I persuade to come here Marlene Dietrich' (or Gigli, or Fairbanks, or René Clair). 'I talk on the telephone to Orson about a musical version of *Around the World in Eighty Days*.'

'Can I print that?'

'Certainly you print it, darling, but it is not for you. That is an evening-paper story' (or 'That is better for the *Daily Mail*'). 'It is so difficult, and I am so exhausted. Last night I talk with Charles Laughton about *Cyrano de Bergerac*. He is trying some new noses. He has gone nuts over new noses. You want to talk to him? We fix it.'

He would stop his prowl and pick up one of the multitude of telephones on his desk. 'You get me at once Charles Laughton,' he would say, and you knew he had got Charles Laughton from the friendly profanation that singed the wires between them. 'That is all right,' he would observe as he put back the receiver, 'we fix it for tomorrow. Don't believe anything that old skunk tells you.'

He always fixed it and we always got our story. Alex knew his newspapers as intimately as he knew his books. I never went to see him and came away empty-handed.

It was wiser to take most of his stories with a pinch of salt. He had far too many plans for all of them to ripen. I have lost count of the number of times he told me, 'So-and-So' (and it was always a different So-and-So) 'will play for us next year Lawrence of Arabia.' London Films never made *Lawrence of Arabia*. Laughton never made *Cyrano de Bergerac*, but he was extremely amusing about the noses. Korda's dream castles were always splendid copy, even when they turned out to be castles in Spain.

The narrow house in Grosvenor Street, which provided London Films with their first headquarters, was so busy and crowded all day long that you could hardly set foot on stairs, or corridors, or in the bumpy little lift, without treading on the toes of some celebrity. There was a waiting-room, to be sure, but except for a torn copy of *Spotlight* and a basket chair that creaked, it was always empty.

People who knew the ropes slipped in through the mews at the back and went straight upstairs to Korda's ante-room. People who didn't know the ropes, but were known to the commissionaire, pushed open the glass door at the front and also went upstairs to Korda's ante-room. It was a small room, in which a dozen made a crowd, and it was always packed with People in the News, most of whom were old friends or eager to be friendly. In the middle of the hubbub sat Korda's secretary, small, grey-haired Miss Fischer, imperturbably tapping at her typewriter and dealing with the telephone in various languages.

Informality was the keynote of 22, Grosvenor Street. Sometimes Korda would push open the green baize door and join the party in the ante-room, leaving the visitor in the office to his own devices. Sometimes, in the middle of a conference, he would fling open the office window and call to some friend in the street below. Opposite No. 22 was the establishment of one of the most fashionable couturiers in London. History records the day when Alex, bored with some trivial business argument, leant out and shouted to Robert Sherwood across the street: 'Don't go in there, Bob! They're bloddy robbers!'

This did not deter the customer, nor was it intended to. It was simply an ejaculation, highly actionable of course, but uttered as a vent for tedium and high spirits. It may have surprised the passers-by in Grosvenor Street, but neither couture nor conference was affected by it.

Alex was what they call 'a masterpiece' for disposing of the unwanted caller, for saying hail and farewell in a single, painless operation. 'Hal*lo*, how are you, old boy?' he would purr, shaking hands as he urged his visitor towards the door. 'I cannot think just now, I am so exhausted. Come and see me tomorrow at five and we will talk. Goodbye.'

And so great was his charm and authority that hardly anyone felt slighted, and almost everybody did come back tomorrow at five.

It was always good copy for a journalist to join the rush-hour crowd at 22, Grosvenor Street. You never knew whom you might meet there, and most people talked freely, as waiting people will.

But if you wanted to learn something about Korda himself you had to meet him on his own stamping-ground. Sometimes, after a late-night run-through of a picture, he would ask a few friends home to supper at his house near Regent's Park.

Alex was at his best in his library at midnight, with a good fire blazing; cold meats and a noble ham on the side-table; whisky, cognac and coffee bubbling in a big percolator. He would prowl softly up and down the room, cigar in hand, talking over ideas for pictures with his brothers and his old Hungarian friend and scriptwriter, Lajos Biro; calling up New York or Hollywood or Paris; discussing books and politics and people into the not so small hours of the morning.

Korda had a multitude of books, in English, French and German; many of them first editions. They were kept on his shelves not for show, but because he enjoyed reading them and liked to have them close at hand.

He had a valuable collection of paintings: half a dozen Renoirs, three or four Cézannes, a couple of Canalettos, a Degas or two, a Monet and several others. But I sometimes think the picture he liked best was a photograph, roughly framed, which he always kept in his office.

It showed a back alley in Paris; a broken fence, with torn papers flying; and a draggled poster, announcing '*Charles Laughton dans La Vie Privée d'Henri VIII*', peeling from the hoarding.

'That is right, that is as it should be,' he used to say. '*Sic transit gloria* . . . a private end to the public life of a notorious film.'

I was in a good position to keep an eye on Korda and his activities. After a few years of making films in other people's studios he decided to build a studio of his own. He bought an old property called The Fisheries at Denham, in Buckinghamshire, a maddening spot to reach by train from London, but only a few miles away from our house in the north-west tip of Middlesex. You could do the journey by car in fifteen minutes; and how useful that was to be when the war brought petrol-rationing! At a pinch you could even walk.

It takes a long time to build a film studio, and Denham took longer than most. Alex was determined not to spoil the character of the place, for he had bought it largely for its woods and water. 'Not a tree shall be touched,' he declared, when first he walked along the river-bank on a wintry afternoon. And he very nearly kept his word.

We had the freedom of the place from the beginning, and often went there and picnicked on a Saturday afternoon. I have always had a passion for old houses in tanglewood surroundings, and, with the curiosity of the odious Mrs. Elton in *Emma*, I liked, of all things, to go mildly exploring.

The Fisheries must have been a friendly place to live in once, deep in the Buckinghamshire countryside. It had a family feel; I think a number of generations must have loved it. The unofficial way we used to reach it was across a humpbacked bridge, and then, parking the car on what is known nowadays as The Verge, through a gap in the hedge into a little coppice, where hazels covered and bluebells carpeted a forgotten dogs' graveyard.

There were headstones with the names of Tim and Bob and Nero and some fifteen other dogs who had hunted and ratted and spent their busy lives at The Fisheries before the First World War. Beyond this touching graveyard you struck the footpath by the river. On your right was the placid water, with its reeds and islets and hundreds of nests of wild fowl. On your left was a fringe of steeply hanging woods, with a fox-hole in the bank. In front was the old house, with its stables and outbuildings. Beyond lay broad acres of pasture land and arable.

As the studios grew, a great deal of the flat land was naturally gobbled up. But the old house itself remained, with a number of home fields and a long stretch of wooded river-bank. We saw them for many years in scores of pre-war British pictures.

For that matter, thanks to television, we can see them still, although films are no longer made there, and the place has been turned into a store for the United States Air Force. Not long ago I.T.A. showed us a revival of *The Ghost Goes West*. Looking at the ruins of Glourie Castle, later to become a Flemish market place for *Rembrandt*, I felt quite sentimental for a moment. *Ehu fugaces! O tempi passati!* Gone, gone, gone with lost Atlantis! Dear, absurd, vainglorious old Denham!

Television showed us *Fire Over England*, and we recognized the meadows beside the river where an extremely nervous Flora Robson, in the stiff robes and ruff of Queen Elizabeth, rode down to Tilbury, and just managed to sit her white cart-horse long enough to harangue the troops before the Armada.

It showed us *The Scarlet Pimpernel*, with Merle Oberon and Leslie Howard, and as I watched the Blakeney coach drawn up in the stable-yard of The Fisheries to carry Marguerite to Dover I idly wondered what they'd done that morning with the cats, all hundred of them, who were grossly pampered by the old and somewhat lonely commissionaire.

Whenever I went there the yard was cluttered up with cats: thin cats, fat cats, old cats, young cats, cats of every shape and colour. They monopolized the place and spurned it too, turning up their whiskers at saucers of canned milk and kipper-heads, loudly demanding fresh sandwiches from the canteen and top milk from the bottle.

It was never a surprise to meet animals at Denham. Apart from the indigenous cats and visiting dogs, both professional and amateur, there was a herd of goats, which had been imported to habitate the ruins of City Square in the Wells film *Things to Come*, and remained there with their offspring for years, perfectly content, and apparently quite forgotten.

At one time there was a resident tiger, and elephants were almost common. They lived in a compound down beside the river. I was told by one old gardener that them elephants was masterbits for fertilizer. His hothouses and nursery beds had never done so good, he said, as when Mr. Zoltan and that other gentleman (Bob Flaherty) were taking that picture they called *Elephant Boy*.

The studio buildings themselves looked gargantuan to me, but the Hollywood architect who came over to design them described Denham as 'just a decent-sized little place, handy, with enough elbow-room to move around in'. A London Films publicist, with greater exuberance, informed a breathless world that Denham's power plant 'generates enough electricity to light the whole city of York'; though heaven knows why it should be required to do so.

There were seven stages, miles of concrete corridors and fifteen star dressing-rooms.

The corridors were memorable for their peculiar smell: a combination of cellar clamminess with hot radiator and varnish. The walls were decorated with what looked like crazy maps of some Underground railway system, with lines, blobs and arrows in assorted colours, directing you to get nowhere fast. Above your head, at intervals, red signs commanded SILENCE, while the air was clamorous with sawing, filing, hammering, the rattle of tea-trolleys and a bable of talk in half a dozen languages.

The star dressing-rooms had the perfection of exhibits in some ideal-home exhibition. Each of them was equipped with bath, shower, telephones, couch for exhausted artists and refrigerator. Picture windows, chastely framed in chintz, gave a view of trimly formal gardens.

These dressing-rooms suggested bedrooms in a luxury hotel. They changed hands, but seldom character. Hundreds of guests passed through them as the years went on, but only a few people managed, or cared, to endue them with a personal touch during their brief tenancy.

Elisabeth Bergner's sanctum always smelt of fruit; she adored munching at ripe apples. Charles Laughton's room invariably had a single vase of flowers, which he brought up from his Surrey garden and arranged most beautifully. I remember bluebells, just enough, no more, tenderly gathered without touching the white of the stem; and a low bowl of very small, sweet-smelling Penzance briers.

Flora Robson was always busy sewing, usually with a niece in attendance, and the floor of her room was littered with materials. She is an exquisite needlewoman with a special turn for patchwork; she likes to cover her own chair and sofa cushions with bits of silk and velvet wheedled from her dressmaker, and embarks without trepidation on a full-sized patchwork quilt.

Marlene Dietrich's V.I.P. dressing-room, used when she was making *Knight Without Armour* with Robert Donat, was specially done over for her with pale wood, blue glass-topped tables, pink satin cushions and a continuous supply of pink long-stemmed roses. There she would receive her courtiers under an enormous hair-dryer, stretching out a white arm to be kissed in continental fashion; and many were the men who came to kiss it.

One very young star, who shall be nameless for obvious reasons, gave me a unique reception when I went to interview her. We hadn't met before, and my name obviously meant nothing to her. I tapped at the door. She called 'Come in!' and emerged from behind the shower curtain completely naked. This embarrassed her more than it embarrassed me. She blushed crimson, snatched a robe, and apologized with what I am sure was utter honesty. 'Oh,' she said, 'I really am most *terribly* sorry. I thought you were a *man*.'

A few miles from Denham, at Iver Heath, another studio was beginning to grow. This was Pinewood, where the Rank Organization makes most of its films today.

Pinewood was an old estate which had come on to the market at about the same time as The Fisheries. Korda had looked it over, but decided against it, because he thought the grounds too formal. Formal they were, but in a pleasing Victorian way, with clipped box hedges, landscaped vistas, broad green lawns and a great deal of sunshine.

The house itself became a social and residential club before they stripped the first turf for the studios. It made an admirable dormy house for film people who wanted to avoid the daily trip from London into Buckinghamshire. A number of the stars who worked at Denham lived there, or became members of the club.

It flourished from the start. The food was good. There was a bar with fruit machine, extremely popular with visitors from Hollywood. There were tennis courts and a swimming pool. There was even a long picture gallery. Charles Laughton, who knew something about painting, and was himself the owner of a big Renoir (the Renoir made a deep impression on me, not because I know anything about painting, but because it was the first time I had seen strip-lighting fixed above a canvas in a private sitting-room), took a wry interest in the fortunes of this gallery.

'Most of the stuff is junk,' he said to me the first time we walked along it, 'but there are one or two good pieces. That's a decent little painting; so is that, and *that*. Watch it, Lejeune, they'll GO.'

They did go. Charles had been in America for months when next we walked together through the crowded gallery. Faded oblong patches in the wall showed where That and That and *That* had hung. Nobody but Charles, to the best of my knowledge, noticed or commented on their disappearance. Perhaps they were legitimately sold. Perhaps not.

The bedrooms at Pinewood may not have been equipped with all *mod cons*, but they were large and quiet. The pride of the club, the most select of all the bedrooms, was the one with the lavatory seat raised on a reredos, commanding a spacious view of lawns and gardens. It was reserved for V.I.P.s like Marlene Dietrich, and I have no doubt was priced accordingly, but I have never quite credited the story that the seat was made of gold.

I found it hard to care for Pinewood as much as I cared for Denham. Perhaps my outlook was coloured by the unfortunate circumstances of our introduction.

Before the old house was turned into a club a few press people were invited out to dinner. It was a lovely summer's evening and I was in good company, driving through the Buckinghamshire lanes with John Betjeman and his wife Penelope. (At that time, briefly, John was film critic on the *Evening Standard*.)

The garden glowed with roses. The sunset was on its best behaviour. There was a romantic young moon and a heady scent of lavender. The dining-room looked a picture, with flower decorations on the one long table. The wines were discreetly chosen and the food was perfect, with the exception of a single oyster. And, unhappily, it found its way to me.

An oddly prophetic conversation which I heard about this time may perhaps furnish a postcript to a chapter on studios and players.

A film was being made of John Galsworthy's story *The First and the Last*, to be called *Twenty-One Days*, with Laurence Olivier, Ralph Richardson and the still comparatively unknown Vivien Leigh in the leading parts. One scene called for a river trip from Tower Bridge down the Thames to Southend. The pleasure steamer *Golden Eagle*, well known to thousands of Londoners, was hired for the day. And from the moment we cast off it rained inexorably.

There was nothing for anyone to do but wait for the weather to clear, watch the grey docks sliding by, read the newspapers, play gin rummy and talk. The talk inevitably came round to the film that M.G.M. was planning to make of *Gone With The Wind*. No casting had yet been announced, but there were hot tips that Paulette Goddard, Bette Davis, Barbara Stanwyck, Miriam Hopkins and other celebrated stars were certainties for the Scarlett O'Hara role.

Somebody turned to Olivier and said, 'Larry, you'd be marvellous as Rhett Butler.' He laughed it off, but the suggestion was not too preposterous; by this time he had an international reputation as an actor.

Someone else ventured that she *saw* Rhett Butler as Robert Taylor.

Others saw him as Gary Cooper, Erroll Flynn and Cary Grant. Discussion of the casting went on in a desultory fashion, until the new girl, Vivien Leigh, brought it to a sudden stop.

She drew herself up on the rainswept deck, all five foot nothing of her, pulled a coat snug round her shoulders and stunned us with the sybilline utterance: 'Larry won't play Rhett Butler, but *I* shall play Scarlett O'Hara. Wait and see.'

17

WARTIME AND LESLIE HOWARD

JUST before Easter in the April of 1936 Mother died. It was bitter cold, with an east wind tearing the ice-pink blossoms from the almond trees. She had been badly shocked not long ago by the news of Russell's death in Australia; he was killed by a ricocheting bullet in a kangaroo hunt. Her heart was none too good, and the doctor had warned her not to over-exert herself.

But she was an independent person and not to be deterred. One day I was working in the garden and she came in to speak to me. She had walked up from the village with a heavy bag of shopping; said she thought she had a little chill, and would go to bed early. The chill turned to pneumonia, and she died a few mornings later; very quietly; the only sound I can remember is the chatter of sparrows under the bedroom window.

Her death was as considerate as her life had been. All her affairs were left in perfect order. In her practical way she had prepared for death as sensibly as she had once planned for family holidays.

For us there was none of that miserable business of going through old letters, photographs and personal belongings. She had kept nothing that was not essential. Her wardrobe and chest of drawers were almost bare. The papers in her desk were sorted neatly, tied up with string and addressed to the relevant member of the family.

Franziska, as the eldest, was entrusted with her old diaries, back to the days in Germany, and from Franziska they passed on to me. I found a packet of letters in my own handwriting, tied with an economical bit of string and labelled: 'C.A.L. Return to her. To burn unread if she likes.' Because we had been so much together the letters were comparatively few.

Life with Mother had never impinged sharply on life with work, although it had made work possible from the beginning. What I missed was the comforting assurance of her presence just across the road, her endless patience with small worries, real or fancied. It was a long time before I stopped listening for the click of her front door, the sound of her sandals on the gravel path, and fell out of the habit of thinking, 'I must ask Mother about that.' But the weekly round of work went on as usual.

Perhaps not quite as usual. A wind of change was in the air. The first thing that it brought was television. About this time the B.B.C. started a transmission service from Alexandra Palace, and there were three eager, happy-go-lucky years for it to grow before the war closed it down.

The new thing fascinated me from the beginning. I liked its intimacy and informality, so different from the glossy public entertainment provided on the cinema screen.

In those days television was as cosy and, in the best sense, amateur as the first sound broadcasts from Savoy Hill. The handful of announcers became our friends. We trembled for Leslie Mitchell when he climbed the tall television mast in a high wind, and shivered with Elizabeth Cowell as she hugged a coat around her and watched Mr. Middleton prodding away at his exposed patch of Saturday garden.

My husband bought a small Bush set at cost price—never ask me how—and neighbours would drop in to look at news or cricket, plays or boxing; for this was before the days when every house sported a television aerial.

We saw Hutton make his record score of 364 runs in the Test match at the Oval, and Bois Roussel flash past the post in the Derby like a streak of black lightning.

We watched Neville Chamberlain step out of the plane at London Airport, umbrella hooked over one arm, waving his famous 'little piece of paper'. That was a splendid afternoon, an occasion to remember; not only because we had seen history in the making but because we honestly believed—or the more trustful of us did—that the Prime Minister had brought back peace from Munich.

Too soon, however, we were forced to realize that Munich was a respite only. A storm was brewing up in Europe, and nobody could stop its breaking. The Americans, who keep their ears closer to the ground than we, had adumbrated war for years. With them, 'Nazi' had become the dirty word that 'Commie' is today; though nobody could make the word sound so despicable as Churchill in his wartime speeches.

Hollywood films of that period were violent with anti-Nazi propaganda. Our own films, always slow to reflect political or social change, went on more or less in the old fashion, but there was a noticeable exodus from the studios. People who were offered jobs in Hollywood decided it was prudent to accept them. People without immediate prospects took a chance, and set off for California while the going was still good.

It isn't really fair to blame these emigrants. Few people *want* to be caught up in war, and conduct in such circumstances must be an individual choice. The only point I should like to make, to explain if I am able, is that it was hard for English people later on to bridge the gap in experience between those who stayed away and those who stayed at home. It is a very different thing to have watched war, however anxiously, from a distance, and to have lived with it as a constant bedfellow. With the best will in the world we never seemed to speak exactly the same language again.

That year after Munich we all felt we were living on borrowed time. We spent it as seemed best to us. I remember, one afternoon at Denham, talking to Ralph Richardson on the set of *The Four Feathers*. While the big blue cyclorama was being lit for Durrance's blind scene, he showed me a picture postcard from his friend Olivier.

Olivier was playing on the New York stage, commuting at weekends to California, where Vivien Leigh was at work on *Gone With the Wind*, just as she had prophesied. He sounded lighthearted and gay, and urged Ralph to come out and enjoy the climate and absurd luxury of, Hollywood.

I asked him if he meant to go, and he replied firmly in the negative. Time was running short, he said, and there seemed no point in wasting precious weeks in Hollywood swimming pools while one could be doing something worth while in the English theatre.

The Four Feathers proved to be one of the first film casualties of the war. Finished and briefly shown in London, it was due for general release on 4th September, 1939. On that day all the cinemas in England closed down. When they reopened, *The Four Feathers* had lost its place in the booking list, and the country didn't see it until a long time later.

I have always felt sorry about this; partly because Ralph's Durrance was one of the best things he had done on the screen; partly because of my own affection for the story. I grew fond of *The Four Feathers*, in its scarlet binding, when I was very young. When the film was on its way I talked to the author about it in his study.

'Mr. Mason,' I said, 'one thing has always puzzled me. 'Why didn't you let the fourth feather be redeemed?'

'To show that nothing in this world is quite complete,' he answered.

The year that followed Munich was a time of unnatural tension. Few of us spoke of war outright, though most of us were thinking of it. We used circumlocutions like 'If anything happens', or 'If the worst comes to the worst'.

Air-raid shelters and sandbags appeared in London streets, and a network of silvery balloons laced the sky. Suburban lawns were sacrificed to dug-outs. Arrangements were made for mass evacuation of children from the cities. Large country premises were earmarked by schools, business firms and Government departments. We were all issued with gas-masks and shown how to use them. There was a run in the shops on black-out material, siren suits and sleeping bags. Selfishly precautious people laid in hoards of canned meat, dried milk, tea, sugar, soap, preserves and whisky.

We all lived on borrowed time in our own way. Tony and I went for our usual summer holiday to Bexhill. One day at the end of August my husband turned up in the car to fetch us home. He said the roads were thick with military traffic, tanks and guns and lorries on the move.

Nothing had happened yet, but something was likely to happen at any moment. Quite suddenly I knew what I must do with my last hour of borrowed time. I went down to the beach and had a solitary bathe. There was nobody in sight along the shore. I am nothing of a swimmer, and an appalling sailor; but the sea, the fact of being in the sea, part of the sea itself, has always fascinaetd me. The sea comes into almost all my dreams, and in the best dream of all I find myself moving with careless ease through temperate water into a golden sunset.

The water was temperate that day, and there was a hazy sun in a pale August sky. I floated on my back for a long time, accepting the benison, and deliberately thinking of nothing at all.

That was the last bathe I ever took. After the war I felt too old for swimming. As I dried myself, dressed, swept the wet sand from the coconut matting, and locked the hut door in what proved to be an act of supererogation, I knew quite well that this was a goodbye.

We never saw that foolish little hut again. It was destroyed not through enemy action, but by the cheerful dilapidations of our own defence troops, who must have had a high old time with their haul of hockey sticks, beach balls, deckchairs, crockery and children's comics, not to mention nice dry wood to feed their fires.

On Sunday morning, 3rd September (and it was such a lovely morning too), just as the bells stopped for matins, the Prime Minister broadcast to the nation the news that we were in a state of war with Germany. Hardly had his broadcast ended when the air-raid sirens set up their banshee wailing. Here it comes, we thought, just what everyone predicted: immediate mass bombing.

It turned out to be a false alarm, but for a long time the idea persisted that congregations of any kind were undesirable. All the cinemas in Britain were closed down for a week. When nothing happened in the next seven days most of them reopened shyly, but a number of the smaller halls stayed dark for good. Nobody was admitted without his gas-mask. You couldn't go to church without a gas-mask. You couldn't go *anywhere* without a gas-mask. The thing became an albatross, our burden and our curse.

The fishermen went down to the sea with that bouncing abomination slung across one shoulder, their nets over the other. Schoolchildren stumbled over the square cardboard boxes as they scrambled in the lanes for blackberries. Housewives bundled them out of their shoppings baskets to make room for apples or a vegetable marrow.

That was in the early days of war, before we tumbled to the fact that all we really had to carry was a *container*. Some of the containers did contain a gas-mask, the vast majority didn't. There is a record of a forgotten case picked up somewhere in East Anglia and found to contain: a piece of knitting and a ball of wool, powder compact, lipstick and mirror, a comb with several broken teeth, a bar of chocolate, some loose change, a flask of brandy and a packet of photographs and letters. There was another gas-mask too, abandoned and distinctly crumpled. On the lid of the box was scribbled the legend, 'WE'VE GOT TO BE PREPARED'.

Many people felt quite sure that war would be the end of the British film industry. As it turned out, they were wrong, but the assumption was a natural one. The studios were in for a hard time, and working conditions became more and more difficult as the years went by.

One man after another was called up. Floors were commandeered for storage or to house the staff of Government departments. Materials were in ever shorter supply. There was an increasing scarcity of timber, steel, paint, canvas, plaster and even such unconsidered trifles as nails and hairlace for making wigs.

But challenge produced results. We learnt to be ingenious and economical through sheer necessity. In the old days a set would be struck and demolished as soon as it was done with. Now nothing was thrown away. Nails were pulled out with care and straightened. Canvas was whitewashed and repainted. Not a stick of wood was burnt; gone were the roaring bonfires that one used to see on studio lots before the war.

Sets were adapted in ingenious ways and used over and over again. A few banisters, a beautifully turned newel post and a dozen risers suggested a fine staircase which in fact led nowhere. The trick in camera work and lighting was to concentrate on the little that *was* there. The trick worked surprisingly well.

Inevitably, our films changed in character. Big, spectacular productions were abandoned; or, like Korda's half-finished *Thief of Bagdad* and his projected *Lady Hamilton*, transferred to Hollywood. Every film that was made had to contribute in some way to the war effort, and although that may seem at first thought a gloomy programme, it did our industry a power of good.

I think it is no exaggeration to say that the war years, with all their hardships and perhaps because of them, marked the richest production period in the whole of our film history. Pictures escaped from the routine novelette pattern, began to pursue a purpose and develop a character. While Hollywood still clung to the old conventions, we got the needed jolt, the shot in the arm.

At Pinewood, under Ian Dalrymple, the Crown Film Unit embarked on a heavy programme of documentary shorts and features. (I abominate the word 'documentary', but let it stand; it is part of the currency of modern language, and everybody knows, or imagines that he knows, exactly what is meant by it.)

A number of the people who worked for Crown had learnt their business at the Empire Marketing Board or the G.P.O. Film Unit with John Grierson, and people who are taught by Grierson stay taught. I know that, because I learnt so much from him myself. In my early years on the *Observer* I saw a good deal of him, watching films in a makeshift little theatre on a first floor in Oxford Street, at the squalid end, near St. Giles's Circus.

Grierson taught me how to look at films and see them whole; how to judge each one on its own merits; not seeking in it for some quality that was not intended to be there. He was a sharp and brilliant critic. His film review, in *Tribune* in the 1930s have never to my mind been bettered by any other writer. As a reviewer he was uncommitted and generous to a degree. He could admire the sweeping spectacle of Cecil B. de Mille with as much zest as he brought to the simplicity of Flaherty's *Nanook* or the purposive strength of the Soviet *Turksib*. He never allowed politics or policy to interfere with his judgement.

Grierson's reputation as a director rests upon a single film, *Drifters*, a study of the North Sea herring fleet. His real importance to the cinema is not as a director, but as a teacher, critic, what one might almost call a *conveyancer* of ideas; one can hardly exaggerate the part that he has played in developing film as a means of quick and lucid communication.

He would have made a master salesman. In fact, he *is* a master salesman. In the old days in the cinema he used to sell us fish, pineapples and New Zealand butter; postage stamps, the night mail or the Pool of London; and we bought them without hesitation. Today, on the television screen in *This Wonderful World*, he is selling us hammer mills, Lippizan horses and Canadian abstracts with the same aplomb. He has trained himself to a fine point as a persuader.

I haven't seen Grierson now for many years, but some time before I left the *Observer* I had an unexpected letter from him.

'Dear Caroline,' he wrote, 'that was a most pretty piece on *Salome*. Quite in the great tradition of movie-writing, and of your own not least. The wonderful trick is to be able to do it all over again in one's old age. Anyway, here's to a lovely flourish of the aged scalpel. What's —— got that the boys and girls didn't have better?'

It was a good letter to have.

When, after the war, the Crown Unit was put down, there was wide and understandable indignation. But sometimes I wonder if it were not the best thing that could have happened. The job for which the Unit had been formed was finished. It had shown the world a true picture of Britain at war: in the air, at sea, on the home front.

Story after story of real life came from its observant cameras. They were simple statements of fact, never exaggerated nor bombastic; but often, without sentiment, extremely moving. They showed us children in the blitz, nights in an underground shelter, the hazardous work of fire-fighting, the plotting and execution of air defence, the care of convoys in the western approaches. They were good films, supervised with authority, and made by skilful and courageous people. We had every reason to be proud of them, and for my part I am rather glad that they ended when their mission ended, with a united nation, and were never involved in the polemics of peace.

Unity of purpose gave distinction to almost all our war films. Even the fictional subjects, played by professional actors, showed much of the same quality, the same directness of behaviour and dialogue. Emergency seemed to beget sincerity in writers, directors and performers. Muir Mathieson has told me how much easier it was to persuade the best composers, such as Vaughan Williams and Sir Arthur Bliss, to compose music for these pictures. At last, in a shoddy world of movie stories, they found themes to stir the imagination; the longest undefended frontier in the world, the George Cross island of Malta.

You could sense a new feeling in the studios; a common doggedness that had not been there before. At Denham, the studio I knew best, there was also a new kind of intimacy. After a bad night of bombing during the heavy winter blitz of 1940-1 people would turn up from their London homes with sleepless faces; a little late, perhaps, because of some fresh crater in the road, but determinedly cheerful. It was good to be together for another day, even if the company had not always been our nearest and dearest.

The English are notoriously bad mixers, but it is difficult to remain on formal terms with people when you are cooped up with them in a tunnel for an hour during an air raid. One of the peculiar features of Denham was its air-ducts: catacombs that ran the whole length of the studio. They seemed to stretch out for ever, and the story goes that Korda, walking along them for the first time with the architect, Jack Okey, suddenly blenched, stopped, caught his companion's arm and said, 'Jack, are you *sure* we have not gone too far?'

In wartime they made natural air-raid shelters, and at the first sound of the alert we were supposed to troop down into them in an orderly manner and stay there until the all-clear.

Work stopped on all the stages when a raid was on, for apart from any danger the noise of guns and aeroplanes made sound-recording impossible. 'Everyone to the ducts' was the wardens' order, and down there in the catacombs one found groups of grips and chippies playing cards, actresses with bags of knitting, extras reading crumpled newspapers, egg-heads propounding theories of the art of cinema and ballet to anyone who would listen.

After a while, though, the catacomb habit was largely abandoned. People who had offices stayed in their offices, or, just to satisfy the wardens, walked in at one end of the ducts and out the other. It was such a long journey that, what with stopping for a word with this person and that person, quite often the raid would be over when you came out in the daylight again.

Memories of early war days at Denham are inevitably mixed with memories of Leslie Howard. I learnt to know him well at that time, and came to be very fond of him.

We had met once, years earlier, briefly and entirely in the way of business. He had just come back from Hollywood, where he had been playing with Norma Shearer in *Romeo and Juliet*. The *Observer* wanted a story about him in his Surrey home; so did the *Boston Evening Transcript*, which reprinted most of it under the headlines, 'Leslie Howard at Ease on an English Estate'.

The 'English Estate' proved very hard to find. It was hidden in a leafy lane near Dorking, but nobody could tell me exactly *which* lane. They knew of only two actors thereabouts, I found: Mr. Sybney Howard, the comedian, and a Mr. Charles Haughton, or some such name, who lived up along there on the hill. (It was May, and Charlse and Elsa's beloved bluebells were in a blaze of glory.)

In the end I discovered that Mr. *Leslie* Howard, the one that I was asking for, was known locally as the mad fellow with the polo ponies. He kept sixteen of them at that time, six newly imported from America with a Californian polo-player and a Texan cowboy to train them.

When I arrived at what was presumably the 'English Estate' I found the lane blocked by errand boys with bicycles, chattering women in aprons, an ice-cream cart, a couple of tradesmen's vans, a string of polo ponies and long, black American saloon flung haphazardly across the road, while what seemed to be the entire Howard household turned out to catch a brown mare who had gone berserk.

Leslie himself, looking oddly improbable to a filmgoer in cowboy chaps, sat his pony in silence and watched while the Texan, with professional cries of 'Ho yo!' and 'Hi girl!', attempted to rope the unco-operative mare. Never, in the gravest of his screen epics, had the actor looked so worried. The other horses were getting too excited. There was a mare in the next field with a young foal, tossing her head nervously, neighing and cantering.

When the brown mare was eventually caught and saddled, Howard disappeared. He had a way of silently disappearing, as I was to find out later. I think it was an escape from instant pressure. Time and again he would be missing from the studio set; discovered at last, usually far away, reading or asleep in somebody's parked car. His comings and goings had an air of vague inconsequence, but when he was caught at last he was entirely at your behest, and could talk about his work with enthusiasm and authority.

His talk, on that long ago May morning, was mostly about Shakespeare. He naturally had a good deal to say about *Romeo and Juliet*.

'I always thought Romeo was a perfectly deadly part, except in the later scenes, when he is something more than just a man in love. A man in love is a stupid thing—he bores you stiff, in real life or anywhere else

—but a woman in love is fascinating. She has a kind of aura. Shakespeare was obviously fascinated by Juliet, and it was the woman he enriched. Romeo acquires something in the late scenes, when he becomes the victim of a political feud, and in his tragic moments he is rather interesting, a kind of adolescent Hamlet.'

It was about *Hamlet* that he really wanted to talk. His mind was full of *Hamlet* at the time. He had plans to produce a *Hamlet* film in what he called a 'dolls'-house set'. The idea was to show the Hamlet family moving from room to room in the castle of Elsinore; to let us watch the cooks preparing the funeral baked meats in one corner, while the Queen was dallying with Claudius in another; to show the marks on the wall where the young prince had been measured as he grew; the casements he looked out of, the familiar stairs he trod. Elsinore, as far as I could understand it, was to be endowed with a special *genius loci*, and become a protagonist in the tragedy.

Leslie Howard's ideas for his screen *Hamlet* were original and exciting, but they stayed just ideas. That was the first and last time I ever heard of them. I cut my visit very short, for Leslie, although full of charm, was clearly absent of mind. Having forgotten the errant mare, he was following the movements of the adolescent Hamlet. I didn't see him again until the war.

Perhaps my first impression was superficial; possibly circumstance had altered character; at any rate, the Leslie Howard whom I came to know at Denham seemed a very different person from 'the mad fellow with the polo ponies'.

He looked a great deal older and a little frail. He had taken to wearing heavy, horn-rimmed spectacles; not always, and never on the set, but often enough to make them seem a part of him. There was still the gentle charm of manner (although one actor that I know insists the gentleness was a façade, and that as a director he was ruthless), but with it a new philosophy and purpose. It was as if the war had shown him where his heart lay; as if his passion to release a *genius loci* had passed from Elsinore to England.

When the airliner in which he was flying home from Lisbon was shot down over the Atlantic in June 1943 the news was received here with as much grief as shock. Perhaps no single war casualty gave the general public such an acute sense of personal loss. Leslie Howard was more than just a popular film star, who had endeared himself to audiences with *Pygmalion, Pimpernel Smith* and *The First of the Few*. He had become in an odd way a symbol of England, standing for all that is most deeply rooted in the British character.

I have sometimes wondered what Howard would have done if he had come back safely from that trip to Spain and Portugal. I had a long talk with him the day before he left. He was in a strange mood; overtired and overstrained; worrying, as he was far too apt to do, about his health. He had just turned fifty, and was acutely aware of it. He talked a great deal about youth, and youth's right to leadership.

He left me with an odd impression that he felt his special job was done. To be sure, he had plans; plans for a film about the Liberty Ship One Thousand and One, built in the Rockies and sailing in convoy to Murmansk; another film about Sir Christopher Wren and the building of St. Paul's Cathedral; another very special one about the *feeling* of the English Downs. He was also toying with a fancy for a sequel to *Pimpernel Smith*, in which Professor Smith would meet a Mandarin. The essential characteristics of the British and the Chinese, he insisted, were curiously alike.

He could have been persuaded to appear in one or other of these films, I don't doubt. At the back of his mind, however, was the idea that it was time for him to stand aside as an actor. The public, he said, wanted young faces, and new voices. He may have been right about the faces, but about the voices—and his was one of the best-loved voices on the air at that time—he was supremely wrong.

I have just been going through my files and found a scribbled note from Robert Donat, dated 4th June 1943. 'How awful about L.H.', it says. 'I'd no idea how much he meant to our business until I realized he'd gone from it altogether. He had such subtlety and delicacy and style and I think he'd have developed into a first-class director.'

Subtlety, delicacy and style, all these; and with them a tremendous power of personal persuasion. I hope that nobody will ever try to film the Leslie Howard story. It would be, for many reasons, not only impertinent but impossible. His son Ronald, who looks so very like him, has properly refused to play the part, and anyone else would be unthinkable.

Leslie Howard was an odd man to encounter in the film business; not at all an easy man to understand; but I am very glad to have known him, however incompletely. He was a rewarding man to meet; he always set imagination working. He was a mass of apparent contradictions. He had the Kipling secret of the Cat Who Walked By Itself, and yet he was a born ambassador. He came, on one side, of Hungarian stock; he knew and loved America; but he was as much a part of England as Kipling's oak, ash and thorn.

WAR'S END AND ARTHUR MACHEN

THOSE were hazardous days for journalists whose functions had been to supply newspapers with art, drama or film criticism; features which could, by no stretch of the imagination, be considered essential to the national war effort. Just as the cinema closed its doors to many films in the first week of war, so did Fleet Street cast out a number of its special correspondents.

I have kept a letter postmarked 5th September 1939, written in Garvin's sprawling hand on the blue paper he always used for private correspondence from his home at Beaconsfield.

'My dear,' it runs, 'I can scarce bear to write this. I have written a dozen miserable letters of the kind already and this is the worst. For want of room and money nearly all the non-political and special features of the *Observer* have to be discontinued at once, and among them films, as well as the theatre, music, art, broadcasting comment and other subjects. In many ways I am as indomitable as ever, but all this part of the dire necessities of war is a heartbreak to the human nature of this editor.

'And you? I have been so proud of you and so fond of you—as much as befits a veteran whose antiquity has seen two Punic Wars. May we resume in happier times.'

As things worked out, we resumed without much delay, for Fleet Street soon discovered that films not only had their propaganda value but were a means of cheering up the troops. So my weekly film piece crept back into the *Observer*, although at half-length and mere pocket-money salary.

Luckily, there was still a good market for studio stories and general articles on England at war in the columns of the *New York Times*. For a year or so I did quite well with these, but as we became more and more involved, censorship made it difficult to send news freely from one country to another.

When incendiaries burnt out part of Denham one was not allowed to mention it. When, driving home from Ealing Studios one golden afternoon in late summer, we found that the sky was suddenly filled with aircraft, grappling and tossing and tumbling, with sounds of gunfire up so high, so far, we were not able to say that we had watched the beginning of the Battle of Britain.

Our reports to New York became more and more skeletal each week. They wanted facts, and we couldn't give them facts. They wanted colour, but the colour was drained from everything we sent. It was plain to anyone with the smallest sense of journalism that This Correspondence Must Now Cease. As a country at war to a country friendly but not yet at war, we could make neither ourselves nor our way of living clear.

The final break came with the *New York Times* when they sent me a nonchalant cable asking: 'What has happened to the English weekend?' They might as well have asked me: 'What has happened to the pterodactyl?'

Since I have been talking about J. L. Garvin, I might as well finish off the Garvin story, so far as it touched mine. To the best of my knowledge, we never met again after we 'resumed' relations as correspondent and editor.

His name must have appeared in the January Honours List of 1941 and I must have written to congratulate him, for I find a characteristic note, dated 14th January 1941, in which he says:

'No sooner a bit upped by the King than downed by the 'flu. There was an awful spate of congratulations. Hundreds of them. The worst was, they seemed uncommon honest too, and so required more attention—which they couldn't have until now.

'I refused the C.H. twice. Why, the first time in 1918, is neither here nor there. The second time in 1929 because they wouldn't do anything I wanted for C. P. Scott, so I swore to take nothing while he lived. What a skein nearly everything is. . . .'

This letter seemed uncommon honest too, and I have kept it, because

I often wondered, and still wonder, why They did so markedly little for C. P. Scott, and I like this high and proud salute from one great editor to another.

Just one more Garvin letter and we shall have done. It is dated 18th June 1941, and brings good news. There is a marked change in style, a fresh spring of energy. Although the Irishman is never far away, the editor is in charge now, and no longer an editor whose grey hairs are almost brought in sorrow to the grave. I notice with amusement that I am no longer addressed as 'My dear' but as My dear Miss Lajeune'; and the spelling seems odd too, considering the long years during which J.L.G. had professed to have watched over me with interested affection.

'My dear Miss Lajeune, Seldom and little are my letters, ceaseless my thoughts. Every week I think how good you are in your work—incomparable in it—and how staunch you are in your character.

'I have pulled the paper round financially, God knows by what drudgery and contrivance together. The life behind my writing life that nobody knows. By pulling round I mean keeping out of debt and a bit on the right side. Anyhow, the conditions are not so gaunt as when the war came. I have instructed Mr. Berridge' (the business manager) 'to send you ten guineas a week for your article as from the beginning of June. I hope it pleases you. I wish it could be more, but there's a length of war to come.'

That was the last communication I ever had from Garvin. The weekly *Observer* lunches had stopped with the war, and I never had occasion to see him in the office. Early in the following year he parted company with the paper.

I have never fully understood the whys and wherefores of the break, which happened within twenty-four hours and sent Fleet Street into pandemonium. Nor have I inquired. 'A blazing row between Garvin and Lord Astor about an Astor article' is the common explanation. At all events, on Friday the paper had an editor, and on Saturday, when it was due to go to bed, it had none.

I believe—I am almost certain—that it was Ivor Brown who stepped at once into the breach and took control. There are few people as trustworthy as Ivor in an emergency. He is a man of tremendous fortitude and loyalty; a great journalist whose talents have never been sufficiently recognized; one who should have been picked out long ago for special honours.

The result of that Friday's whirlwind was that Garvin left his chosen people and the paper that had been his lifework. Several other people, feeling strongly, left with him. Those of us who stayed were now working directly for the Astors, under a series of temporary editors, with the understanding that young David Astor would presently take charge of the paper.

That didn't worry me. I did all my writing at home and was in no way involved in office politics. Besides which, I had always got along well with the Astors. With the departure of Garvin, one couldn't help feeling that Fleet Street had witnessed an historic exit; the last of the Great Editors. But it never crossed my mind to leave the *Observer*, and I was to stay there as film critic for another eighteen years.

I always skip the war chapters in other people's memoirs, so I shall make my own chapter as short as possible. It is, I am afraid, a confession of utter funk. From the wail of the air-raid sirens on that first Sunday morning until V.E. Day I lived in a state of perpetual strain and terror.

This was very wrong and stupid of me. I ought to have been thankful that neither of my menfolk was of an age to join the Services: my husband was too old, my son much too young. (Although there was always the mother's dread, 'Suppose it doesn't end in time?')

I ought to have been grateful, and indeed I was, that we lived far enough outside London to miss the full horror of the bombing; but we saw and heard enough from sixteen miles away to stretch nightmare imagination to full capacity.

We could hear the rumble of the guns at Dunkirk, and watch the smoke from burning oil-vats cover the sky with an orange pall. You'll remember that it was a fine, hot summer, one of those rare, perfect English summers with dew on the morning grass and hardly a movement in the air. It should have been lightsome and beneficent. Instead it was heavy and full of presage. 'Good things of day begin to droop and drouse.'

I remember working feverishly in the garden on a long border choked with ground elder, with the absurd notion that if I persisted long enough to dig out all the roots, stop it creeping up on us, I could somehow check the advance of the German troops along the Channel coast. But, as any gardener who has struggled with ground elder could have told me, my hopes of winning that campaign were slight.

Every night after the Battle of Britain the German planes came over, and there was an alert which could last anything up to six hours. We were within earshot of at least a dozen different siren systems, covering Herts, Bucks, Middlesex and even, when the wind was in the right direction, Surrey and Essex, all sounding off at different times. We also had a naval gun which ran up and down our railway line. The noise was deafening.

The only nights, from the late summer of 1940 until the end of the war, on which one could count on undisturbed sleep were Christmas Eve and Christmas night. In an ironically sentimental way the Germans were punctilious about observing the Christmas truce. Sleep on most other nights was sleep in spite of thunder.

We had no air-raid shelter of our own, but our kind next-door neighbours let us share the amenities of theirs. During the first winter blitz we used that dugout a good deal. Like most suburban shelters, it was a clammy and inadequate affair, sunk in the clay soil a few feet below the level of a rockery, with a sagging canvas bunk and two hard wooden benches, but it did give an illusion of security. I used to scramble through a gap in the privet hedge, with an armful of rugs, a sleepy, reluctant small boy and our old West Highland terrier.

Boy on bunk and dog on rug very soon went to sleep again. Connie and one of the women neighbours usually joined us. The men would stand outside and watch the sweeping searchlights and the dog-fights in the sky. Listening to the heavy, relentless drone of bombers and the ack-spit of our ground defences, we guessed which city was to be the 'target for tonight'. Birmingham? Manchester? Liverpool? Coventry? Or the other way, by the north-south route—using Harrow Hill as a signpost—London?

One night the ground shook as a big bomb fell beside the golf club a few hundred yards away. Another night they dropped a basket of incendiaries into our garden, and within minutes the rose-beds seemed to be crawling with A.R.P. persons, advancing on hands and knees with strange extinguishers, retrieving bits and pieces of foreign matter for daylight examination.

These were the nearest 'incidents' we had, although we were directly beneath the bomber lanes into and out of London. After that first year we rarely used the dugout. Hospitable though it had been, it was not a reasonable shelter. There was no drainage, no heating and no means of ventilation. The rains poured down the steps and seeped in through the walls. Many a morning I had to wade into it in rubber boots and bale out at least six inches of water. The canvas of the bunk rotted with damp. Risk of pneumonia seemed more formidable than risk of bombing.

My husband despised it and our son hated it, grumbling dreadfully when he was woken up, bundled into a dressing-gown and taken, yawning, into a nasty cold hole through a nasty cold garden. So it was decided to let him stay in bed, after which he slept peacefully through the heaviest raids.

It is easy, I think, to make too much of the strain to which children were exposed in wartime. The majority of normal children *enjoyed* their war. It was exciting, an adventure of its kind.

The city children who had been evacuated to nice safe places in the country could hardly wait to get back home again; to play among the rubble of bombed streets, spend nights in the chummy atmosphere of Tube shelters and share their parents' meals of tinned salmon, chips and beer after their experiences of country diet. 'They give us nothing but cooked food to eat,' one of them was heard to complain.

Franziska returned to me, a few years before she died, a letter which our son wrote to her in the middle of the bombing. It begins with a spirited drawing of 'ME feeding CABBAGE to a COW' in a field behind the house. It goes on, nonchalantly:

'Two more craters (really huge ones this time) have appeared on the Golf Course throwing tremendous blocks of earth in all directions! ! ! One of them uprooted a tree.

'A land Mine hit Eastcote the other night and four houses went up into the sky and have never been seen again (Daddy says they have literally vanished). At Wealdstone for a mile along the High Street there is nothing but wreckage. There is an awful lot of wood in a house.

'Our newsagent has been killed in his shelter by an Archie shell. His wife was also killed.

'A pub and shop have been destroyed on Batchworth Heath. Several bombs fell behind Merchant Taylors'. We have a Naval Gun near us, not to mention many ordinary guns. Love from Tony.

'P.S. There seems to be quite a lot of wreckage at Eastcote.

'P.P.S. Our milkman's wife and daughter have been killed. He and his son are seriously wounded.'

Is that the letter of a frightened child? I don't think so. Callous, no doubt, but most children are callous except where their intimate affections and perhaps where animals are involved.

The war slipped easily off the shoulders of the young. It was a heavier burden for their elders. There was so *much* of it, one strain after another. First the dread of invasion, then the nightly bombing, then the flying-bombs, day and night, and after that the rockets.

During the flying-bomb period I took to sleeping in the garden. It was warm weather, and I fixed myself a mattress in the summer house. With the door wide open I could watch the procession of glowing killer-bugs go by, almost nose to tail some nights, like traffic on an arterial road.

I felt much safer in the garden. All my life I have suffered from a stupid kind of claustrophobia, due perhaps to choking nights of asthma in childhood. I easily grow panic-stricken in the middle of a crowd, and can hardly endure a room with all the windows shut. For years I had to steel myself to travel in the Underground, and would walk miles to avoid a journey in the rush hour. In cinemas and theatres I always choose an outside gangway seat, and even in old age prefer my own legs to other forms of locomotion.

The buzz-bombs didn't really frighten me as long as I was out of doors. The rockets were different. To my mind the V.2s were the most dreadful of all war weapons. They were mysterious; the first we ever heard of them was a rumour of a strange crater that had appeared somewhere in Bayswater or Notting Hill. They were unpredictable. No alert could be given. They slew without warning, at any moment of the day or night.

The rockets came when we were all worn out and had very little resistance left. A few years ago there was a misguided attempt to show us a film called *I Aim at the Stars*, about the German scientist who invented the V.2. He was presented as an idealist whose work had been twisted and used for evil purposes, a misjudged and estimable person.

The whole film made me shudder, and I said so in print. There was an impulsive response from readers who shared my feelings. Typical was the letter of a London woman who wrote about the rockets: 'It was the worst time. I said goodbye to my husband and daughter each morning and didn't know if I should ever see them again.'

The end of the war in Europe came only just in time for the raw nerves of many of us. For a week or so it had been apparent that the end was near. But somehow there was no glow of victory. Most people were too tired to care.

Tony and I went up to London on V.E. Day. For some vague, clouded reason it seemed the proper thing to do. Hundreds of thousands of other people had the same idea, and we all found ourselves drifting in the same direction: towards Buckingham Palace.

An immense crowd had gathered outside the Palace by two o'clock. It was an orderly and sober crowd, strangely quiet, except for the rhythm of the rising chant, 'We want the King—*we want the King.*'

We had not very long to wait. Before loyalty had time to stale there was a movement behind the curtains of the Palace windows. They were drawn back, and the King and Queen came out on to the balcony, with Queen Mary and the two young Princesses. They took a number of curtain-calls, and the response from the crowd seemed more than ordinarily affectionate, warm and sincere.

When the balcony windows had closed for what was obviously the end of the matinée performance, we decided to walk back to Piccadilly through St. James's Park. Just before we reached the park, in a quiet side street, we had to slip quickly on to the pavement to avoid a big open car that was coming towards us. In the car was Winston Churchill, driving to the Palace. He looked unutterably weary, and tears were running down his cheeks. He stood up in the car and gave the 'V' sign to us.

Good enough is enough, I felt; now let's go home. We had to fight our way into the Underground at Piccadilly. Half the population of England, it seemed, was streaming up to London for the evening.

I had a sudden flash of memory: Manchester on Armistice Day in November 1918; the university students whooping it up in a grand victory procession; and the girl that was myself then slinking home by way of the back streets, crying for no reason that I could explain, with a wild desire to get away from everybody.

The north-bound trains on V.E. Day were almost empty. Everyone who was travelling at all was travelling to town. It was good to get home to the quiet of Pinner Hill, and later on, when blackout time arrived, to realize there was no blackout any more. Like many other people, we turned on all the lights and flung the curtains wide that night. It was our form of celebration.

There was a quiet thankfulness for release from pressure. Lovely to be able to open your front door and let the light stream out along the garden path. Lovely to go to bed without the lullaby of sirens, to know that tonight there would be no rockets.

But even in our gratitude we knew that we had lost something. The war in Europe was over, for the moment, but to many older people the peace brought no sense of lasting security. There was too much to be remembered, too much still to be determined. Never glad, confident morning again.

There was one pleasure that the war did bring, and that was the chance to explore the countryside on foot, meeting no motor traffic for mile after mile. The air smelt sweet then, and walking was a pleasure.

Here, in the north-west tip of Middlesex, we are not far from the foothills of the Chilterns; within reach of some really unspoilt country places, or what were unspoilt places twenty years ago.

In those days Tony was a day boy at Merchant Taylors' School. Almost every Saturday, after lunch, we would take the train 'up the line' for several stations and set off on a new exploring expedition. I was a good walker then. Tony is a great walker still. We tried to find a fresh place every week. We climbed the heights above Great Missenden and Wendover. We dropped down through the beechwoods to the little River Chess, where it flows placidly through water-meadows fringed with flag iris, beside great fields of mustard flower, as dazzling a gold as I have ever seen. We found remote farmhouses where they could still give us tea and scones and honey; and came home laden with bags of blackberries and apples, catkins and fir-cones, sometimes an old book from the stalls in Aylesbury market. They were very happy afternoons.

On one of our weekend walks, in September 1943, we formed a friendship, which was to enrich our lives for the next four years, with Arthur Machen and his wife Purefoy.

It began as Tony's story, so I will let him tell it in his own way, from an article he wrote not long ago for the *Aylesford Review*; which, largely due to American interest, was bringing out a special Machen number.

'We only knew Arthur Machen in the last period of his life: the years when he lived in retirement on the first floor of a small square red-brick house in the wide High Street of Old Amersham; a very old man, cut clean off from the world; lovingly cared for by his wife, but with few visitors and fewer luxuries; dressed, whenever he walked down the village street, in an inverness cape and black hat, with a white mane of hair just touching his collar. We got to know him for the best of reasons; because we wanted to know him. . . . I've always liked strange stories and, having recently discovered some of Machen's in dusty old second-hand editions, I was curious to know what manner of man it was who hinted at such dark things, whose mind dwelt so lovingly on half-remembered rituals and the powers which might linger among the foxgloves and hawthorn around some mossy stone, who wrote in flowing prose about lonely parts of Roman Wales and the still lonelier country which stretches away to the north of Oxford Street.'

During the summer holidays, for what reason none of us can now remember, my husband and Tony and I had lunch in town with John Betjeman. The conversation came round to strange stories and mystic rites, and Tony asked Betjeman if he had ever heard of Machen.

'Rather,' said John. 'I know him well. He lives at Amersham, not far from you. Why don't you go and see the old gentleman? I'll give you a letter of introduction. He'll be delighted.'

So, to take up Tony's narrative again:

'A few weeks later my mother and I walked down from the railway station through the autumn woods to the village of Old Amersham. We found the house and rang the bell. Machen opened the door himself, looking dishevelled and surprised to see us. I'm sure he'd made little of Betjeman's letter and had no idea who we were. But he received us with great courtesy, gave us tea and talked to me as one gentleman to another, both men of the world, equal in age and understanding.'

Tony was quite right about Machen's bewilderment. A few days later I had a letter with an Amersham postmark, forwarded from the *Observer* office, in handwriting that we were soon to know well.

'Dear Miss Lejeune,' it ran. 'If Betjeman's script had been easier and my sight better, we should have been enabled to say the pleasant thing, which is also the true thing; that we have admired your *Observer* work for many years past. It is a great feat to get a hearty laugh out of the Films once a week without fail.

'I hope that you and your son will manage to repeat your visit. If you could contrive to call somewhere near 6 p.m., "they" open then. 'I remain, Yours sincerely, Arthur Machen.'

To this was added a touching postscript by his wife:

'May I associate myself with this apology? All my husband said was, "There are two young people—friends of Betjeman's—in the sitting-room." When I came in I took you for brother and sister!'

That afternoon was the first of many meetings with the Machens. My husband and Tony and I would go over to Amersham every month or so, and give them lunch or dinner at one of the old town's coaching inns. Arthur used to sit by the fire, puffing away at an evil-smelling pipe, while Purefoy smoked equally evil-smelling cigarettes which she rolled herself.

He was splendid company all the time. He took conversation seriously as an art. When he raised his hand and announced, 'Literary anecdote!' he dominated the room. People at neighbouring tables would hush and listen; with cocked eyebrows, with smiles half hidden, always with delight in this strange character.

At one time he had been an actor in Frank Benson's company; not, I imagine, a very good actor; probably a glorious ham. But, like everyone who ever worked with Benson, he knew how to 'project', and very odd it was to hear him talk of theology and roll out his magnificent Church Latin in what my son describes as 'a voice like a great bell booming above the local chatter of turnips and tractors'. 'I can't part with my beloved Latin tags,' he used to say, 'as dark with antiquity and as well worn as old farmhouse furniture.'

The thing he missed most in his retirement was what he called 'good company'. He had never been able to accept the wireless or cards as a substitute for talk. 'Cards,' he once said, 'cards are a confession of inability to maintain conversation.'

He never told the same story twice, which was remarkable in an old man, and he had a great fund of stories; some of them strange, some comical, some dramatic, some deeply moving.

One Machen story stays most vividly in my mind, and although I have set it down in print before, I feel that in any account of our family friendship it must be told again. On a certain December in the worst days of the war I made up my mind that this year, writing for a Sunday newspaper, there should be no Christmas article. What was the use, I thought, to speak of peace on earth, goodwill toward men, to people whose sons and husbands were lost, or prisoners of war, or far away from home; to wish good cheer to the bombed, the anxious and the lonely?

And then there came a letter from Arthur Machen in his square, scholar's hand, recalling the story of the shipload of pilgrims who were due to get to Bethlehem on Christmas Eve. 'A great storm arose,' he wrote, 'and a clever man who had somehow found his way aboard, said in a jeering fashion, "It will be a pity if we don't get there by Christmas Eve, won't it?" An old peasant with a white beard quietly replied. "It is always Christmas Eve at Bethlehem." '

Machen died in 1947, at the age of eighty-four, and I will leave Tony to write the last note about him, as he wrote the first:

'I was away in the Navy when he died', he says. 'I remember hearing it announced on the radio. I thought of him as I'd seen him last, walking away arm-in-arm with his wife down the quiet High Street, in his old Inverness cape and the quaint black hat, with his white hair lying like a halo on his collar. I remember too something he'd once said to Purefoy, when she was worried about dying. He said: "Oh, I don't know, I think you may find it a very refreshing change." '

19

CLIVEDEN AND HORSES

It was about this time, as the war ended, that I began to know the unique, the astonishing, Nancy, Viscountess Astor.

I had met her several times before the war, for it was the Astors' custom in those days to invite the whole of the *Observer* staff, including the printers with their wives and children, for an annual outing in the summer to their home at Cliveden.

Coaches were laid on from Tudor Street. A big marquee was set up on the lawn below the terrace. Lunch and tea were served on trestle tables. A band played resolutely, and there was a choice of entertainment for the guests. They could roam at will about the grounds, take boats on the river, watch an office cricket match or join a conducted tour of the famous Astor stables. At the end of the day Lady Astor would give great bunches of summer flowers to the printers' wives: sweet peas, iris, paeonies, tall spires of delphinium.

At those first meetings I was terrified of Nancy Astor. She was so small, so vigorous and vivid; her tongue was so quick; her reputation as a holy terror in the House of Commons was so widely established. She had a knack with clothes, and somehow her plain cotton frock and shady hat looked much more distinguished than the bits and pieces of finery that most women had added to their persons.

Later on, when I came to know her better, fright gave way to intense respect, and out of respect grew genuine affection. I discovered her warm heart and tomboy sense of humour. She was a born mimic, like her niece Joyce Grenfell. 'Joyce is good, but nothin' like her mother yet. Her mother was brilliant. We're all mimics in our family. I can imitate anybody.'

She could, too. She would come back to Cliveden from the House of Commons, pause on the terrace, push her hat askew and give a diabolic imitation of her fellow Members. You could see the way they walked; their stance as they rose to speak; the folds of flesh, the pompousness, the vacillation and all the mannerisms. Then she would do the politicians' wives, and that was even more devastating.

There was no cruelty in Nancy Astor's nature, but she was impetuous, prejudiced and wildly indiscreet. She had no time at all for fools and upstarts; she spoke out what she thought in bold, unmitigated terms. She made no secret of her abhorrence of drink and her belief in the capacity of women, whom, as the mother of five sons, she considered more responsible than men. But she was a great listener to other people's troubles. She listened thoroughly and in silence, which is a rare accomplishment, and when practical steps were necessary she always took them.

I could tell you many stories of her kindnesses to strangers, some of them war casualties who appealed to her after vainly seeking redress elsewhere, but to do so would be a breach of confidence. One story I can tell, though, because it is my own, and I am still touched and amused whenever I remember it.

During the war years I had to go into our local cottage hospital for an operation for varicose veins. One day, when I was recovering, Matron came into my room in a great flutter and said that Lady Astor had telephoned and announced her intention of paying me a visit that afternoon.

Nancy Astor's mistrust of the medical profession was well known. She was an ardent Christian Scientist, and made no secret of the fact. The stir in our little hospital was considerable. Matron herself and several Sisters found me an interesting case that afternoon. My Scots doctor dropped in for an unexpected call. All of them wanted to take a look at this remarkable and feral woman.

The visit was a riotous success. Lady Astor was in her best 'kidding' mood and jollied them along. She made an instantaneous hit, particularly with the doctor; for although she thought she preferred what she called 'wimm'n', she was better at understanding men.

Before she left, having really made the day for the staff of our small hospital, she pressed into my hands two objects: a copy of the works of Mrs. Baker Eddy and a sealed envelope. In the envelope I found a cheque for ten pounds, to be spent on taxis when I got back to work; presumably in case my trust in Christian Science should prove unequal to the strain.

I went to stay at Cliveden for the first time in July 1947. I find an invitation from Lord Astor which runs:
'Dear Miss Lejeune, If you are coming to Cliveden for the *Observer* party on Monday the 21st, I wonder whether you would like to stay with me for the Sunday. This would be more restful than attempting to come down on the Monday. Most of the house is still closed, so I am only able to offer a room to a few of our prospective guests. You, who have been connected with the paper for so long, have a high priority on this list. Best wishes, Astor.'

This was the first of several visits. I fell in love with Cliveden once and for always, and still keep visiting there in my dreams. It was heaven in summer when the gardens were in full bloom. I remember snipping off dead heads in a rose garden carpeted with dwarf iris and mauve violas; looking down from a heathery height, through a cunningly landscaped cutting in the woods, to the reaches of the Thames far below, curving in silver smoothness towards Maidenhead.

But it was heaven in winter too, and I can well understand why the present Lord Astor, whom I had grown to know as 'Bill', chose Cliveden in the snow as one of his first subjects when he took to watercolour painting.

There was an unforgettable weekend when Nancy Astor, in her peremptory way, decided that I was tired and ought to have a change. She swept me off to Cliveden at an hour's notice, and gave me a small, charming suite in one of the elegantly curving wings. You reached it through a baize door from the hall, along a service passage and up a winding stair. At the foot of the stair, to my intense delight, I found one of those old-fashioned batteries of bells, swinging on curved stems like question marks, bearing the labels, 'Blue Room', 'Pink Dressing Room', 'Her Ladyship's Room' and so on.

I had a private sitting-room with a crackling fire, a tiny bedroom and bathroom (with a Bible beside the bed), and a wonderful view across the snow-covered lawns that sloped under their thick white blanket towards the river. The rooms were brilliant with sunshine reflected from the snow. There was early-morning tea in bed, breakfast beside the fire, the morning papers, a typewriter in case I felt the urge to work, and a low bowl of bright flowers on the table.

Cliveden was always full of flowers. The big hall and drawing-room were massed with them. The air was heady with the mixed scent of flowers and burning logs, and behind this the scent, as intoxicating in its own way, of hundreds upon hundreds of books in old, seasoned-leather bindings.

It was the Astors' custom to entertain a small house party at weekends, with several members of the family and a sprinkling of celebrities from the newspaper and political worlds, both English and American. Like most people I had heard dark rumours of 'the Cliveden Set' and the plots that were hatched in that great house at weekends. Perhaps by the time I became a guest the plots were over; perhaps I didn't notice what was going on; perhaps, even, there were no plots. It all seemed quite innocuous to me.

The one thing that did strike me as a little odd was the carafe of fruit-cup on the table in the hall. Nancy Astor, as you know, was a rabid teetotaller, and although she would serve wine with meals on certain occasions, and allow her sons, not without comment, to drink their beer at table, she was insistent that soft drinks only should be set out for thirsty guests. That carafe of fruit-cup in the hall was deemed to be non-alcoholic, but it was ripely matured and well fermented, and I'm sure she had no notion of its potency.

On Sundays there would be a large lunch party, when visiting delegations to England would be entertained. I remember one Sunday lunch with about twenty coloured clergymen at table, though who they were I never have discovered. In the afternoon the unflagging Nancy led them off to tour the grounds and visit the fine Canadian hospital which had been built there during the war.

Evenings at Cliveden were the nicest times, when the house party was very small and there was no formality. I remember one Saturday evening in particular. Lady Astor was wearing a plain black velvet dress with just a single jewel at the throat. I thought to myself how lovely she must have been as a girl. How beautiful, with her fine bones and bright eyes, she was still.

I can see her sitting on the floor after dinner beside the fire, with an attaché-case open beside her. Hidden behind the lid was her Christian Science Bible, which she was reading and marking for the next day's service all the time she talked. Sometimes she sang. She would burst into comic congs or negro spirituals or half sing, half tell a story in her soft Virginian voice. But she went on swiftly marking the Bible with slips of paper in the appropriate places. I was sitting just behind her, and I think nobody else could see.

Those early weekends at Cliveden, when Viscount Astor was still well and vigorous, had another fascination. He was a passionate student of horse-breeding, although he never put a bet on any horse. It was his custom to hand out sheets of paper to his house guests, on which were typed the list of mares in the Cliveden stud who were due to foal next spring.

We were asked to suggest names for the expected foals; names which would combine those of the dam and the sire by whom she had been covered. The Astor horses were celebrated for their clever naming, and the exercise was as challenging as a crossword or a jigsaw puzzle. Nor was it easy, for the names must never have been used before, and prolific sires such as Hyperion were beginning to become real teasers. There was a concession in Hyperion's case, which helped a bit. The word 'Sur' was permissible in a combination.

Before we left Cliveden on Monday morning all the lists were collected and taken to Lord Astor by his manservant. The editor of *The Times*, the late Barrington Ward, was particularly clever at this game, I remember. I myself was enormously proud when one of my suggestions was adopted. That was Ash Blonde, by The Phoenix out of Miss Minx. Ash Blonde turned out to be a pretty filly, who won several small races, proved later to be a useful brood mare and earned a respectable sum of money for her owner.

That was my introduction to the world of horse-racing and horse-breeding, which has since become one of my favourite hobbies. My interest, of course, is purely academic, combined with the very common desire to have an occasional flutter.

From a practical point of view I know nothing whatsoever about horses. I have never ridden a horse in my life, and until I went to Cliveden, and walked round the stables and paddocks with Bill to see the mares and foals and yearlings, my personal relations with the horse had been confined to offering a lump of sugar to the grey who pulled our milk-cart.

As a child I had never been allowed to sit in front, beside the driver, when we went for country outings in a pony-trap, because they said the hairs would give me asthma. As for betting on a horse-race later, the idea would have scandalized my relatives. I was brought up to think of gambling in any form as a sorry waste of time and money, if not an invention of the devil.

My husband, with his Quaker background, holds much the same opinions, so it was not unnatural, I think, that after several years of marriage I should have decided to go out in a small way and cut a dash. At first my bets were confined to half a crown each way on the Derby, which someone in the film business would lay for me. Presently I found an ally in the family. On one of our summer hoildays at Bexhill I discovered that my brother-in-law Laurence liked to pore over the racing columns of the *Daily Telegraph*, and was in the habit of putting a few shillings on a horse when he went out to buy the fish and vegetables.

This struck me as a pleasant holiday activity, and I was always ready to add another shilling to his wager. Unfortunately, Laurence, although a master-hand at bridge, was not a very clever picker when it came to horses. So on the whole we lost, but it added a spice of excitement to the holidays, and I began to take an interest in horses and courses which has never left me.

At Cliveden I got my first glimpse of the fascinating study of breeding: the crossing of classic lines to produce the best sprinters, stayers and middle-distance horses. The Astors were far too considerate as hosts to indulge in stud talk in front of indifferent guests, but both Viscount Astor and Bill were only too pleased to answer questions and give information if you showed that you were really keen to learn.

It was their hobby and their joy, as it was soon to be of the youngest son 'Jakie' (the Hon. J. J. Astor, whose name as an owner and steward of the Jockey Club now appears so often on the race cards). When I first met Jakie he was in the Commandos, a rakish young scallywag with a scarred cheek, whom I barely knew, but admired from a distance as a figure of wartime romance.

David, presently to be my editor, was indifferent to the problems of the Astor stud. I think he was indifferent to horse-racing as a sport. You asked him about a horse, and, smiling, he put the question by. (David has always been a ready smiler; partly from natural kindness of heart, and largely, I believe, to cover a certain diffidence in himself.) 'I'm afraid I know nothing at all about it,' he would say; 'you must ask my brothers.'

Bill was always eager to talk. His admiration for his father ran very deep, and in more ways than one he had learnt a great deal from him. It was fun to go with him to the paddocks where dozens of yearling colts and fillies were kicking their heels, running and nudging and jostling one another in a purposefully antic way.

I saw for myself the difference that two months can make in the development of a yearling colt, as some early March-born veteran tossed his proud head and lorded it over the more backward May youngsters. I was shown the points to look for in a racehorse, and even began to recognize—or think I did—certain family characteristics in classic bloodlines.

'That bay's a Court Martial,' Bill would tell me. 'There goes a Niccola del'Arte. We haven't tried him as a sire before; we'll have to wait and see; I'm still reserving my opinion. What? You like that little chestnut? He's the new Hyperion colt. The image of the old man, isn't he?'

That I was unable to say, because at the time I had never seen Lord Derby's little champion, although I had wagered half a crown each way on him in 1933, the year he won the Derby.

But I had followed his career with interest, as the schoolmasters say. I thought his name very beautiful; in fact it was the name, in the first place, which led me to that dashing disregard of money. As the years went on, and I noticed that his sons, daughters and grandchildren collected prize after prize, Hyperion had grown into a hero in my mind; a legendary hero, like Pegasus, or the piebald in *National Velvet*, or Roland, who brought the good news from Ghent to Aix.

I am not a 'fan' by nature. I don't collect autographs. I have never, even in the green days of my youth, decorated my bedroom wall with 'pin-ups' of actors and film stars. I wouldn't cross the road to look at one of the stage, screen or television celebrities whose names, in heavy type, adorn the gossip columns of our newspapers. Receptions for film stars always left me cold, just another job to be done, or avoided if possible. But as time went on, my longing to meet this horse star, person to person, became compulsive.

In the end I got my wish. In 1954 I was writing a regular monthly feature for *Good Housekeeping* magazine, with a fairly free choice of subjects. I suggested to the editor that it might be nice to have an article about the Derby for the June issue. Perhaps, since this was meant to be a 'personality piece', an interview with the great Hyperion, who was celebrating the twenty-first anniversary of his own Derby triumph?

The editor approved. The Astors' stud manager put me in touch with the manager of the Stanley House stud, and a day was fixed for me to go to Newmarket. My friend and fellow-journalist Paul Holt offered to drive me down. It wasn't entirely altruism on Paul's part. Like all good journalists, he could smell a story half a mile away, and jumped at the chance of meeting the great Hyperion.

Here I must divagate for a moment and say something about the Holts, who are new characters in this story. Paul at that time was writing a weekly film column for the *Daily Herald*, as well as extremely elegant pieces for *The Tatler*. He and his wife Estelle were both mad about horses. She had once been secretary to a racing tipster, and had mopped up a good deal of useful knowledge about the racing world.

I became a frequent visitor to their flat in Kensington. I got into the habit of drifting back there with Paul after a morning press show on the big racing days of the flat season. Estelle was wonderful at whipping up a lunch at short notice. Risotto and a great bowl of salad were her main standby; she cooked risotto like an angel.

After lunch we would collect and telephone our last-minute bets after the draw had been announced, and we would listen to the race on radio or watch it on television; sipping white wine from tall, chilled glasses, and smoking, in our excitement, far too many cigarettes.

Those were foolish but very happy days, and although they didn't last long, I still recall them with a vivid pleasure. Paul died quite suddenly a few years later. Estelle gave up the London flat and vanished, with a tape-recorder and a typewriter, on a strange, nomadic tour of the Far East. I haven't seen her since, but she has kept in touch with me most faithfully. Perhaps it would be more accurate to say she has continued to remember me. With the best will in the world you can't really keep in touch with somebody who sends you loving picture postcards with no address other than Vietnam or the Taj Mahal.

However, in March 1954 there was no shadow of these changes. Paul drove me down to Newmarket, through rich brown ploughland just beginning to show green. It was exciting, as we got near Newmarket, to see the various strings of horses out at morning exercise; to go into a pub for lunch and find the walls lined with sporting prints, the talk exclusively of horses. It made you realize you were in the heart of the racing country, and gave a meaning to the description of Newmarket as Headquarters'.

We found our celebrity at home in his loose-box; a chestnut head poked over the lower half of the stable door, contemplating the world with curiosity. Hyperion, they tell me, had always been an inquiring horse. He liked to know everything that was going on around him. In his old age he liked to amble along the road, ears pricked, and watch the people and the traffic. As a youngster he had a habit of suddenly stopping dead in his tracks, standing and gazing for minutes on end into apparent vacancy.

His trainer insisted that when he did this he was never to be hustled; let him take his own time to come out of his trance. When I first heard this story I took it with a grain of salt. Now I have learnt by experience that it can be true. The Cairn terrier we have now has exactly the same habit. In the middle of a walk he will stand quite still and stare. Nothing but brute force will make him move until he has satisfied his curiosity about the thing he sees: something quite imperceptible to human beings.

Hyperion was born and spent his entire life at Lord Derby's stud, and a very happy life it was. Everybody at Newmarket loved him; he was one of the most cherished local characters. He never lacked for visitors; they came from all parts of the world. Even in his retirement loyal friends would send him hampers of Cox's Orange Pippins (his favourite fruit), carrots, peppermints and sugar. Nor should he be forgotten in the years to come. The sculptor, John Skeeping, has cast a life-sized bronze model of this brave little horse, which will be found in a grove at the entrance to Lord Derby's stud, with the simple words, 'Hyperion, 1930 to 1960'.

'Little' is the first word that springs to mind when one thinks of Hyperion. His pocket size, compared with his immense achievements, was quite startling. As a yearling he was so tiny that few people thought he could be trained or raced at all. When he grew up he stood just fifteen hands and one inch high. Only that single inch separated him from pony-racing.

He was unbelievably gentle for a stallion. The lad (fifty years or thereabouts) who 'did' him took me unconcernedly into his stall, and encouraged me to pet and pat him, as one would handle a large, patient dog. He nibbled sugar in a gentlemanly way, and softly explored the crevices of my hand to find out if there were any crumbs he had missed.

To be sure, he was a veteran in the middle twenties by this time, and there was a sprinkling of grey in the brown mane and tail. But he was still performing occasional stud duties in the private paddock outside his stall. The lad thought it unrefined to mention it before a lady, but Paul Holt told me later that he had been shown a grassy mound in the paddock known as 'Hippy's Hill', from which the small champion could better accommodate the large mares who came to visit him.

A couple of years before Hyperion died his name led to a fierce altercation between Gilbert Harding and myself during a recording session of the radio programme *These Foolish Things*. If you ever heard the series you'll remember that certain sounds were broadcast, and then Roy Plomley would turn to the panel and say, 'Well, what does that sound remind you of?', whereupon each member produced some anecdote.

On this occasion the sound had something to do with racing, and while the other panellists spoke their pieces, Gilbert, who was sitting next to me, scribbled something on a sheet of paper and passed it over. What the gist of it was I cannot now recall, but I know the name 'Hyperion' was written in Greek characters, with some idea, I fancy, of confounding me, for that was Gilbert's little way. Happily, I had not mugged up two books of the *Odyssey* for nothing in order to pass responsions, and somehow the correspondence developed into a lively argument about the life and death of animals.

I wrote that I didn't like to see animals stuffed after their death. He wrote back: 'Better than being butchered alive for foreign horsemeat.' 'Taxidermy,' I replied, using my own best Greek characters, 'seems a humiliation to an animal's soul.' Furiously he scribbled: 'ANIMALS HAVE

NO SOULS.' I disputed this with passion, adding: 'If there are no dogs and cats, horses and birds in heaven, I don't want to go there.'

I shall never know what he intended to reply, for at that moment Roy Plomley called on me for an anecdote, and our interesting correspondence came to an abrupt end. I have always thought this a great pity.

I have devoted so much of this chapter to my hobby of horse-racing that perhaps it might be as well to let the subject run its course. By now the thrill of racing had 'got a holt' on me, as old Herring used to say about the bindweed in the garden.

I began to study books of form, become familiar with the styles of jockeys, notice at what meetings the shrewdest trainers placed their horses, talk Horse seriously with John Hislop, then the racing correspondent of the *Observer*, and enthusiastically with my film friend 'Tibby' Clarke, who wrote the scripts of *Hue and Cry*, *The Lavender Hill Mob* and other Ealing pictures, and had played truant from boyhood to go racing.

Apart from the day when Tibby took me to Hurst Park—and that was a snap decision after another recording of *These Foolish Things*—I never went to race meetings myself, finding it cheaper, and on the whole more informative, to watch them on our television set.

There was one exception to this rule, however. During my last years on the *Observer* I got into the habit of taking my holiday in September, and would spend a few days at Brighton during the last summer meeting. I stayed at a small hotel near Black Rock, much patronized by actors; having been introduced to it by Margaret Johnstone and her husband Al Parker, when I was spending a weekend with them in their Regency dolls' house in Wyndham Street.

I enjoyed every moment of my visits there, and used them to the full. I would get up at half past six, before the hotel was stirring, except for a night porter in shirt-sleeves, who bade me good morning with surprise. I liked to walk a couple of miles before breakfast, buying the newspapers on the way, and sit on the tide-washed shingle between the two piers, smelling clean salt air and fish market and a faint tang of creosote from upturned boats, and watching Brighton's innumerable cats on their morning perambulations.

Later in the day the front began to smell of car exhaust, disinfectant, perspiring bodies and fried fish-and-chips, but by that time I was back in the hotel, surrounded by newspapers, picking my fancies for the day's racing. After lunch the manager and his wife, who were both horse-mad, would run me up to the track in their little car, and I would spend a deliriously happy afternoon losing money.

It always seemed to be fine weather when I went to Brighton. September can be the loveliest of months, and it was glorious to be up there on the race-course in the heady air, with the mown grass smelling like a garden party, the sloping shoulders of the downs in front of you; behind and far below the blue cut of the sea.

The jockeys' silks showed up like coloured flags. The pavilions were always massed with flowers, and there was something at once homely and romantic about the *nearness* of everything: the runners parading in the paddock, the winning enclosure so small that you had the illusion of being within nudging distance of the horses and their riders. I didn't much care whether I won or lost. I was happy just to be there, a member of the meeting.

Not many racing people stayed at my hotel, but Lester Piggott was a regular guest. The manager's wife made a great pet of him. She had known him since he was a shy and rather speechless boy, immersed in 'comics' between studies of the books of form.

He was still shy and far from talkative, but was growing up to have a mind and will of his own. Few people noticed him, because he was so quiet, but sometimes a whisper would float around the staff, 'Lester's in a mood this morning.' 'He hasn't got a mount.' 'He wants breakfast in his room, just an egg.'

Once he came down to dinner and sat at the table next to mine. The military man who was with him at the table introduced us, and I got the impression that Lester was far from pleased. His greeting was punctilious enough, but his manner was unlike that of any boy I had ever met before. It was impossible, one felt, to penetrate that wall of shyness, deafness and professional security.

He volunteered little to his companion and nothing at all to me. Our tables were set close together, and it was a most embarrassing meal. Presently, when I saw he had the whole of a vanilla ice-cream to get through (he had sent away the one with nuts) before we could expect a merciful release, I asked what seemed to me a harmless question about his rides abroad.

'Mr. Piggott,' I said, 'doesn't it worry you having to fly to the continent at weekends for a single race on a strange mount?'

He looked me straight in the face for the first time and put me in my place with a reply which I have never forgotten: '*Nothing* worries me.'

20

RECREATION OF A FEUILLETONIST

ONE of the occupational hazards of writing any form of memoirs is the tendency of the mind to wander. It moves in no orderly, chronological way, but by leaps and bounds. You force yourself to remember one thing, and that reminds you of another thing. You concentrate on one passage of your life, only to find that it leads directly to a different passage. Before you know what has happened you are years ahead of—or sometimes years behind—the point of departure from your story.

My divagations about Cliveden and horses have carried me almost to the eve of my retirement. Now I must scramble back to the days of the late 1940s, when I never, *never* looked at the selections in the racing *Standard*, and was reviewing five, six or seven films a week, as a very busy critic of the cinema.

The war had ended. The habits of civil life were gradually returning. Most of us took it for granted that the cinema would flourish widely now that the blackout was lifted, actors and craftsmen were drifting back into the studios and materials were freely available again.

We were right in our estimate. A period of great prosperity for the trade set in. The threat of television had hardly raised its ugly head. Bingo and the twist, ten-pin alleys, even rock-'n'-roll, were still a long way off. A new generation was flocking to the pictures. But the pattern of the screen was changing.

During the war years, under constant harassment, the British cinema had enjoyed its day of glory. It would be nice to say that this golden age continued in the years of so-called peace, but it would not be true. The challenge had produced the men; the men, the pictures.

Complacency has always been the curse of the film trade. Wardour

Street, like Hollywood, looks at the world through technicolored spectacles. It has a talent for self-hypnotism, and has forced itself to believe implicitly in the genius of its stars, the magnitude of its epics, the pulling power of its publicity and the pure art of its posters.

Hollywood has inspired our industry from the beginning. Only during the war years had we enjoyed an enforced independence. It was clear that the end of the war must mean the beginning of a new boom in English-speaking pictures, and just as clearly that the United States would be the main source of supply.

In Wardour Street quantity matters more than quality. The box-office, not the critic, is the measure of success; although a 'rave notice' or even a 'good write-up' is not to be despised. It did not take long for our little industry to be absorbed as junior partner in the vast transatlantic corporation, and, while maintaining a kind of independence, lose its entity.

The character of our films began to alter. There was no longer any need for them to speak of England; they had only to speak the English language. The Crown Film Unit, its wartime purpose served, was forthrightly disbanded; its veteran corps of directors, writers, editors and cameramen allowed to drift away to other jobs; a number of them, ironically enough, to television.

The loss of the Crown Unit was a real loss of organized talent, although, as I have said before, there were grounds for relief that its official status was not used as a platform for peacetime propaganda.

It was a sad day, too, when Denham, once the humming centre of our industry, was handed over to the U.S. Air Force as a storage depot. Alexander Korda moved to Shepperton, where he appeared to be as active and enterprising as ever. But those who knew him best discerned the difference. With this final exile from the studio he had created (he once described Denham to me as 'my best production'), half the heart seemed to have gone out of him.

He began to look tired and grey. He lived mostly in a penthouse suite at Claridge's, where he was kneaded by a masseur every morning and ate less than ever. A slice of lean ham and a hot peach would constitute his luncheon, when he remembered to take any.

He made some expensive errors of judgement. The most expensive was *Anna Karenina*, a major flop, with Vivien Leigh, Ralph Richardson, and the hapless Kieron Moore flung into the part of a Russian aristocrat, which was sheer torture to the young Irish actor whom the women's magazines liked to describe as 'The Boy from Skibbereen'.

The Korda enterprises, too, were apt to get no further than the paper stage. I have lost count of the number of versions of *Lawrence of Arabia* that were now scheduled, with a different player each time in the title role. There were more advanced plans for a musical version of *Around the World in Eighty Days*, to be directed by Orson Welles, with himself in the leading part. They came to nothing, but were typical of Korda, who knew and cared little about music, but sensed, with a showman's perspicacity, that musicals were in the wind.

Korda may have seemed to be a waning power in the post-war years, but if the film industry thought they had done with him they were mistaken. Not long before his death he struck out with the shrewdest thrust of all. He decided to give the 'world première' of Olivier's *Richard III* on American television, a hook-up right across the continent.

'I want,' he said, 'that my film should be seen by as many people as possible as soon as possible. That is the right way for modern times. We cannot beat television, so we should embrace it.' And so, not for the first time, he enraged the industry, and remained an independent and lively challenge to the end.

In an attempt to recall what was happening to the cinema in the years soon after the war my mind is immediately confronted with the image of a poster showing Marilyn Monroe: colossal, supine, in the minimum of clothing, stretching from side to side of the Niagara Falls.

Miss Monroe was certainly happening, in no small way. And now I come to think of it, most things at that time began to S-T-R-E-T-C-H, as they say in the advertisements for stockings. There was also a horrid tendency for objects on the screen to Leap Out At You.

Thank heaven the days of Leaping Out are over, at least for the time being. You can go to the cinema today without danger of a lion landing in your lap, a blazing building toppling into the stalls or a clutching hand stretched out from the screen to throttle you. No longer are you forced to perch a pair of cardboard spectacles on your nose, the better to enjoy the horrors of 3D. The craze for 3D has passed by; so far as I can discover, unlamented.

The stretching business is another matter. I'm afraid that it has come to stay. Films are growing bigger and noisier every year. The audience has become a captive of the monster screen. Speakers to right of us, speakers to left of us, speakers in front of us volley and thunder. Syrupy theme songs trickle down our backs, and the Voice of God is embarrassingly apt to issue from a grating above the doors marked 'Gentlemen' and 'Ladies'.

Amongst the films I remember with most pleasure from the years soon after the war are the Ealing comedies *Hue and Cry*, *The Lavender Hill Mob* and *Kind Hearts and Coronets*; *The Third Man*, with those tantalizing zither tunes which sounded all the same but were really quite different; the splendid Westerns *High Noon* and *Shane*; and *State Fair*, the only musical which Rodgers and Hammerstein wrote directly for the screen.

I doubt whether *State Fair* was a big box-office success in England. Like the book from which it was derived, it was a piece of homespun. I think that's why I took such a fancy to it. It made me think of summer holidays and summer frocks; long, velvet twilights and the friendly smells of pig, preserves, pickles, sunripe berries and home baking.

Directly after the press show I went to Charing Cross Road and bought the sheet music of 'It's a Grand Night for Singing'. For years I used to bash the tune out on our old piano and make a spirited attempt to sing it when everybody was out of earshot.

It was a wonderful song to let yourself go with, lying right under and within the compass of the voice. Rodgers and Hammerstein were to catch the same magic again in *Oklahoma* with 'Oh, What a Beautiful Morning!' That is the way that song comes naturally; words and music indivisible; sung speech, phrased melody. The need for accomplishing some such form of dual expression was the beginning of the art of opera. It is the secret of Noël Coward's most persuasive numbers, the joy of *lieder* singers, and the spring of folksong to the present day.

What else was happening in those years after the war? Danny Kaye was happening, and so was Gregory Peck, over whose dark good looks fans used to swoon as presently they were to swoon over the hips and dimples of Elvis Presley.

Ava Gardner and Rita Hayworth were the Liz Taylors of their day to gossip-writers. A fair-haired, elegant girl called Grace Kelly caught the enterprising eye of Alfred Hitchcock. One heard a good deal of Alec Guinness and Jack Hawkins, and Kenneth More was well on the way towards becoming one of the Top Ten Money Making Stars in Britain.

The name of power behind the scenes was that of J. Arthur Rank, who supplied the trade with everything it needed, from films to roll them in the aisles to carpets in the aisles for them to roll on.

I say 'behind the scenes' advisedly. To the ordinary people of this country a tycoon, even a tycoon with a title, means next to nothing. In spite of all the gossip-writers' efforts, success in big business doesn't impress them. Nor does expenditure by others of vast sums of money. When they think about money at all it is in terms of rates, railway fares, the sharp rise in the cost of vegetables, the appalling price of fish this weekend.

When they come away from seeing a film the only names they carry home are the names of the stars. They can always tell you who was in it, hardly ever who produced, directed, wrote or distributed it. To them a film is valued at two and fourpence or perhaps four and ninepence; certainly not a million dollars, or whatever round sum the industry wants them to believe.

I am inclined to think this is a matter in which the English proletariat is unique. I find that people in other countries are far more production-minded; they know the people who makes the films almost as well as the stars who appear in them.

Quite recently I asked a regular British filmgoer, by no means a fool, what she could tell me about J. Arthur Rank. 'Say that name again,' was her reply. I said it again, very slowly and carefully. 'Oh, *that* man!' she cried, a great light dawning. 'Something to do with films, isn't he, like Hitchcock?' So much for the stature of a tycoon.

One of the first and most durable effects of peace was to introduce Italian films to England. Perhaps I should say reintroduce, for some of us could still recall *Gabiria* and *Quo Vadis* from the silent days, and Rome had sent over the odd film or two before the war; very odd films indeed, we used to think them, with their thick, heavy make-up and wildly operatic acting.

Few people had taken Italy seriously as a film-producing country, but now we were obliged to change our minds. Alexander Korda brought to London a film called *Rome—Open City*, directed by one Roberto Rossellini. Korda was dubious about the chance of that grim film in England, but he liked it very much himself and thought we ought to have a chance of seeing it.

His doubts were justified. *Open City* did no money business at the box-office. But it served its purpose as a pathfinder for other Italian films. By the time we had seen *Vivere in Pace*, *Shoeshine*, *Bitter Rice* and *Four Steps in the Clouds*, soon to be followed by *Bicycle Thieves* and Anna Magnani in *The Miracle*, we were no longer in any doubt that Italy was a film-producing country.

It became fashionable to discuss Italian neo-realism at parties, along with French films such as *Les Enfants du Paradis* (another Korda import), *La Ronde* and Cocteau's tantalizing *Orphée*.

I was careful not to join in talk about neo-realism. In later years, for the same reason, I was careful not to join in talks about the *nouvelle vague*. The reason is simple: I had no notion what the terms implied, except that some directors were doing more exciting work than other directors. A man did once take the trouble to explain to me just why the new wave of films was so important, but it proved to be a wasted labour. By the time he had finished his explanation they were announcing a second, newer wave.

Why bother to label a film 'New Wave' or 'Neo-Realistic'? Either the fact is evident or it isn't. What matters is the film itself, and the spirit in which it is apprehended. In the eager chatter of the post-war generation we recognized the ring of voices from another post-war generation: the young people of the 1920s, who were all agog with enthusiasm for the 'New Wave' of *their* time; only they called it *avant-garde*.

It had been exciting to write film criticism in those days. It was exciting to write film criticism now. One was sharing an experience with an eager and responsive public; the people who were soon to band themselves together into film societies and ardently support the National Film Theatre. It was a privilege to be able to tell them where to find the films one guessed they would enjoy, and fortunately at that time there was no shortage.

The screen, like June in *Carousel*, was bustin' out all over. After the first Italian films came films from Sweden, Greece, Japan, India, Russia, Poland, Czechoslovakia; while the French cinema could always be relied upon to supply the unexpected at the proper moment.

Specialist theatres multiplied and did thriving business. Film societies sprang up like mushrooms in all parts of the country. English people seemed quite ready to take subtitles in their stride. We learnt the trick of scooping the printed words up at a glance, then concentrating on the pictures and what we could understand of the dialogue. Dubbed versions, made for the English-speaking market, were powerfully resisted. In this country we have never cared for dubbing.

Foreign-language films were a success, without prejudice to the priority claim of bigger, brighter and brassier English-speaking pictures. The trade still looked to Hollywood for its main supply; and on the whole its faith was justified. Commercial films, whatever their deficiencies, did well; musicals did splendidly. As I heard a leading member of our industry explain to Archbishop Temple after an informal lunch at Lambeth Palace, 'You've got to think in terms of box-off., my Lord.'

Like many middle-aged people, I had a burst of sudden energy about this time. My mind seemed to quicken as the physical pace slowed down. I did a good deal of broadcasting and lecturing and an immense amount of writing. At one time I was reviewing films for four different periodicals, under my own name or a pseudonym. (My favourite pseudonym was Charles MacLaren; somehow that man forced me to write well.)

I produced a book called *Chestnuts in Her Lap*. I use the word 'produced' instead of 'wrote', because it consisted mainly of reviews which had already appeared in the film columns of the *Observer*. It was a very casual book, intended for light bedtime reading; in marked distinction to a solemn book called *Cinema*, which I had contrived in 1931, covering the great names of silent films, and predicting a bright future for the newcomer Walt Disney, creator of the 'Silly Symphonies' and Mickey Mouse. *Chestnuts* did well enough to justify a revised and enlarged second edition. What pleased me most, I think, was to hear later from Service people that it helped to fill the gaps of films they missed while posted overseas.

The cinema by no means monopolized my energies. I had a spell of reviewing detective stories for the *Observer*, and for a year and a half was television critic as well as film critic for the paper. In addition to these professional jobs, I suddenly found myself producing plays for amateurs.

This happened quite by accident. I had never been particularly interested in amateur theatricals. Like most people, I had been bullied by friends from time to time into buying tickets for some local show, and spent a cramped evening on a narrow chair, from which it was impossible to see the stage (but perhaps this was a blessing), assisting at a zealous performance of *Quiet Weekend*, *Tons of Money* or *See How They Run*.

The accident happened one Sunday evening in March 1947. My son was off next day to join the Navy for his National Service, and I suppose I was in a vulnerable mood. The telephone rang and Tony answered it. The call was from one of his school-friends, so I paid no attention until I heard him say, 'I really don't know, but hold on, I'll ask her.'

He covered the transmitter and turned to me.

'It's Michael Rogers, Mother. He's at a meeting of the Northwood Players. They're in the middle of a play and the producer has suddenly dropped out. They want to know if you'll take over.'

'What, *me*?' I gasped. 'I don't know the first thing about producing plays.'

'Mike says that doesn't matter, he can help. He seems to think you'll do it because you're interested in young people. You'd better speak to him yourself.'

I went to the telephone and told it yes. As I said, I was vulnerable that night. And that's how I became involved with amateur drama.

The idea was to oblige a friend of Tony's by finishing one play. But things didn't work out as planned; they seldom do. I was counting up the other night in bed, and found that during the next few years I produced something like twenty plays. I had found a recreation.

The Northwood Players were all young people in their late teens and early twenties. They rehearsed each Sunday evening in the classroom of a local preparatory school. The first Sunday that I went there I was almost in despair. They were all so cool and confident, and there seemed so many of them.

The one that frightened me the most was a tall, good-looking girl in Wellington boots, who was introduced to me as 'our professional'. Her name was Dinah, and she went up to London every day to study speech and drama at the Royal College of Music. I can't imagine why. I'm sure she had no intention of going on the stage. She certainly had no desire to teach. I don't think she knew what she wanted, except to marry a good-looking young army officer whom she had met during an 'Excuse Me' dance. In the end, after years of emotional ups and downs, she did marry him.

I grew to be very fond of Dinah, perhaps because we were alike in many ways: impulsive and temperamental, with the same sort of follies. But at these first rehearsals the girl scared me stiff. She talked so glibly about mime, projection and pear-shaped vowels ('How now brown cow?') She knew all about the pitfalls of the player: 'blocking', 'crossing' and 'upstaging', malevolences of which I had never heard.

What I had said to Tony was quite true. I didn't know the first thing about producing plays. I had no notion how to plot a scene; how and when to move the characters about the stage. I still looked at a play from the spectator's point of view, and was bewildered by the sudden change to seeing everything in a mirror image, in which audience right suddenly became stage left.

I was a middle-aged ignoramus among knowledgeable youngsters. I couldn't let them know how little I did know. The problem was to learn fast enough to maintain authority without letting the ignorance obtrude. It was quite a poser.

There were other problems. The play the company was doing was *Pink String and Sealing Wax*; a 'period' piece which calls for skilful dressing; bric-à-brac, dozens of small pictures on a busy wallpaper, gas brackets, plush, wax flowers under a glass dome, repp tablecloth with fringes and mantel cover with bobbles.

That sort of dressing can be hard to find if one is particular and wants everything just right. The stock in the furniture-hire departments is limited, and latecomers may find themselves out of luck if several amateur societies are doing 'period' pieces at the same time.

We happened to be out of luck over *Pink String*. It seemed there had been a heavy run on Victoriana and Edwardiana. I solved the problem by going straight to my old friend Michael Balcon, head of Ealing studios, and telling him about our troubles. 'I think we can deal with that,' he said, and gave me the run of Ealing's property department. There I found everything I wanted: delightful baubles, calculated to give nostalgia to any elderly member of the audience. If it had nothing else of quality, I knew that *Pink String* would have at least a perfect set.

A much severer problem was the plotting. My predecessor had left off at the point where a breakfast table laid for six had to be cleared and disposed of to leave the stage free for action. It was plain that the actors would have to move the stuff themselves; and getting rid of six chairs, a table and all its fixings, without holding up action or dialogue, was quite a problem for a novice.

I spent two anguished evenings working out the moves with counters. When the same moves worked out on the stage with human beings it seemed like a small miracle. It also proved to be my doom, of course. After that there was no help for it. I had to go on experimenting with plays.

Any reader who has had much to do with amateur dramatic societies knows how easy it is to become entangled, how very hard to break away. Amateur drama, to its victims, is compulsive; almost a form of slavery. I know, because I was enslaved for several years, although at the time I thought I was mistress of the situation.

In spite of the success of *Pink String and Sealing Wax*, I never felt really happy with the Northwood Players, nor did they with me. They had played together for too long, always under a young producer, to welcome the intromissions of a middle-aged stranger.

After one more production we agreed to separate. That, of course, was the moment when I should have abandoned the whole thing for good. But, of course, I did nothing of the kind. A few of us decided to start a company of our own. There were very few of us at first: my friend Dinah of the Wellington boots and five or six of the boys.

We had soaring ambitions, but no base to work from and no funds at all. In order to raise some, I persuaded the directors of Pinner Hill Golf Club, of which I was a member, to let us give a performance one evening in the ladies' lounge and take up a collection. As an added attraction, Michael Wilding promised to be present as my guest. He had once enjoyed a passing dalliance with a girl who lived on Pinner Hill, so the place had pleasant associations for him; also he is a naturally kindly fellow.

The lounge (their word, not mine) had a deep Victorian bay window, which we turned into a stage. We railed it off with curtains wheedled out of the captain's wife by the captain's pretty daughter. It was a tiny stage, of course, but served for a small play. The small play we chose was *Rope*, with a five-minute curtain-raiser diplomatically starring the captain's pretty daughter, and introducing guest artist Michael Wilding, shooting craps with the stagehands.

Rope is a horrid play, I agree; but for our purpose it had a number of advantages. It is short enough to cause no great physical discomfort to an audience, even if the chairs are hard and tightly wedged together. It can be played with effect in a constricted space. It needs no scenery, no special costumes. The only essential furnishings are a chest which can be used as a supper table, a window, a telephone and a couple of chairs.

We borrowed the chest from Gilbert Wilkinson, the cartoonist of the *Daily Herald*, who was a member of the golf club and one of our first friends on Pinner Hill. The window was there already. The deep bay was our cyclorama. A dummy telephone was easy. The chairs came out of the bar and dining-room. By courtesy of the head greenkeeper we were able to add a touch of realism to the storm scene which builds up in the second act. A hosepipe from the ninth green was fixed to play against the windows, while Mike Rogers crouched in a bunker and shook a 'thunder sheet.'

After the play the captain's daughter and her younger sister went through the audience taking up a collection. They carried beer trays from the bar stamped with the brewers' trademark, a red hand. Nobody escaped them. Nobody had the courage to refuse them. They came back with their trays piled with silver as a result of this artless exercise in blackmail.

Now we had a little cash in hand as well as the nucleus of a company. Soon we also had a place to work in. For a nominal rent we obtained the use of a derelict building topped by a mouldering tower in the grounds of the golf club.

The tower (it has been demolished since), built of yellow brick and roughly hexagonal in shape, was obviously some sort of a Victorian folly, and a familiar landmark hereabouts. There are two towers like it in the near neighbourhood. The story goes that they were first used by three eccentric brothers who liked to climb to the tops and signal to each other every morning.

During the war our tower, which was topped by a flagstaff and distinguished by a chime of bells, silenced during the blitz, was used by the Home Guard and as a spotting station. After the war, the landings on the spiral stairs were used as love-nests by teenagers from the new town through the woods. The place was ostensibly locked up, and I had the only key. But the love-birds found their own ways of getting in. They never interfered with us, except that it was irritating to find a kettle missing one week, then a couple of chairs, then our only cherished oil-stove. I managed to retrieve most of our possessions, once I had discovered what was happening, but I did resent the dirty scarves and handkerchiefs they left behind.

Beneath the building was a tunnel, dating from a much earlier period than the tower itself. This part of Middlesex is honeycombed with subterranean passages, leading no one quite knows where, and blocked every few yards by earth-falls. Some people say our tunnel was a priest-hole, or some sort of escape route in times of trouble. Later it was simply used by rats, bats and spiders, who didn't encourage strangers to explore.

The ground floor of the building, where we worked, had been a storage room for apples when I first knew it. Later it became the golf professional's shop, then the ladies' locker room, then a place for parking trolleys. By the time we gained possession it was fit for nothing but mad actors. It was infested by dry rot, wet rot and every kind of rot. The roof leaked malignantly. The floorboards were rotten. The clammy, whitewashed walls sprouted the most repellent fungus.

All the same, it was a place of our own, and we thought ourselves lucky to have found it. There was electric light, which was all right when juvenile delinquents had omitted to break open the fuse-box and throw away the fuses. There was an ancient, coke-burning stove of sorts, which warmed one corner of the room quite nicely once the smoke had cleared. There was even a wash-basin with rusty cold water and a semi-blocked-up drainpipe.

We built, painted and stored all our scenery there, and rehearsed there every Sunday evening, except when the rain was dripping in at more than half a dozen places. The golf club supplied us with tea and sandwiches at sixpence a head. The boys went over to the kitchen and carried it across on heavy iron trays. Each Monday morning I would go up to the tower, rake out and relay the stove, sweep the floor, collect and wash up the tea-things. For quite a time I honestly enjoyed it.

The plays themselves were given in a hall in Pinner used by several amateur societies. Our first production was nothing less formidable than Cocteau's *The Eagle Has Two Heads*, in which Eileen Herlie had just scored a big success in London.

Eileen was under film contract to Korda at the time, and I knew her fairly well and liked her very much. When I told her what we were doing she couldn't have been kinder. I took my two young leading players up to see her one Sunday afternoon in her London flat, and she gave them all sorts of tips about the way to handle the trickier bits of business (though heaven knows all the business in *The Eagle* is tricky).

She came to watch the first night too, and that almost provoked a catastrophe. Dinah, who was playing the Herlie part, suddenly spotted her in the front row, and at the end of the first act came off in near hysterics. I found her sobbing and shaking in the ladies' dressing-room. 'I can't go on,' she wailed. '*She's* there. In a *pink hat*. Watching *me*. I tell you, Mrs. T.' (they always called me Mrs. T.), 'I'm sorry, but I *can't* go on.'

In despair, I went and told Eileen. She was wonderful. She took off the offensive pink hat and came quietly backstage with me. 'I know,' she told the sobbing Dinah. 'That's a terrible scene to play, twenty minutes on the stage alone. I always felt shaky at the end of the first act. But, do you know, you're giving me so much pleasure? I've played the part hundreds of times, but this is the first time I've ever been able to sit and watch the play. I want to see what happens next. I'm fascinated.'

Dinah wiped the eye-black off her cheeks and gawked at her. 'You mean it's *all right?*' she said. 'You really want to see what happens next?'

'I do indeed,' said Eileen. 'I'm enjoying it so much.'

Dinah gave her a wan smile and played the next two acts like the soldier's wife she was presently to be. Eileen watched hatless for the rest of the performance.

This was only the first of many kindnesses we received from people I had come to know through films. We did a couple of Noël Coward plays, and Noël was always generous with tips. It was he who taught me never to plot a scene with a fireplace upstage centre ('They'll be speaking lines with their backs to the audience') and always to put a drop of water in the ashtrays, so that cigarette stubs would go out instantaneously. He gave sound advice, too, on the lighting and tempo for comedy; and solemnly warned me, however much I might feel tempted, not to let amateurs speak dialogue so that the lines overlap.

I always did my best to persuade some film star to put in an appearance at one of our performances. The possibility was never advertised, but came to be well known, and did a power of good in selling tickets.

At various times we had as guests Anna Neagle and Herbert Wilcox; Margaret Johnston; Margaret Leighton; Nadia Gray, not much known in England at that time, but later to become conspicuous by her performance in *La Dolce Vita*. Michael Wilding came along one evening, bringing with him a glamorous but aloof Marlene Dietrich, who went to no great pains to hide her natural boredom.

I shall always be grateful to Michael Denison and his wife Dulcie Gray, who happened to be with us on the dreadful night when all the lights went out, and the electrically controlled curtain stuck halfway and thereafter refused to budge an inch.

I went round to the front of the house and explained our plight to Michael and Dulcie. They didn't hesitate an instant. They followed me up on to the stage, sat one at each end with legs dangling, and for the next fifteen minutes entertained the audience with accounts of their own most dreadful experiences in the theatre. They answered questions, exchanged backchat, signed autographs, jollied everyone along and kept the whole hall happy until the electricians had the trouble fixed.

The Tower Players flourished for several years and earned quite a local reputation. Of course, we had our good plays and our bad plays. *The Heiress, Love in Idleness*, Priestley's *Eden End* and, strangely enough, *The Glass Menagerie* came off very well. We had a surprise smash hit with the American nightclub gangster and melodrama *Broadway*, for which Gilbert Wilkinson adorned the whitewashed walls with clever broad cartoons in charcoal.

I admit that our version of *The Guardsman* was not in the same class as the Lunts'. We should never have tackled Bridie's *The Black Eye*, and our attempt at *Pygmalion* was a dismal one. My own idea for a Shaw play had been *You Never Can Tell*, but this had to be abandoned because we hadn't enough good actors for the men's parts, and all the women were determined to play Dolly, the soubrette part, and no other.

However, there was a recompense for this failure. I had written to G. B. Shaw asking for permission to do the play, and got back a letter from Ayot St. Lawrence in his spiky handwriting.

'Dear Miss La Jeune,' it began. 'How jolly to get a letter from you, the most famous feuilletonist since I was in that job myself!'

That was, of course, the sentence I have cherished, but I should like to quote some more for the benefit of fellow-amateurs.

'I have done everything in my power,' G.B.S. goes on, 'to help amateurs and societies like yours.

'When I began they were charged £5 5s. 0d. which could be paid only by little groups of silly ladies who thought they could "do Mrs. Patrick Campbell's part" and gentlemen who had the same delusion about Wyndham's or Tree's or Alexander's, just what they couldn't do, the amateur's only chance being in unfashionable first rate and classical plays which will hold an audience if only read intelligibly and audibly by presentable people who cannot act and had better not try much.

'I banished all this from my practice. When a handful of enthusiasts pawned their last shirts but one to perform a play of mine in a village school with admission front row a shilling and the rest twopence, and the receipts were ten shillings, I took sixpence (5%), touching my hat and hoping for a continuance of their kind patronage.

'The other authors, being arrant snobs, would not condescend to take pennies and clung to the old five guinea fee, which naturally did not bring much to them with me in the field. The agents objected because my small fees were not worth collecting; but they had my big fees to console them; and the small ones mounted up through their propaganda of theatre going. What began in the village ended in the Haymarket and Shaftesbury Avenue.'

The letter ends with a characteristic outburst. 'You can tell your first informant' (somebody had assured me that the Shaw plays were not available for amateurs) 'not to be a damned fool. Does he suppose I live on air? I get round about £300 a year from amateurs.'

How wise G.B.S. had been in advocating 'unfashionable, first-rate and classical plays' for amateurs I discovered when we entered for a Festival of Amateur Dramatic Societies at Harrow. The rules demanded one-act plays, or single acts from full-length plays, presented in a way that would be both comprehensible and comprehensive.

Our entry was the last act of Ibsen's *Ghosts*. We used a skeleton stage. Windows and doors were suggested by arches of steel scaffolding, wound round with a twist of red Victorian velveteen. We had a minimum of furniture and as close as we could get to a dramatic use of lighting.

I wrote a condensed introduction of 'The Play Till Now', simplifying the several characters and their problems at the point of curtain rise. This was spoken by a narrator on a darkened stage, as he moved from point to point presumably lighting lamps. When he withdrew we had (we hoped) the drama stated and a tableau set: a sitting-room in the

Alving house with Mrs. Alving and Regina at the window watching the glow of burning in the sky.

I thought it a pretty good attempt myself, and the adjudicator from the British Drama Leauge apparently thought so too. In his summing-up, both that night and on the last night of the Festival, he went out of his way to be complimentary about *Ghosts*. The memory of his words, 'Production bang on', still fills me with a childish pride.

The trouble with any dramatic society which starts life as a project by enthusiastic young people is that young people grow up so fast. They go to college; they graduate; they get jobs and leave home; they get married; they become doctors or solicitors; they drift away one by one.

After a few years almost all the original members of the Tower Players had left us. The worst shock came with the news that Michael Rogers, who was as keen about flying as he was about music, mathematics and metaphysics, had been killed in a solo flight in a jet plane. Mike was a friend of long standing; a good boy through and through; a wise and kind and thoughtful boy. It was he who had cajoled me into this business in the first instance, and it never seemed the same without him.

The new company had a number of talents, but the feeling of confidence and unity had vanished. Rehearsals became a strain. It was largely my fault, I can see it now. I expected from comparative strangers the same loyalty and enthusiasm that I had once received from friends. I tried them too high; there were mutterings in corners, and in the end it seemed wisest to dissolve the company. After a momentary smart I realized it was the best thing that could have happened. With that severence I had lost a burden just as much as they had; for all things pass, and old people have to grow up too.

WRITING FOR TELEVISION

During the months when I was reviewing television as well as films for the *Observer*, I spent a good deal of time at the B.B.C. studios at Alexandra Palace—this was just before the move to the present studios at Shepherd's Bush—getting to know people and learning something about the business.

I know there are purists who frown on any sort of fraternization between critics and artists. Book reviewers, they say, ought not to mix with authors; drama critics should shun the company of actors; music critics should avoid musicians; film and television critics should never, never visit studios.

I have no patience with this attitude myself, even if it were possible to sustain it in the personality-pursuant conditions of modern journalism. For a critic, or an artist for that matter, to immure himself in an ivory tower strikes me as both contemptuous and contemptible.

Critics and artists can learn a great deal from one another, without any loss of professional integrity. The best of each kind know this. In my experience no actor worth his salt resents fair comment from a writer whose opinion he values; although, being human, he may feel sore about it for a little while. And a critic who allows friendship or personal dislike to cloud his judgement and come before his duty to his readers has no business to call himself a critic at all.

So in order to learn more about my business, about which I knew singularly little, I often climbed the steep hill to 'Ally Pally', just as I had done in television's nursery days before the war, and made a number of new friends there.

It was an old friend, George More O'Ferrall, who introduced me to

Michael Barry, a clever producer of plays who was soon to become head of Television Drama. He was a long, dark Irishman with a bony face, who took his job with a seriousness at time approaching anguish. He could laugh with a kind of schoolboy abandon, but the laughs came infrequently; he was a natural worriter and fretter.

We haven't met now for several years; not since he was temporarily seconded by the B.B.C. to work in Irish television. But I can see him vividly as I write, striding along a windy street to the R.A.C. Club, where he often gave me tea; preoccupied and blind to his surroundings; briefcase in hand, head thrust slightly forward, forehead puckered in a frown of worry. I can also recalled the sinking feeling in the pit of my stomach when, talking about television with a fine, careless rapture, he dashingly and dangerously drove me home.

It was Michael Barry who encouraged me to try my hand at writing television plays. By that time I had finished my spell as the *Observer*'s TV critic. It was becoming too big a job to double with another. David Astor had given me the choice of reviewing films or reviewing television. Somewhat to his surprise, I think, and certainly to mine, I had elected to stay with my old companion, the cinema.

Better the devil you know than the devil you don't know, was an adage that possibly affected my decision. Perhaps, too, I sensed subconsciously that a relapse into armchair viewing might accelerate the onset of old age in a woman well into her fifties. Rightly or wrongly, I chose films.

Now that I was free of the necessity of reviewing or ignoring my own work, I jumped at the suggestion of writing television plays. For some reason the idea of writing a film script had never appealed to me; probably because I knew too well that the original story teller of a film finds little of his work left in the final version. But television is a different thing from films. The playwriter remains the writer; his story is seldom mangled; the dialogue is more or less his own.

Not being gifted with an original story mind (I have never, since the days of the penny exercise book, been able to resolve plots to my satisfaction), I started with adaptations of other people's stories. I excused it to myself by saying that they were all good stories that would bear repetition, and perhaps bring to modern viewers a hint of the magic that had caught me long ago.

In the next couple of years I wrote three serials for television. Each of them ran for six weeks at peak period on Saturday night. The first was a collection of Sherlock Holmes short stories: *The Empty House, A Scandal in Bohemia, The Red-headed League, The Dying Detective, The Reigate Squires* and *The Second Stain*. I chose the stories that seemed most readily adaptable to television, with a minimum of location shots and change of scene, although it nearly broke my heart to leave out my favourite *Silver Blaze,* and the incident of the dog in the night-time.

As it happens, we were lucky to be able to put the series on the screen at all. At the last minute we learnt that the copyright had not been cleared, and that the television rights in all the Holmes short stories were on the point of being sold to America.

The series had been announced in the *Radio Times*; I had written a piece about it for *The Listener*; the cast was engaged, the half-hour booked for six weeks, and the first episode was in rehearsal.

There was near panic in the studios. A B.B.C. lawyer hopped on the first plane to Rome to see Adrian Conan Doyle and plead for a special dispensation for these six stories. Mercifully, his plea was successful and we got the series through. What the eye doesn't see, the heart doesn't grieve over, and I doubt if many people but myself were aware of the amount of dialogue from other stories in the omnibus which slipped in under the cloak of the permitted six.

Dialogue was no trouble in the case of Conan Doyle, for almost everything that Holmes and Watson say is pointed, characteristic and beautifully in period. We found a very different state of affairs when we came to our second serial, a version of John Buchan's thrilling but oddly neglected novel *The Three Hostages.*

The novel has almost all the qualities that one looks for in a serial: a story full of action, human interest, suspense and natural 'cliff-hangers' for the ends of episodes. But oh dear me! the way the people talk! There is hardly a line in the whole book that you could give an actor. The phrases have no character, no rhythm, no spontaneity. There is no flesh and blood in them at all. As Lady Tweedsmuir, Buchan's widow, said to me when we were discussing the story, 'John never could write dialogue.'

I found I had to invent most of the lines in *The Three Hostages,* and again in our third serial, a version of A. E. W. Mason's historical romance *Clementina*. This has always been my favourite Mason book, much closer to my heart even than *The Four Feathers*, but I am told that it has long been out of print, and hardly anybody seems to know it.

If it were famous for nothing else it deserves recognition as the book which first told readers how to barricade themselves into a room without a key, by the simple device of wedging a tilted chair under the handle of the door. As a child, I had a splendid time demonstrating the dodge to all and sundry, and I take a poor view of the tendency to set door-knobs too high and make chair-backs too low in modern houses.

Clementina is an eighteenth-century cloak-and-dagger story about the adventures of four Irish mercenaries, who undertake a journey beset with hazards, by coach and on horseback, from Innsbrück to Italy, to bring the Polish princess Clementina to marry James, the Old Pretender. It is a bitter-sweet story full of intimations of romance, but as I found when I came to work on it, the romance is implicit and rarely spoken. It was a challenge for a script-writer to put Mason's intimations into words which would be clear, speakable, moving and true to the pattern of the story.

Writing these television scripts was a challenge altogether, but I enjoyed every minute of the work. It was an adventure into the unknown; so much to be learned, so many changes to be understood, so many new tricks to be mastered.

Writing for television is different from any other kind of writing. In my ignorance I had thought of a television script as something very like a play, written out with dialogue and stage directions. I quickly found how wrong I was. Here you are writing for the camera and the microphone; you are making a blueprint for the architect, who is the producer. Certain practical things must be grasped firmly from the start. The cast should be kept as small as possible. The sets should be few and compact. There is a strict limit to the number of sets that can be built on a single studio floor, and very little drama short of Shakespeare rates two studios.

Then again, one must consider the time it takes for an actor to move from one set to another, particularly if a costume change is involved. It doesn't do to end a scene on one character and immediately introduce him in the next scene. This can be done in films, where the scenes are probably shot on different days, if not weeks apart, but not in live television.

The writer learns in time how to sneak a leading character out of shot before the end of a sequence. ('Let Holmes go. Hold Watson.')

If this proves impracticable he can bridge the scenes with a short film sequence. (Traffic in a London square, figures skulking in the heather, police cars chasing fugitive, or simply 'Enormous Close-Up of Hand Inserting Key in Lock'. This is one of television's favourites.) These linking shots can be accompanied, when necessary, by off-screen, pre-recorded voices. There is no genius in their invention. It is simply a matter of practice and common sense.

Once the script is accepted, the writer's main task is done, although he may be consulted later at rehearsal stage over minor alterations to the dialogue.

Even after years of broadcasting it isn't always possible for a writer to know exactly how a line will 'speak', particularly if he is unfamiliar with his players. I always made a point of attending two or three of the early rehearsals in order to get to the know cast and hear for myself how the dialogue was working out. I found it paid handsomely. Sometimes I could help the actors; very often they could help me. It was not unusual for some old, experienced actor to suggest a sudden bright amendment. 'Do you mind if I change this?' he would ask me most meticulously. He was nearly always right.

I learnt a great deal about dialogue from these old professionals. As time went on I found myself adapting the original author's dialogue far more freely, and it was pleasant to be told by some player at the end of a passage of my own invention, 'Your lines are so much easier to speak than his.'

Rehearsals for the average television play start a fortnight before transmission. Only the final rehearsals take place in the studio; the others are held in one of the many out-of-the-way and unexpected B.B.C. rehearsal rooms scattered through the west and west central districts of London.

They vary little in essentials. A big, bare room, with no furniture except a number of chairs ranged round the walls for the actors, and a couple of small and rather rickety tables. Camera positions are marked on the floor by the stage manager in different coloured chalks: white, blue, pink, mauve, criss-crossing in mysterious triangles. Chairs are arranged to represent walls, windows and doors; and since anything from half a dozen to a dozen set-ups may be fitted, back to back, side by side, on to this single practice stage, the whole thing looks to a layman like some complicated maze; one of those flat mazes without hedges which, so long as you play fair, are just as difficult to unravel.

The two things that struck me most when I went to my first rehearsal (it was somewhere in the labyrinth behind Tottenham Court Road) were the general sense of hush, and the soft, almost catlike movement. The big room is curiously quiet. Players waiting for their scenes sit silently outside the chalk-lines, marking their scripts or reading the midday edition of the evening papers. The actors in the scene being rehearsed read or speak their lines at something under normal conversation pitch. As a rule they use no properties, but mime the raising of a glass, the writing of a letter, the ringing of a bell. Their passage from one group of chairs to another, representing a change from set to set, is noiseless and extremely rapid.

The producer, once he has given his players their positions for each scene, moves swiftly from shot to shot, placing himself in the position of the camera. He uses a viewfinder, or extemporizes one with his fingers. The cue to start action is not given in words but by the dropping of an arm. During actual transmission this is done by the studio manager, who receives his orders from the producer through his headphones. A television player must learn to watch for these silent and all-important cues out of the corner of his eye, without apparently looking for them.

On the day before the broadcast, sometimes not until the day itself, the play moves out of its makeshift rehearsal rooms on to the stage of the studio where transmission will take place. For the first time the camera crew see their scripts; the actors see their sets and properties. The early part of these studio rehearsals is mainly for the benefit of the technicians, with the actors more or less fulfilling the role of stand-ins. Later in the day they get their one chance of a complete run-through with cameras. The best that can be hoped for, a producer once told me, is nine minutes of full camera rehearsal for every three minutes of running time. If any tricky passage overruns, some other passage of the play must go without rehearsal.

At the time scheduled for transmission the cast stands ready on the stage, watching for the flicker and gradual settle of lights high up on the wall which signal 'Vision On', 'Sound On'. The stage manager is standing ready with the prompt script. The studio manager has called for absolute silence. He raises his hand. Somewhere at the far end of the stage the roller captions (main titles and subtitles) begin to turn. The grams., with the opening music, are faded in. The studio manager drops his hand. The action starts. The play is on the air, and millions of viewers in their homes—dinner over, evening drawing in, attentive people, indifferent people, eager people, critical people—are settling down to watch it.

Everyone who loves the theatre knows the thrill of the moment when the house-lights face, the floats come up, the curtain rises and the play begins. But the opening of a television play has a special sort of thrill. For at that moment, and not until then, the real play begins to be created. It is the unique job of a television producer, as distinct from producers in the theatre or directors of films, literally to talk his play into life.

High above the studio floor is the producer's gallery; a small, glass-walled room from which he can see the actors below, and at the same time watch the monitor screens in front of him. There are two of these screens, side by side. The one on the right is the actual transmission screen, which shows the same picture as the viewer is watching on his screen at home. The one on the left is the preview screen, on which the producer can see the set-up waiting to be taken over by the next camera.

He gives his directions through a microphone to the studio manager and the men behind the cameras on the floor below; to the tele-cine operators, who are usually housed in the basement; to the vision mixer in the gallery, and to the girl in charge of 'grams.'. Second by second, shot by shot, he brings the play to life; directing, cautioning and encouraging.

'Camera Two, it's all yours now.' 'Camera One, pick up the girl, never mind the man.' 'Keep on that hand, Two, he's going to use it in a minute.' 'Take her nose out of the left of the frame.' 'Sorry, I'm afraid I'm rattling you, I'll leave you alone now.' Oh, a *beautiful* track; that was a honey.'

This impromptu method of creating drama is an extraordinary test of nerves, skill and resourcefulness, and hardly seems to be the ideal way of producing a masterpiece, since every first transmission must be something in the nature of a dress rehearsal. In the days when the

B.B.C. made a practice of repeating their Sunday-evening play on Thursday it was remarkable how much more smoothly the show came over at the second transmission.

Both producers and actors would warmly welcome more time for rehearsals with cameras. But even in its present imperfect state 'live' drama is infinitely preferred by many viewers, myself included, to transmissions of films finished and canned months, years or often decades ago. Live drama, immediate reporting, is what television is for; what makes it an individual and exciting medium. We like to know that what we see is happening here and now before our eyes, that we are assisting, in the French sense, at a human drama; that we can beat the newspaper to a bit of headline news, or watch a play before the critics tell us what to think about it.

Perhaps instinctively I have always enjoyed television most for the very things that distinguish it from my own occupation, the cinema: its spontaneity, lack of polish and revision, and the chance that the unforeseen may interrupt at any minute. Nowadays, when so much of the material is pre-filmed and edited, television has become a less exciting thing.

After *Clementina* I did one more play for television, an original which my son and I wrote together over Christmas called *Vicky's First Ball*. The story was so slight as to be almost non-existent. It was the atmosphere that we wanted to catch. The idea was to give the impression—a little humorous, a little tender, a little nostalgic—of a young girl's feelings at her coming-out ball, in the days when Strauss waltzes were all the rage and Mr. Tennyson's 'Maud' an admired poem.

I was rather fond of *Vicky*, and have sometimes toyed with the idea of turning the short play into a short novel. But toying is not the same thing as doing. It never has been done, and I don't suppose it will be, any more than the television play of Galsworthy's *The Dark Flower* which Michael Barry and I so often discussed as a joint proposition.

The times are not right for this sort of wholehearted romance. By the middle of the 1950s, when *Vicky* appeared, a change was already in the air, affecting every kind of writing.

Romance was out of fashion; sentiment had become, all of a sudden, a contemptible word. To write successfully you had to be 'committed', which mean socio-politically committed. To be committed to an idea, an individual design, the telling of a good story, or to that quality which Professor Joad used to describe as truth-and-beauty, was not enough.

Sometimes it seems to me as if the only quality admired in modern writing, or playmaking, or film-making, is truth-and-ugliness. This, for some reason, is described as realism; as if nothing could be real that is not sordid, disagreeable or violent.

To look back in anger was the code of the middle and late fifties. It was discovered, with relief and relish, that nobody was a malefactor; he was simply maladjusted. Whatever he did wrong was the result of his upbringing; of social underprivilege and parental misunderstanding, the unfairness of things generally. The mixed-up kid became the popular hero, and it was the proper thing to be a rebel, with or without a cause.

There is never any harm done in giving complacency a healthy airing, and I have a real respect for writers like John Osborne and John Braine, who had the courage to do so in the first place. But the trouble with honest reformers is that they invariably attract less honest satellites, on the principle of 'Big fleas have little fleas, Upon their backs to bite 'em'. The film industry, freed suddenly from conventional restraint, leapt at the chance of turning 'realism' to advantage, and being as sordid as it could.

Sex, horror and violence began to pervade the cinema. To be scrupulous was to be a cissy. The British Board of Film Censors was busy handing out 'X' certificates, and by the less reputable companies these certificates were highly coveted. For a time 'X' equalled box-office (and let nobody ask how many children under sixteen managed to get into the cinemas and see the programmes).

It was a shortsighted policy on the part of the film industry. The audience of rowdy youngsters whom the 'X' film attracted to the cinemas was far outnumber by the steady patrons who began to stay away. Box-office receipts dropped ominously, and every week, it seemed, we read in the papers of another picture-house that was forced to close through lack of custom.

The trade blamed it all on television, naturally. It was the easiest way out of a predicament. The trade has never been quick to appreciate the real reason for its failures. Never has it been able to recognize its own vulgarity. I treasure a remark made to my friend Dilys Powell by Nicholas Ray, director of *The King of Kings*, after a distinctly cool reception of his picture by the London critics. 'I guess,' he said, in explanation, 'that they are not hep enough to the times of Christ.'

22

IT'S NEVER TOO LATE TO BEGIN

BY THIS time I was over sixty and had begun to realize that I was growing old. I dozed off easily—we are a sleepy family—and often had a job to keep awake during the afternoon's picture. I found too that I was stopping to take breath halfway up the stairs to the dress circle, and saying 'You go ahead' to the young critics who came leaping up the steps behind me.

I found the daily journeys up to town a weariness, and resented the long hours that had to be put in at lunchtime. I had no London club, could not afford the prices of the quiet restaurants which I preferred and spent most of my lunch-breaks on a bench in the Southwood Memorial Garden of St. James's Church, sharing my sandwiches with the pigeons.

I can see now that, without consciously realizing it, I was losing my appetite for the cinema. Gone were the days when one met the challenge of each week with zest, hoping that something wonderful would happen. There were still films that I enjoyed, of course, and others that I admired without enjoyment; and I worked harder than ever on my Sunday column, trying to atone with clarity and justice for what it lacked in inspiration.

When a critic reaches this state of mind he should be thinking of retirement, for he is no longer giving full service to his readers. But I was obstinate; habit died hard; I knew my work was conscientious, even if it were no longer spirited. I shall go on until I'm sixty-five, I thought, and then retire and draw my old-age pension.

It wasn't to work out that way, however. One morning in the autumn of 1960, when I was sixty-three, I had a long letter from David

Astor, saying, in the gentlest way possible, that he felt the time had come when my column should be handed over to 'a younger person'. He was quite right, of course, and, looking back on it now, I hold his decision in nothing but gratitude. But at the moment it was a shock. I had been on the *Observer* for thirty-two years, and never known any professional life other than reviewing for the cinema.

I wrote my last article for the *Observer* on Christmas Day 1960. I was glad that Christmas should have fallen on a Sunday that year, for I had always tried to keep my Christmas articles distinct from the other fifty-one; to use them for a special message to my readers. That year I had a very special message, which was to bid them all goodbye; and add, as we were taught to say at the end of children's parties, 'Thank you for having me.'

At first I felt oddly lost without the *Observer* and my weekly column. It was strange to wake up on Thursday morning and realize that this was not press day any longer but just a day like any other in the week. I could hardly believe that I should never again ring up to correct proofs on Saturday morning, or jump into a taxi and tell the driver, 'The *Observer* office, 22, Tudor Street, under the clock.'

It took me some time to understand that the break was final. The editor and trustees of the paper couldn't have been kinder. They gave me an informal little dinner at the Waldorf, at which Nancy Astor herself was present, as well as Bill and David, and I was asked to choose my own guests. After dinner Sir Ifor Evans, the chairman, presented me with a generous book of gift vouchers on Harrod's, and I had a splendid time buying luxuries that I had never been able to afford before.

I bought linen sheets and pillow-cases, plump down pillows to prop myself up in bed when I had asthma, a wheelbarrow with solid pneumatic tyres, several tins of Baxter's pheasant, partridge and grouse prepared with wine, a soft black evening dress, an enormous red leather handbag, a camel-hair coat and several pairs of stockings; and at the end of the year I still had a few vouchers over.

All this was princely, but it wasn't work; and it was the feeling of belonging to something, of a regular responsibility to my paper, that I missed. For a time I had a faint hope that the *Observer* would invite me to write some book reviews, or a general article, or perhaps take over the film criticism when my successor, Penelope Gilliatt, was away on holiday. But that never happened.

I am glad now that it didn't happen. It would have spoilt the new pattern of life that was beginning to emerge. Once the habit of a lifetime had been broken I discovered that I was no longer thinking about films. I was thinking about books and gardens and race-horses; what would happen when the Gilbert and Sullivan copyright expired; how hard I should prune the roses.

I did write a few reviews of films for a monthly magazine, but found I hated half living in this ghost-world, and decided to give it up. Without seeing all the new films, I found my sense of judgement was impaired. Without writing about them every week, I found that work was slow and words no longer came freely.

I learnt a lesson about retirement that was certainly true for me, and might be a help to many other people. When you finish with a job it is wiser to make the break complete. Cut off the old life, clean and sharp. If your mind is tired that is the only way. If your mind is lively you will soon find other interests.

One day, about a month after I had left the *Observer*, I read in the papers that Angela Thirkell was dead. This was a sad blow to the many thousands of people who had read and re-read and loved her Barsetshire novels. They had been my bedside reading for more than thirty years, and every year I waited eagerly for the appearance of 'the new Thirkell'.

Mrs. Thirkell was a friend of the Garvins, and I had known her, not intimately but pleasantly, for quite a long time. We used to send Christmas cards to each other. I have just found a note from her tucked away between the pages of *What Does It Mean?*, acknowledging a rather fetching bit of Victoriana with moss roses and a fringed silk border, which I had discovered in a back-street junk shop.

'What a divine piece of rubbish and thank you a thousand times. And in what perfect preservation—an enchanting period piece. I am hoping to go to U.S.A. early in Jan., partly to do a few "talks", NOT a lecture tour which would kill me straight away in a week, but to worthy societies in Boston and places where I have friends. If you were in town between now and then WOT LARX, but I hope for your sake you won't be as it is HELL and one can't move a step without being trodden on. I should IMMENSELY like to see you again and have a good gabble.'

Our 'gabbles' were mostly about her characters; their past, present and future. 'Francis Brandon has gone sour on me,' she'd say; or, 'I think I'll send the Robin Dales to another part of Barsetshire, I'm getting rather tired of them, such nice, dull people;' or, 'Mr. Adams' children will be part of the county some day, I don't think Heather's ever will.'

I once told her she was running short of marriageable girls, and suggested that she brought back Lettice Watson's daughters, who had been packed off to Yorkshire at the end of *Marling Hall*. She considered the idea for a moment and then said firmly, 'No, I don't feel they are nubile.'

When I asked her if she meant George Halliday to marry Edith Graham she said on the whole she thought not. 'He's too old for her, and the poor fellow needs to marry money. I shall find him a nice, rich daughter of the Upper Clergy who is interested in farming,' and proceeded to do so in *A Double Affair*. I could never persuade her to tell me which was her favourite character. The most she would say was: 'Well, I've always been fond of Lydia. She's very happily married to that nice Noël Merton, and I think he'll go far.'

In the newspaper reports of Mrs. Thirkell's death it was stated that she had left 'an unfinished novel'. It was also made clear that there was no likelihood of its publication. This seemed to me quite maddening. To think that somewhere there was lying around some part of a new Barsetshire story, and none of us would ever read it. What a pity! What a waste! All those delightful and familiar characters left hanging in mid-air; their stories unresolved; after twenty-eight books, the saga uncompleted. It seemed wrong.

One night I had a sudden thought and said to Tony, 'Do you think they'd let me finish it?'

'Finish what!' he said.

'The last Angela Thirkell. The one they say won't ever be published.'

He laughed and said I could but ask. So I got in touch with Hamish Hamilton, the publishers, and managed to persuade them against their judgement to let me have a try. I can only suppose that they had written the book off as a dead loss, and any attempt to retrieve it was worth considering.

When the typescript first came into my hands I was almost in despair. Mrs. Thirkell had written five chapters, less than half a book, and left no notes, no hint at all of the way she meant the story to develop. I am inclined to think she didn't know herself. She was an ill woman at the time, and friends have told me that she was despondent about the book, which had been hanging fire for nearly a couple of years. She had even been heard to say, 'How I wish somebody would write it *for* me!'

At that time the story was called *The Vicar's Daughter*, and I fancy the conclusion was to have been a marriage of convenience between Sylvia Gould and old Lord Stoke. But Mrs. Thirkell's original choice of title had been *Three Score and Ten*, and in the changed circumstances it seemed the proper thing to bring the old title back, enlarge the scope of plot and end the series with an all-Barsetshire celebration party which would pay tribute both to Mrs. Thirkell and to Mrs. Morland, her *alter ego*.

For a couple of weeks I soaked myself in the atmosphere, the idiom and the characters of the twenty-eight existing novels. During that fortnight I read no other books than Angela Thirkell's. I got so that I was thinking and talking instinctively in her language. Then, with the beginning of Chapter 6 and with these things in mind, I spun the rest out of my own imagining.

I invented Robin on the pattern of his father Tony Morland, in *High Rising* and *A Demon in the House*, in order to activate the plot and keep it on three levels: the children, the romantic adolescents and the older people whom we had so long known and loved. I wanted to leave readers with the feeling that nothing was finished, only a golden chapter ended; that life in Barsetshire would go on tomorrow as it had been yesterday, and everyone could dream it for herself.

Three Score and Ten is really Mrs. Thirkell's book. She inspired every word of it, and I am happy to have had so many letters from readers, many of them in America, where the author was well loved, saying that they can't find where 'the join' comes in.

It was the most exciting work I ever did; in an odd sort of way at once an adventure and a labour of love. I wish I could know that Angela Thirkell herself would have been pleased with it and said 'WOT LARX'. I can only be sure that she would be glad if it pleased others.

IT'S NEVER TOO LATE TO BEGIN

One day, when I was passionately involved with *Three Score and Ten*, there came an unexpected letter with a Durham postmark. The University of Durham expressed the hope that I would accept an Hon. D.Litt. at the July graduation ceremony.

I had to read the letter twice before I could believe my eyes. I knew nobody at all at Durham, yet apparently they had heard of me. It was the first time, to my knowledge, that such a degree had been conferred on a film critic. I was scared to death at the thought of all the pomp involved, but couldn't very well refuse the honour.

So on an early July day in the second week of Wimbledon I travelled up to Durham and was duly invested with the degree of Doctor of Letters (*honoris causa*) 'at a Congregation holden on 7th July 1961'.

The Public Orator said polite things about my career as a writer, and as we walked in slow procession from the Great Hall of Durham Castle, where the ceremony was 'holden', to the afternoon service in the Cathedral, I was much comforted to find beside me the sturdy figure of that kind and brilliant little man Dr. Kudwig Guttman, head of the hospital for paraplegics at Stoke Mandeville. Having listened to his citation, and knowing something of the miracles he had performed for patients, I felt very humble. Here was someone who had clearly earned a degree *honoris causa*. We talked about Germany in the old days, about some relatives of mine whom he was certain he had met, and a little about shyness. I don't suppose Dr. Guttman ever realized what a support he was to me.

But oh! how thankful I was, after the service, to be able to discard my fine doctor's robes! 'Scarlet cashmere sleeves and front, faced with old gold satin, with soft black velvet square cap. Hood, scarlet cashmere, lined with old-gold satin.' What a glory! What a splendid piece of dressing-up! But oh how dolorously heavy for a stout, elderly woman on a hot midsummer afternoon!

Apart from the formalities of the ceremony—and in an awed way I enjoyed those too—my short visit to Durham was a thoroughly happy experience. I don't know what I had expected to find there; mile after mile of slag-heaps and coal-fields, I rather think; factory chimneys, blackened approaches and a pall of smoke hanging over everything.

I was certainly not prepared for the green hills and leafy valleys, nor for the quiet, sudden little station, almost a country halt, where the London express seems to discover a platform accidentally and stops for

247

a moment to spill out a few passengers before pursuing its real journey to somewhere else.

I had shied at the idea of staying at an hotel, for as I grow older I have become more and more allergic to the amenities of hotel life: the tightly curtained bedroom with windows that are loth to open; the comfortable sprung beds with slippery quilts and insufficient pillows; the public promenade towards the nearest lavatory; the bath (if you are lucky enough to get one) which was certainly not built for bodies either long or stout; the healthy unvarying breakfast menus; the overloaded and expensive dinner, which offers no charm at all to guests perversely inclined to retire to their room early with a glass of milk.

My aversion to hotels brought me the greatest luck at Durham. For two days I was the guest of Miss Marjorie Williamson, principal of St. Mary's College, and 'one of our nicest dons', as the Registrar assured me on the telephone.

Miss Williamson was a wonder. I don't know how she put up with me so patiently at that busy time, with degree day for her students, a party for their parents, decorators in the kitchen and builders at the bottom of the garden.

Only a woman in a hundred would have undertaken the added responsibility of a guest in such circumstances. Yet she was waiting at the station to meet me, carried me off to dinner in her little car, mothered me throughout the ceremony, showed me the lovely old cobbled streets and gracious houses of the cathedral quarter (they made me think of Rye and Bath and Stratford, and often of Jane Austen), and, above all, gave me a quiet and friendly house to rest in.

I had been sorry to leave my Pinner garden, which was in the full flush of its first summer roses. But the gardens of St. Mary's Hall were full of roses too, and in my bedroom I found a great vase of velvet Crimson Glory and Pink Picture.

The bookcase beside my bed was full of detective stories, and there were three splendid pillows to encourage reading. The windows looked out across a valley to the Castle and the Cathedral, whose chimes marked time sweetly and remotely through the July dusk. The air smelt clean and fresh, with a hint of recent rain, the sky was mackerel, a soft young Geordie voice was bidding somebody good night and there and then I fell in love with Durham.

Before leaving I was asked to sign the visitors' book. I opened it at the last entries, which read quite simply 'Elizabeth R.' and again 'Elizabeth R.'. The Queen and the Queen Mother, it appeared, had both been recent visitors to St. Mary's Hall. I modestly turned over a fresh page before writing: 'Caroline A. Lejeune'. I have signed my name a goodly number of times in the course of a long professional career, but never in such exalted company.

This would seem to be the proper place to bring my story to an end. We have already travelled a long way from the tall, yellow house in Manchester, and the child who slammed tennis balls against a wall and told herself tales of infinite adventure.

There has been nothing particularly adventurous about my life, but it has been a busy and a happy one, and I look back on it with pleasure. I have made some good friends, met many interesting people and enjoyed my work in films; even if, like most journalists, I have loathed the specific labour of setting words down on paper.

Retirement has come at the right time for me. I doubt if I should have been a useful critic for much longer. I find that I don't miss films as I should miss, say, books and music. What I miss most, perhaps, is the stimulus of readers' letters. Every critic gets these by the hundred; from all parts of the world; from readers old and young; verbose or laconic; indignant, grateful, informative, reminiscent and inquiring; from them he learns to know the people that he writes for.

The *Observer* has a wide overseas circulation, so my mail was heavy, varied and continuously fascinating. What surprised me most was the large number of correspondents who appeared to read the column without having any particular interest in the cinema.

In one of my reviews (*The Big Country*) I mentioned a painting which had caught my fancy at an exhibition of modern American art, but whose name escaped me; an impression of a girl lying in the long grass on a bare hillside, looking up towards a solitary house in a vast, lonely landscape. For weeks afterwards I was inundated by letters about 'Christina's World', enclosing reproductions in black-and-white and colour, describing the writers' own emotions on a first encounter with the picture.

This is the sort of correspondence that makes a writer's life an endless joy. Sometimes he wonders what he has done to earn it. I often wondered what I had done to deserve my readers. The warmth of correspondence after I said goodbye to them on Christmas Day of 1960 entirely overwhelmed me. I had expected a few letters from old pen-friends, but there were nearly two thousand of them; some perplexed, some indignant, some apologizing for presumption because 'I have never written to a critic before', but all of them generous and individual.

Most of my letters have been answered and decently destroyed a long time ago, but I still keep a few which for some reason amuse, delight or touch me. I have saved the one from five soldiers in North Africa who want to know, in order to settle a bet, what sort of person I really am. Am I a smart, streamlined woman who scoffs at everything, or a prim, schoolmarm type who likes to keep a class in order? Or am I, in reality, a man and not a woman?

Perhaps my favourite letter comes from a reader who says that she and her husband are in the habit of reading and discussing my reviews each Sunday. 'Yesterday,' she writes, 'I found our four-year-old son building a gasometer with his bricks. Every now and then he stopped to admire the effect, and I heard him muttering: 'It's good. Lejeune says it's good.'

In one family at least I stand a reasonable chance of being remembered as a constructive critic, and a gasometer is no mean memorial in its fashion.